Praise for *An_____*

"Epstein forcefully showcases the collateral damage of myopic American foreign policy that obsesses about terrorism everywhere—even in Uganda—to the detriment of all other considerations. *Another Fine Mess* chronicles how American foreign policy driven by short-term security concerns results in long-term crises and an entrenchment of authoritarian rule in the process. An important and prescient cautionary tale."

— Brian Klaas
Author of *The Despot's Accomplice*

"As her new book reveals, Helen Epstein is an eloquent advocate of human rights and democracy for Africans, as well as a courageous critic of how U.S. aid supports oppressive dictators like Yoweri Museveni in Uganda."

—William Easterly
Author of *The Tyranny of Experts* and *The White Man's Burden*

"For decades, Western policy-makers have hailed Uganda's Yoweri Museveni as a benign autocrat, a charming African Bismarck and trusted partner in the fight against Islamic fundamentalism. *Another Fine Mess* reveals a far darker side to this key African ally, while exposing the cynicism at the heart of American policy in Africa's Great Lakes region. This gripping, iconoclastic, angry book raises a host of uncomfortable questions."

—Michela Wrong
Author of *Borderlines* and *It's Our Turn to Eat*

"A sizzling indictment of Uganda's current strongman and of the American policy in Africa that supports his corrupt regime with generous foreign aid."

—*Kirkus Reviews*

Another Fine Mess
America, Uganda, and the War on Terror

COLUMBIA GLOBAL REPORTS
NEW YORK

Another Fine Mess
America, Uganda, and the War on Terror

Helen C. Epstein

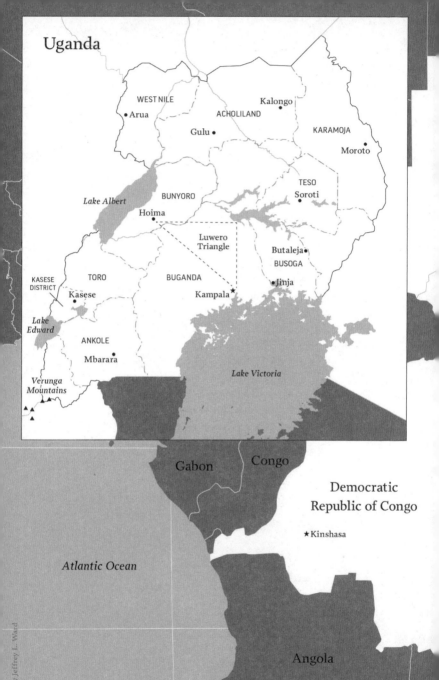

Egypt

Saudi Arabia

Sudan

Red Sea

Khartoum ★

Eritrea

Yemen

Djibouti

★ Addis Ababa

South Sudan

Ethopia

Juba
★

Somalia

Baidoa
•

Uganda

Beni
•

Kampala
★

Kenya

Mogadishu
★

NORTH
SIVU
Goma •

Rwanda

Kigali
★

★ Nairobi

SOUTH
SIVU

★ Bujumbura

Burundi

Tanzania

Indian Ocean

Zambia

Mozambique

Malawi

Published by Columbia Global Reports
91 Claremont Avenue, Suite 515
New York, NY 10027
globalreports.columbia.edu
facebook.com/columbiaglobalreports
@columbiaGR

Library of Congress Control Number:
2017945484
ISBN: 978-0997722925

Book design by Strick&Williams
Map design by Jeffrey L. Ward
Author photograph by Petr Petr

Printed in the United States of America

Love and gratitude to Pete for bearing with me.

Acknowledgments

Kiwanuka Lawrence Nsereko was born in 1968, a few years after Uganda's independence, and grew up in a rural village. As in many Ugandan households, children were expected to summarize newspaper stories, church sermons, school lessons and neighborhood goings-on for their elders in the evenings. Lawrence must have excelled at these monologues, because his fine oratory skills made him an invaluable partner in the writing of this book. Every incidental question—Was it 1989 or 1990 when so-and-so happened? What was the name of the village where you were arrested?—elicited a story with details of personalities, motivations, actions, parallel events, background and priceless commentary.

For their courage and insights into Ugandan politics, I particularly wish to thank Kizza Besigye, Winnie Byanyima, David Sejusa, Paul Ssemogerere, Zoe Bakoko Bakuru, the Otunnu

12   brothers—Ochoro, Ogenga, Amii Omara- and Olara—and numerous other Ugandan friends whose names I dare not print.

I also gathered much wisdom from Uganda's many fine journalists working inside and outside the country, including Daniel Kalinaki, Charles Onyango-Obbo, Eriasa Sserunjogi, Rod Muhumuza and the reporters at the *Monitor* and *Observer* newspapers.

American and European diplomats who tried to do the right thing, even when this was not possible, were an inspiration to me.

For discussions, I am extremely grateful to Bill Easterly, Steve Hubbell, John Ryle, Nuruddin Farah, Maria Burnett, Leslie Lefkow, Boniface Musavuli, Remember Miamingi, Pagan Amum, Alex Papachristou, Jesse Ribot and Jean Stein.

Milton Allimadi, Jonathan Fisher, Filip Reyntjens, Peter Rosenblum, Shaka Ssali, Harry Verhoeven and my father Jason kindly commented on an early draft of this manuscript. It is much improved, thanks to their efforts. Any remaining errors are obviously mine.

Uganda is not a country that typically hogs the headlines, and I am extremely grateful to a number of editors for helping me tell its story. Versions of some chapters originally appeared in the *New York Review of Books* where I had the great luck to work with editor Bob Silvers. He didn't look like a radical, but working with him sometimes felt less like collaboration than conspiracy. Without ever being partisan or doctrinaire, he was profoundly and instinctively sympathatic to those who were too weak, or too oppressed to speak for themselves. I am also grateful to Hugh Eakin of the *New York Review Daily*, Vera Titunik of the *New Yorker Online*, Gemma Sieff of *Harpers*, and Muhammed Ademo of Al-Jazeera.

This book would not exist had Nick Lemann, Camille McDuffie and Jimmy So of Columbia Global Reports not approached me for a book on public health in early 2015 and then put up with many changes of direction since. My agent Anna Stein of ICM was a patient, wise and generous counselor throughout.

Research for this book was supported by the Open Society Foundations, New York University's Development Research Institute, the Pulitzer Center for Crisis Reporting and the New York Review Foundation.

Finally, thanks and love to Jake, Dad, Judy, Susie, Sam, Natalie and Thomas.

CONTENTS

TIMELINE

UGANDA

300 BC–300AD
The territory now known as Uganda settled by various migratory groups from central and eastern Africa.

1300s
Buganda kingdom established.

1840s
Arab traders arrive in Buganda.

1860s-70s
British and French explorers and missionaries arrive in Buganda.

1890s
Baganda Protestants, Catholics and Muslims engage in a series of wars for supremacy.

1894
Uganda formally becomes a British Protectorate.

1962
Uganda granted independence; Milton Obote becomes prime minister.

1966
Obote orders Army Commander Idi Amin to attack Kabaka Mutesa II's palace. Kingdoms abolished the following year.

1971
Obote toppled by Idi Amin.

1979
Amin toppled by Tanzanian troops.

1979-80
Various governments installed and overthrown.

1980
Obote wins election amid rigging accusations.

1981
Yoweri Museveni and Andrew Lutaakome Kayiira establish rebel groups and declare war on Obote's government.

1985
Obote toppled by army officers Basilio and Tito Okello.

1986
Museveni's National Resistance Army topples the Okellos and takes power in Uganda. A quarter of his army comprises Tutsi Rwandan refugees.

1986
The National Resistance Army commits atrocities against the Acholi and Teso people in northern and eastern Uganda, respectively. Various rebel movements emerge.

1987-9
President Museveni makes three trips to Washington where he meets President Ronald Reagan and H. W. Vice President George Bush.

1988
Joseph Kony establishes the Lord's Resistance Army and terrorizes the people of northern Uganda.

1991-4
Uganda funnels clandestine military assistance to both the RPF and John Garang's Sudan People's Liberation Army (SPLA).

18

NOVEMBER 1994
Uganda begins clandestine training of Congolese rebels who will eventually form Laurent Kabilia's Allied Forces for the Liberation of Congo (AFDL).

1990s – PRESENT
Uganda becomes notorious for corruption. Billions of dollars vanish and virtually every Ministry is affected, including Health, Finance and the Prime Minister's Office. Donors continue to support Museveni's regime with ever more generous aid packages.

2001
Museveni wins his second presidential election, amid allegations of rigging. Opposition leader Kizza Besigye flees to exile.

FEBRUARY 2006
Museveni wins a third presidential election. Opposition again cries foul, alleges rigging. Two senior security officials later confirm the election was rigged.

2008
Joseph Kony flees Uganda and peace returns to the north for the first time since Museveni came to power in 1986.

2011
Museveni wins a fourth election, amid allegations of rigging. Non-violent protests are met with brutal security crackdown; at least nine unarmed demonstrators are killed.

2011-12
Parliament begins investigation into management of Uganda's oil sector.

DECEMBER 2012
MP Cerinah Nebanda dies under mysterious circumstances.

FEBRUARY 2016
Museveni wins a fifth election. For the first time, European election observers cry foul. Opposition leader Kizza Besigye arrested for the fiftieth time.

RWANDA

1988
The Uganda-based Rwanda Patriotic Front (RPF), led by Tutsi officers in Uganda's army mobilizes to topple the Hutu-dominated government of Rwanda.

OCTOBER 1990
The RPF invades Rwanda from Uganda.

1990-4
Civil war in Rwanda.

APRIL 1994
President Juvenal Habyarimana's plane is shot down in Kigali. Genocide against Tutsis commences.

JULY 1994
The RPF takes over Rwanda, more than one million Hutu refugees flee to Tanzania and Zaire.

SUDAN

JUNE 1989
Colonel Omar El-Bashir, backed by Hassan Al-Turabi's National Islamic Front, topples Sudan's Prime Minister Sadiq al-Mahdi.

1989-2005
Civil war devastates southern Sudan.

2005
Sudan and the SPLA sign peace agreement

2011
South Sudan declares independence. Rampant government corruption ensues.

2013 – PRESENT
Civil war breaks out within South Sudan. Museveni sends troops to prop up President Salva Kiir Mayardit with tacit U.S. consent.

2017
UN and other observers accuse President Kiir's troops of genocide against ethnic groups suspected of rebel sympathies.

ZAIRE/CONGO

1994-6
Hutu militants in Zairean refugee camps mobilize to retake Rwanda.

NOVEMBER 1996
Rwanda's army invades the Zairean refugee camps and herds most refugees home. Thousands flee, and are tracked down and slaughtered by Rwandan soldiers.

MAY 1997
The AFDL, assisted by the Rwandan and Ugandan armies, topples Zairean leader Mobutu Sese Seko. AFDL leader Laurent Kabila assumes power and renames the country the Democratic Republic of Congo.

1998
Rwanda and Uganda reinvade Congo and begin supporting myriad rebel groups who fight among themselves and against the Congolese army and local militia groups

1999-2003
The Ugandan army occupies Ituri region, killing thousands and looting some $10 billion in gold, timber and other natural resources. Rwanda becomes the world's leading exporter of Coltan, necessary for the manufacture of modern electronics. Most of this is also looted from Congo.

2000s
Rwandan/Ugandan backed rebels, including CNDP and M23 continue to wreak havoc in eastern Congo.

SOMALIA   19

1993
American-led UN relief mission ends in disaster when two Black Hawk helicopters are shot down and eighteen U.S. servicemen are killed.

2004-2006
Islamists and Ethiopian-backed secularists battle for power in Somalia.

JUNE 2006
The Islamists take power in Somalia; Museveni briefs his generals about forthcoming mission to Somalia.

CHRISTMAS 2006
The Ethiopian Army, with U.S. assistance, invades Somalia and topples the Islamists.

2007-PRESENT
Uganda sends African Union peacekeeping troops to Somalia. Al-Shabaab, formerly the armed wing of the Islamists gains support and takes over large parts of the country. Ugandan troops, supported by the U.S. and Britain, continue to battle Al-Shabaab to the present day.

Introduction

Every gun that is made, every warship launched, every rocket fired signifies, in the final sense, a theft from those who hunger and are not fed, those who are cold and not clothed. This world in arms is not spending money alone. It is spending the sweat of its laborers, the genius of its scientists, the hopes of its children. . . .This is not a way of life at all in any true sense. Under the cloud of threatening war, it is humanity hanging from a cross of iron.

—Dwight Eisenhower

I've been a public health consultant for over 20 years. In Rwanda, I carried out field research among villagers too frightened to speak to me for fear that government spies would report them if they complained about ethnic discrimination. In Ethiopia, I met listless, starving children in villages denied sufficient food aid because of suspected anti-government sentiment. In Uganda,

I interviewed mothers whose children had died of malaria because the president's cronies looted foreign aid programs meant to pay for medicine and bed nets. Most of the humanitarian programs I worked on were supported by U.S. tax dollars, but they were no match for the U.S.-backed tyrants who caused the problems in the first place.

The fine work of humanitarians alone won't make poor countries prosper. A nation is built on shared expectations that laws will be followed; that rights won't be trampled; that killers will be punished; that doctors and teachers will be paid what they are owed. If we fail to maintain these fragile promises, even the U.S. would collapse, for those obligations are the foundation of development itself.

In recent years, the East African nation of Uganda has become notorious for warlord Joseph Kony's killing fields, and for a government that attempted to criminalize homosexuality. In fact, Uganda's history is far more interesting, not least because of its role in America's calamitous War on Terror.

The story opens as the Cold War was ending and Washington awoke to growing anti-Western sentiment among Muslims throughout the Middle East. In the Horn of Africa and its nearest neighbors in eastern Africa, a new political map based on a revised vision of national security took shape. Before long, articles listing the fraction of Muslims in different African countries began appearing in policy journals, along with warnings about "lawless bazaars" in diamond and other gemstone markets, and rumors of an underground trade in yellowcake from the continent's uranium mines.

In trying to comprehend this perceived threat, the U.S. and its allies—wittingly, and otherwise—formed military partnerships with African dictators who, while promising to fight

22 terrorism, stoked up six wars in eastern and central Africa that left millions dead and fueled the rise of the vicious Somali terrorist group Al-Shabaab. This book explores how this happened, providing another glimpse of the post-truth world that brought us the Iraq war and other crises in the Middle East and beyond.

Uganda's Yoweri Museveni has been the eye of this storm. Since his rebel insurgency took power in 1986, his government has received over $20 billion in development assistance, an unknown amount of classified military aid, and $4 billion in debt relief. At the same time, Uganda's benefactors have allowed Museveni to shape events to serve his own bloody ambitions. The result has been mayhem in Rwanda, Congo, Sudan, South Sudan, Somalia, and Uganda itself. This book isn't a comprehensive history of these interlinked wars, which have been ably covered by others. Here I focus on what we know about how Museveni either intensified or created these conflicts *de novo*.

Museveni's genius has been to capitalize on Western ambivalence about Africa's capacity for democracy and self-determination. Thus, with America and Europe's blessing, he used our generous foreign aid to turn Uganda into a military dictatorship dressed up to look like a democracy. Uganda has a Parliament, a court system, a lively press, and a pyramidal elected governance structure at the village, district, and regional levels. But these institutions operate at the mercy of a far more powerful paramilitary structure of Museveni-appointed Resident District Administrators, District Internal Security officers, Village Defense Committees, and a shadowy network of unofficial security organs that control their own arsenals, override the decisions of elected officials, and close NGOs, newspapers, and radio stations deemed unfriendly to the regime.

Uganda is not North Korea; many Ugandans openly express political opinions. The latest corruption scandals, the poor state of public services, and the peccadillos of ruling party politicians are widely covered in the media. But denouncing the president himself or members of his family, speaking out or reporting on serious human rights abuses, or simply becoming too politically powerful can land you in jail on trumped-up charges, or far, far worse. Wise Ugandans censor themselves.

Museveni's strategy resembles the "100 Flowers" campaign of his boyhood hero Mao Zedong, who in 1956 encouraged China's citizens to express their opinions of the communist regime and then sent the "rightists" who did so critically to prison labor camps. This enabled Mao to flush out the most dangerous "counter-revolutionaries" as cheese in a mousetrap eliminates mice. What for Mao was a one-off experiment is for Museveni a continuous policy of exposing dissent and then silencing it by paying off or harassing his most articulate and courageous critics.

The arrest and torture of dissidents is done quietly. In early morning phone calls, government thugs intimidate editors and journalists to ensure the gravest abuses receive little attention. Uganda's insecure intelligentsia assures Western diplomats that stories of abuses are mere rumors. Aware that overt military rule would hurt his image internationally, Museveni dons a trademark floppy hat and civilian clothes and justifies the brutality of his security forces to donors with the claim that the opposition is planning to "riot" or commit terrorist acts. During elections, towns across the country fill with tanks, teargas trucks, and lines of soldiers in riot gear carrying machine guns. Security personnel fill out multiple ballots and poll results are routed electronically through computer

24   networks run by operatives who alter vote counts so that
       Museveni invariably wins.

       In January 2017, two researchers presented data suggest-
ing that Americans and Europeans born in the 1980s are far less
likely to say that living in a democracy is "essential" than their
grandparents' generation was. I hope those young people, so
complacent about the freedoms their elders fought for on the
killing fields of Europe and the streets of Birmingham, Alabama,
will read this book and think again.

The Cold War was almost over when Yoweri Museveni's rebel
army seized power in 1986. From its ashes, an old ideology was
being reborn and its specter darkened the triumphal atmosphere. The adherents of militant Islam had dreams of Empire,
but they were neither of a workers' nor consumers' paradise;
they were bound together not by citizenship, but by a common
creed and violent conception of justice and honor. Militant
Islamists had their own schools, hospitals, and charities, their
own courts and systems of trade, their own ways of choosing leaders, their own customs concerning gender and sexual
behavior, and their own militias. Their economies were based
on shadowy, trust-based exchanges of gemstones and weapons. The focus of militant Islamist hatred was America and her
allies: their support for the Israeli occupation of Palestine; their
links to the corrupt Saudi Royal family; their military presence
on the soil of Muslim nations; and their decadent culture which
fostered complacency about all of the above.

       For its devotees, militant Islam seemed like a cure for a
fractured world where the interests of the poor and weak were
trampled by American might and greed. For Washington, this
frightening movement, responsible for ever-bloodier terrorist

attacks against Western and Israeli targets, posed a security
conundrum. The terrorists didn't come from a world they knew,
in which monolithic enemies with clear ideologies faced each
other with enormous weapons drawn but seldom used. These
new enemies weren't represented by states; they were everywhere and nowhere, and their weapons were deadly, portable,
and used without hesitation.

In Africa the stakes were high: an estimated $24 trillion
worth of unexploited oil, gold, diamonds, cobalt, uranium, and
coltan, the raw material for cellphone and computer chips. Much
of this loot lay underground in Uganda's neighbor Congo—or
Zaire, as it was known between 1971 and 1997—that vast, poorly
governed country at the heart of the continent. During the Cold
War, these resources were kept out of Soviet hands by U.S.-
backed thugs such as Zaire's Marshall Mobutu Sese Seko and
the militaristic Apartheid regime of South Africa. But the fall
of the Soviets shifted the kaleidoscope, turning former enemies
into friends and vice versa. South Africa would soon be free,
and the aging and increasingly addled President Mobutu was
growing closer to Sudan, where a new Islamist government was
recruiting militants throughout the Middle East to expand their
own sphere of influence.

In order to confront this new threat, Washington's security chiefs designated two new types of enemy: "state sponsors
of terror"—nations whose governments provided sanctuary
to terrorist groups—and "failed states." Articles about Africa
written by security officials give the impression that the
authors are describing not societies and cultures with histories
going back millennia, but anarchic wastelands where terrorists
lurked amid clans, cattle, and dust. In Africa, that meant Sudan
and Somalia, respectively.

26   As in the Cold War, proxy armies would be needed. Officially, U.S. policymakers would say Africans needed to fight their own battles; in reality, Africans would be fighting ours. Wedged between Congo/Zaire, with its enormous mineral wealth, and eastern Africa's Muslim fringe, predominantly Christian Uganda occupied a crucial geostrategic position. Its leader Museveni was a brilliant military strategist, whose ragtag rebel group had famously toppled Uganda's much stronger national army.

Since then Ugandan troops have served as a doorstop against what American national security officials see as potential Islamic militant advances across Africa, with troops at one time or another in Sudan, the Central African Republic, and Somalia—as well as Rwanda and Congo, where they removed regimes that although not themselves Islamic, were potential allies of Sudan.

To many Americans and Europeans, the resulting conflagrations—the Rwanda genocide, the Congo wars, the Sudanese civil war, Joseph Kony's massacres in northern Uganda, the gruesome Sharia amputations in Somalia—must have seemed like distant storms having nothing to do with us. But U.S. advisers and military officials were involved in some of this violence, at times arming one side against the other, at other times doing nothing until tensions built up and then downplaying abuses by our allies, including Museveni.

In 1989, an alliance of military officers and hardline Islamic militants took power in Sudan, and with help from Iran, began plotting to export Islamic revolution across Africa. Sudan's new leaders gave sanctuary to Osama bin Laden and the head of Egypt's Islamic Jihad, and permitted others, including the assassins who killed Egypt's speaker of Parliament in 1991, to be trained on its soil.

Shortly thereafter, Uganda's army began receiving assistance from the U.S. to train and equip the Sudan People's Liberation Army—or SPLA—a rebel group that had been battling the government in Khartoum on and off since the 1950s. In retaliation, Sudan's leaders began funneling weapons to notorious rebel leader Joseph Kony, who has since been indicted by the International Criminal Court on charges of crimes against humanity. The result was more than a decade of war that decimated the people of northern and eastern Uganda and southern Sudan who were caught in the crossfire.

The most disturbing example of U.S. involvement in Museveni's warmongering was the horror that erupted in Rwanda on April 6, 1994. Over three months, hundreds of thousands of Rwandans were murdered in the most rapid genocide ever recorded. The killers used simple tools—machetes, clubs and other blunt objects, or herded victims into buildings and set them aflame with kerosene. Most of the victims were Tutsis, who comprised about 14 percent of Rwanda's pre-genocide population. Most of the killers were of majority Hutu ethnicity.

The Rwanda genocide has been compared to the Nazi Holocaust in its surreal brutality. But there is a fundamental difference between these two atrocities. No Jewish army posed a threat to Germany. Hitler targeted the Jews and other weak groups solely because of his own demented beliefs and prevailing prejudices of the time.

The Rwandan Hutu genocidaires, as the people who killed during the genocide were known, were also motivated by irrational beliefs and prejudices, but the powder keg contained another important ingredient. Three and a half years before the genocide, an army of Rwandan Tutsi exiles known as the Rwandan Patriotic Front—or RPF—armed and trained by Uganda, invaded Rwanda and set up camps in the northern

28   mountains. Hundreds of thousands of mostly Hutu villagers
        fled south, citing killings, abductions, and other crimes in RPF
        occupied areas.

        The RPF represented hundreds of thousands of Tutsi refu-
        gees who had fled their country in the early 1960s. For centuries
        before that, they'd formed an elite minority caste in Rwanda.
        In a system perpetuated by the German and Belgian colonizers,
        they treated the majority Hutu peasants like serfs, forcing them
        to work on their land and sometimes beating them like donkeys.
        Hutu anger simmered until shortly before independence in
        1962, and then exploded in brutal and bloody pogroms against
        the Tutsi, who fled to neighboring countries. In Uganda, a new
        generation of Tutsi refugees grew up, but they soon became
        embroiled in the lethal politics of their adoptive country. Many
        naturally allied with Ugandan Tutsis and the closely related
        Hima—Museveni's tribe—many of whom were opposition
        supporters and therefore seen as enemies by President Milton
        Obote. After Amin overthrew Obote in 1971, many Rwandan
        Tutsis moved out of the border refugee camps. Some tended the
        cattle of wealthy Baganda; others acquired property and began
        farming themselves; some married into Ugandan families, and a
        small number joined the State Research Bureau, Amin's dreaded
        security apparatus that inflicted terror on Ugandans. When
        Obote returned to power in the 1980s, he stripped the Rwandan
        Tutsis of civil rights and ordered them back over the border or
        into the refugee camps. Those who refused to go were assaulted,
        raped, and killed and their houses were destroyed.

        As the end of the Cold War drew near, the plight of the Tutsi
        refugees finally came to the attention of the West, which began
        pressuring Rwanda's government to allow the refugees to return.
        At first, Rwanda's President Juvenal Habyarimana refused.
        Rwanda was among the most densely populated countries in

the world, and its people, dependent upon peasant agriculture, needed land to survive. The population had grown since the refugees left, and Rwanda was now full, Habyarimana said. However, by August 1990, international pressure had forced him to agree, in principle, to a negotiated return of the refugees. Unfortunately, the Tutsi refugees, dreaming of their lost dominion, were no longer interested in negotiation. They wanted power, not just passports. They invaded Rwanda two months later.

During the three and a half year civil war that preceded the genocide, Ugandan operatives supplied the RPF with weapons in violation of the UN Charter, Organization of African Unity rules, a UN Security Council Resolution, various Rwandan ceasefire and peace agreements, and Museveni's own promises.

The U.S. embassy in Kampala monitored the traffic in weapons and personnel between Uganda and the RPF inside Rwanda but did nothing to stop it; nor did the George H. W. Bush or Clinton administrations impose sanctions on Uganda such as foreign aid cuts or an arms embargo. On the contrary, U.S. foreign aid to Uganda nearly doubled during this period. In 1991, Uganda purchased ten times more U.S. weapons than in the preceding forty years combined.

As Rwanda's increasingly weak Hutu-dominated government reluctantly acceded to the RPF's demands for power, Hutu extremists who had long feared a Tutsi onslaught from Uganda roused the population using the specter of a return to a time, still fresh in the memory of older people, when the Tutsis made them feel like slaves in their own country. Four months before the genocide, the CIA accurately predicted that panicked Hutus could unleash extreme violence, resulting in up to half a million deaths. By then, the Rwandan government had been rightly subjected to an arms embargo. However, the Clinton administration continued to arm Uganda, which continued to arm the RPF.

30   By July 1994, hundreds of thousands of people had been killed, the vast majority of them innocent Tutsis who had nothing to do with the RPF, including children and even infants. The hatred the Hutu extremists unleashed represents the worst that human beings are capable of. But in considering what led to this disaster, it's important to bear in mind that the violence wasn't spontaneous. It emerged from a century or more of injustice and brutality on both sides, and although the genocidaires struck back against innocents, they were provoked by heavily armed rebels, supplied by Uganda, while the U.S. looked on as tensions mounted. In the years that followed, President Clinton has repeatedly apologized for failing to support a UN force to end the genocide; neither he nor President H.W. Bush have ever apologized for allowing Uganda to create the conditions that their own CIA maintained could lead to genocide.

    The Rwandan army was no match for the RPF, and as the rebels advanced on the capital, more than a million Rwandan Hutus fled into neighboring Zaire—now known as the Democratic Republic of Congo—and settled in enormous refugee camps only a few miles from the Rwandan border. Most were women and children, but at least 30,000 of them were members of the former Rwandan army and militia groups that had carried out the genocide. With help from Zaire's President Marshal Mobutu Sese Seko they began arming themselves to re-take their country. Because the genocidaires blamed Uganda for their problems, they also formed alliances with Sudan-backed anti-Museveni rebels camped in eastern Zaire.

    Tensions between Uganda and Rwanda on one side, and Zaire and Sudan on the other had been building for years, and a crescendo was not long in coming. In 1996, the new Rwandan army, now known as the Rwandan Patriotic Army, or RPA, invaded the camps and herded most of the refugees back to

Rwanda, where they live under Tutsi domination to this day.
Hundreds of thousands of others fled deeper into Zaire and on
to other countries. In the years that followed, Rwanda's largely
Tutsi army tracked thousands of them down in the jungles of
Congo, and even on the streets and slums of other countries,
and killed them in cold blood. We'll never know who was innocent and who was an ex-genocidaire. The aim was vengeance,
not ethnic extermination, but there's little doubt that the killings amount to war crimes.

When Comrades Go to War, a detailed account of the
Congo conflict by political scientists Philip Roessler and
Harry Verhoeven, describes how U.S. Special Forces provided
advanced training for the lethal commandos that would carry
out these attacks only a few months later, but there is no evidence that the Americans knew what the commandos were
about to do. Then the RPA, along with the Ugandan army and
a new rebel group known as the Alliance of Democratic Forces
for the Liberation of Congo (or AFDL), which had been created, trained and armed by Uganda and Rwanda, marched to the
Zairean capital Kinshasa, toppled Mobutu, and installed their
own man, an addled Marxist and former kidnapper and gemstone trafficker named Laurent Kabila as president of Zaire.
He renamed the country Democratic Republic of Congo and
quickly fell out with his Rwandan and Ugandan backers, and
war resumed in 1998. Kabila was assassinated in 2001 and
replaced ten days later by his son Joseph. Although atrocities continue even now, the worst of the war was more or less
over by 2003, by which time hundreds of thousands—perhaps
millions—of people had died in what scholars now refer to as
Africa's Great War.

For five years, Museveni's army occupied a huge mineral-
rich swathe of Congolese territory, where his generals looted

32   some $10 billion worth of gold and other natural resources while backing proxy militias who massacred and raped thousands of Congolese.

In addition to the mayhem he created in Rwanda, Congo, Sudan and northern Uganda, Museveni also provoked or worsened at least two other African conflicts. In 2006 Museveni helped persuade the Bush administration to assist Ethiopia's brutal invasion of Somalia that nearly flattened the capital Mogadishu, causing more than half the Somali population to flee. The invasion provided the notorious terrorist group Al-Shabaab, until then a relatively small band of thugs, with the moral fervor to attract massive Gulf support, expand its ranks and metastasize into a full-fledged member of the Al Qaeda terrorist network.

Then in 2014, Uganda joined the South Sudan civil war on the side of the nation's ruthless president Salva Kiir Mayardit, greatly prolonging that conflict, at the cost of thousands of lives. Humantiarian groups and UN diplomats called for an arms embargo that would have effectively censured Uganda's intervention, but they were overruled by President Obama's National Security Advisor Susan Rice. Kiir eventually won the war and his army then proceeded to "eliminate" pockets of resistance around the country. Anyone suspected of disloyalty was in severe danger, and innocent men, women, and children were massacred. As famine loomed in 2016, the UN Human Rights Commission warned that the country was on the brink of genocide.

Museveni's contacts with Washington began early. Between 1987 and 1989, he met with President Ronald Reagan three years in a row, visited Reagan's California ranch, and hired a public relations firm run by Reagan's son-in-law Dennis Revell. Such close and frequent intercourse with U.S. presidents is unusual for any African leader, let alone a greenhorn, as Museveni was then. He has since had far more contact with high-level American and British officials than any other living African leader, and Western policymakers continue to publicly applaud him as a peacemaker, even as his army wreaks havoc in much of eastern and central Africa.

What explains this strange infatuation with Museveni? Is it just "Muddling in Bumbledom," as British historian Christopher Hamlin calls policymakers' all-too-human tendency to make mistakes when faced with situations they don't understand?

Or is it something else?

Here's what I think: all across Africa, elders still entertain children with fables about the powerful elephant, the angry lion, and the dopey hyena. The principal hero is always a weak but shrewd little creature—usually a hare or small antelope— who outsmarts them all with cunning and trickery. The stories are rooted, wrote the distinguished Africanist Alice Werner, in a deep conviction that the strong must not always win; the underdog must also have his day. When it comes to post–Cold War U.S.–Africa relations, Museveni has modeled himself on the wily, clever hare, and cast America's national security officials as the dim-witted lions, elephants, and hyenas. Whether they know it or not, he manipulates them at his pleasure by playing on their fears, and then leaving them flummoxed and humiliated in the midst of pandemonium they helped create but don't understand, while he leaps unscathed from one briar patch to the next.

In 1990, Museveni insisted he didn't support the RPF invasion of Rwanda; he then pretended his army didn't invade Zaire and had nothing to do with the toppling of Mobutu or the ongoing slaughter in the east of that country. In 2006, Museveni joined the George W. Bush administration as it waded into yet

34   another quagmire, this time in Somalia. In exchange for placing
      Uganda's army in the midst of this deadly and seemingly unwin-
      nable war, Museveni's government has since collected hundreds
      of millions of dollars; in 2014, Museveni claimed to be sending
      his army into South Sudan to protect and evacuate Ugandan
      civilians when in fact he was sending it to prop up the cruel dic-
      tatorship of President Salva Kiir Mayardit. In every case, the U.S.
      government could have tried to stop him, but did not.

      Most Americans think Africa is a low priority in Washington,
      but since 1997, the Africa staff of the National Security Council
      has tripled, and long before 9/11, the Pentagon began planning a
      network of military installations right across the continent from
      Somalia to Senegal. Now known as the U.S. Africa Command,
      or Africom, it is part of the global garrison created by the U.S.
      after the Cold War that today spans much of the northern hemi-
      sphere. A description of Africom was first shared publicly in a
      2000 article in the military journal *Parameters* in which Navy
      Commander Richard Catoire pointed to the predominance
      of Islamic cultures north of the Sahara and the mineral rich
      expanses of central Africa, which he characterized as a vast dys-
      topia of warlords, arms dealers, and humanitarian tragedies.
      "U.S. policy alone," he wrote ominously, "may not secure all of
      America's regional interests." A permanent military force would
      therefore be needed.

      Today, the 60 or so Africom bases, camps, compounds,
      port facilities, fuel bunkers, and other sites are predominantly
      manned by local African militaries, but can accommodate U.S.
      forces when necessary. They conduct drone strikes, counter-
      insurgency drills, and intelligence gathering. When asked the
      purpose of all this, Africom officials typically point to humani-
      tarian missions: tracking down the notorious warlord Joseph

Kony in the Central African Republic, or trying to rescue the schoolgirls kidnapped by Nigeria's Boko Haram militants. However, Africom officials themselves admit that their main aim is to preserve "the free flow of natural resources from Africa to the global market." Kenyan journalist Christine Mungai calls Africom a "hippo trench": Hippos attack some 3,000 people a year and Africans living near lakes sometimes build trenches around their gardens because hippos can't jump. In this case, the hippos are Islamic militants, or anyone else who might be interested in Congo's precious natural resources.

Uganda is a crucial transport and logistics hub for Africom, which maintains at least three installations in the country, at Entebbe, Kitgum, and Kasenyi. Year after year, Museveni's U.S.-trained army has proven highly effective in crushing nascent democracy movements, both in Uganda and in other countries. There appears to be no policy to restrain Museveni or other African tyrants from using America's large and growing military assistance to repress the aspirations of their people for democracy or rein in a tyrant's ambitions to plunder and destabilize other countries. The political implications of this are chilling.

In 2009, a wave of protest spread from Iran to the Arab world. It then crossed the Sahara desert, inciting uprisings against autocratic leaders in Burkina Faso, Burundi, Senegal, and the Democratic Republic of Congo, as well as in Uganda. No one knows what set it off, but one of the triggers may have been the election in November 2008 of Barack Obama, whose hero was Abraham Lincoln and whose most famous campaign speech honored those who "through protests and struggle, on the streets and in the courts, through a civil war and civil disobedience and always at great risk . . . [narrowed] that gap between the promise of our ideals and the reality of their time."

36   One person who took notice of Obama's election was a stocky, bespectacled 40-year-old Ugandan journalist named Lawrence Kiwanuka Nsereko, who lived in a second floor apartment in a run-down building near Vassar College in Poughkeepsie, New York. Lawrence had been fighting to bring democracy to his country since he was 14 years old. He'd been a child soldier, a reporter, an editor, a democracy activist, and a political candidate. He'd seen his newspaper offices ransacked, his party headquarters torched, friends and colleagues killed. He'd been arrested and tortured and narrowly escaped assassination himself. But he wasn't giving up now.

After Lawrence fled Uganda in 1995, nearly every physical copy of *The Citizen*, the newspaper he worked for, was destroyed. Two copies of each issue had been sent to Uganda's main university library, and others were stored in the newspaper's offices, but my own efforts to find them 20 years later nearly proved futile. The offices no longer existed and at the university, one librarian after another told me he had never heard of the publication. But during and for a few years after the Cold War, the U.S. government microfilmed nearly every periodical in the world; copies of many issues of *The Citizen* are stored in the Library of Congress, where I found them in 2015. Eventually, a courageous Ugandan intellectual made additional copies available to me in Kampala. In order to see them, I had to meet him at night and hide behind a bookcase. He would not tell me why such precautions were necessary, but as I turned the pages, I realized they told an extraordinary and little known story about some of the worst humanitarian tragedies since World War II.

Along with others, Lawrence witnessed the early moves in this brutal game and tried to warn Western diplomats. The journalists' efforts made no difference. The administrations of Reagan, George H.W. Bush, Clinton, George W. Bush and, alas, Obama as well, continued to provide Museveni with vast amounts of foreign aid, more open trade arrangements, and a quiet but steep increase in military assistance. Throughout the years of mayhem, decisions concerning the deployment of Ugandan troops would be made by Museveni alone or in consultation with U.S. national security officials, often without the democratic niceties of parliamentary or public debate. As long as Museveni cooperated, or appeared to cooperate, the U.S. and other Western nations ignored his corruption, rigged elections, and outrageous human rights abuses against Ugandans, Sudanese, South Sudanese, Rwandans, Congolese, and Somalis.

The reasons why U.S. security officials allowed Museveni to get away with this are known only to themselves. The rest of us may conclude, along with one of Lawrence's journalist colleagues, that Museveni simply "bewitched the Americans." The purpose of this book is to try to break that spell, for it is part of an escalating global paroxysm of violence in which states, rebels, militants, deranged individuals and over-zealous police and soldiers now vie daily for the bloodiest headlines.

There is a solution. Every nation on earth has signed on to the simple provisions of the Universal Declaration of Human Rights: States must never kill, torture, silence, or otherwise abuse their own citizens or those of other nations, ever. In 1989, America renewed its promise, broken during the Cold War, to fight for the realization of human rights wherever we have influence. Then, in a turn astonishing for its cynicism, one president after another broke it yet again by backing tyrant allies, funding rebel armies, invading other nations without cause, and ignoring the interests of people in much of the Middle East, Africa

38 and South Asia—while claiming to be acting in the name of democracy.

This militarism has set a moral tone for the world, inciting others to rebel, retaliate, or simply join in the chaos. It affects every one of us. The only way to stop it is to renew the pledge— and stick to it this time—to work continually for the human rights of everyone, everywhere.

The many Ugandan politicians, activists, journalists and others working still for freedom will never succeed without a shift in U.S. policy. Martin Luther King could not have ended Jim Crow had the Cold War not forced the U.S. to confront its shameful racist policies; Nelson Mandela could never have brought down Apartheid had the end of the Cold War not heralded the Soviet Union's decline. The heroic Ugandans described in this book need a similar shift, in this case American recognition that the War on Terror has not only failed, it has become itself a source of terror.

Africa's future matters. It is home to over one billion people, a number expected to quadruple in the next 90 years. Some African economies are already among the fastest-growing in the world, and the continent will soon become the source of much of the world's oil. But Africa can also seem like a perennial heart of darkness, wracked with hunger, poverty, and war without end.

But what if the story is different? What if the darkness is in our own hearts—as Joseph Conrad himself suspected? What if Western leaders' naïve dealings with African strongmen short circuits the power Africans might otherwise have over their own destiny? What if the aid we give sometimes entrenches corruption, impunity, brutality, and terror? What if our policymakers' singleminded focus on Africa's natural resources and other strategic interests is itself at the root of the continent's lawlessness? What if the condescending assumption that poor people of color are incapable of self-government and are more tolerant of oppression is wrong? What if the belief that Africa's politics are naturally more emotional and its wars more spontaneous and primitive than ours blinds us to the damaging effects of our own foreign policy? I didn't set out to ask these questions, but after many years working in various African countries, I couldn't get them out of my head.

How Your Taxes Support Corruption and Dictatorship in Uganda

U.S. foreign aid to Uganda comes from three main sources:

The U.S. Agency for International Development—or USAID—supports NGOs. This money is closely audited and relatively difficult to steal.

The U.S. Department of Defense supplies the Ugandan military with cash, training, equipment and weapons. Information about DOD projects is classified. U.S. taxpayers are not entitled to know how much money is spent on what.

The World Bank and other multilateral organizations like the Global Fund for AIDS, TB, and Malaria directly fund Uganda's general and/or sectoral budgets such as health, transport, education and so on. This money is intended to pay teachers, doctors and nurses; build roads and run ministries. It is seldom audited, is relatively easy to steal and has been the subject of numerous multi-million dollar scandals involving high-level Ugandan officials.

40 **A Note on Sources**

Political repression and the destruction of records and archives make covering recent African history particularly challenging. The inspiration for this book came from reading old copies of *The Citizen* and other Ugandan publications, whose reporting, in retrospect, has turned out to be remarkably accurate. Reporting these stories at the time took enormous courage.

In much of Africa, local scholars and journalists are often dismissed as politicized and untrustworthy, especially if their views are at odds with U.S. policy. This is not only unfair; it is also dangerous, because while local sources may have interests, the well-groomed spokespersons for the West's autocratic allies do too. Even journalists in the supposedly free world are subject to subtle government influence. In 2010, Yale economist Nancy Qian found that during the Cold War, major U.S. news outlets including *The New York Times* and the *Washington Post* were significantly less likely to report on human rights abuses committed by developing country governments that were U.S. allies than those considered Soviet-leaning. In some cases, the State Department's Human Rights Bureau downplayed our allies' abuses; in others, editors and journalists knew they risked being denied access to government briefings and insider tips if they didn't toe the U.S. government's line. There's no reason to think such mechanisms stopped operating after the Berlin Wall fell.

The failure to consult and take seriously local dissident sources like *The Citizen* has led many Western diplomats, journalists and academics to deny the existence of Museveni's torture chambers; to assert that Museveni's election victories are uncontroversial, to claim that Ugandan rebel groups have no legitimate grievances against Museveni's government, to maintain that the atrocities in northern Uganda were the fault of the deranged warlord Joseph Kony alone, and to commit other deadly blunders described in this book.

Uganda's Origins: From Many, One and From One, Many

A king, good or bad, will go the way he comes, for he will never rule over your laughter and your tears.

—Ejigayehu Shibabaw

Lawrence Nsereko's father Joseph was a Ugandan aristocrat. His suits bore not a single wrinkle, and although his accent was poor, his English grammar was impeccable. His pompous habit of correcting others earned him the nickname *Mungereza,* meaning Englishman in the local Luganda language. Joseph's grandfather had been a collaborator during the early years of colonial rule, and in exchange for ensuring the locals complied with British policies, he received a large tract of land, much of which Joseph eventually inherited. Some was used to grow coffee for export; some was reserved for family gardens—maize, yams, beans, bananas—some was used for grazing cattle, and

the rest was rented. Joseph also owned some grocery stores, so
money came in easily.

Joseph had at least seven wives, perhaps more—Lawrence
isn't sure. Some of the women lived together in the same house;
others lived on their own, but they shared everything and all of
them referred to Lawrence and each of his more than 40 brothers and sisters as "our child." Lawrence moved around from the
house of one co-mother to another, usually, he says, depending
upon who was cooking chicken, his favorite food. When one co-
wife's maize patch ripened late, she would notify another that
she was taking some from her garden. No one asked permission
or kept accounts. Joseph would sometimes bring babies home
"from wherever," Lawrence says now, presumably the product of
one of his numerous affairs. Lawrence's co-mothers would raise
these children as their own as well.

Today, Lawrence puzzles over this arrangement. There was
great animosity among the co-wives in many other families.
Sometimes Lawrence's last and youngest co-mother could
be cantankerous as well, but the others never seemed angry,
either at Joseph's philandering, or at each other. Only two of
his co-mothers remain alive, and if he ever manages to return
to Uganda, he'd like to ask them what they were thinking. All
could read and write, but they seemed immune to modern
individualistic competition. When AIDS began spreading in
the 1980s, Lawrence, by then an adult, moved his biological
mother Agnes into a modern house some distance from his
father and the others, hoping to protect her from the scourge.
After a year, she sold the house and moved back in with a
co-wife.

Lawrence's family was nominally Catholic, but Joseph knew
that his philandering ways prevented him from taking Holy

44   Communion. "I can't afford for you to be sinners too," he told his children, "So you must all go to Heaven and pray for my soul." Every Sunday he sat on a stool outside the church and looked in through the window to ensure all his children took the wafers and wine.

Lawrence's people were Baganda, Uganda's largest tribe. When British explorer John Hanning Speke first arrived in Buganda—as the Baganda call their territory—in 1862, he found a vast, well-organized kingdom ruled by a Kabaka (or king) named Mutesa who could recite the names of his forebears back 32 generations. Mutesa was advised by a prime minister known as a Katikiro and an appointed parliament of chiefs known as a Lukiiko. Below them were clan heads, known as Bataka, and below them peasants and at the bottom, slaves captured during raids on neighboring tribes. The Kabaka's palace was a huge circular dome crowned with a magnificent shag of grass thatch. Ordinary people lived along straight roads in gracefully constructed houses made from woven reeds and wore hazel-colored draperies fashioned from the inner bark of the ficus tree pounded until it was as soft as felt.

Because of Buganda's isolation, the economy was virtually static. The only way to elevate oneself was through warfare: conquering others and demanding tribute, looting ivory, livestock, and slaves and occupying land. The ivory and some of the slaves were sold to Arab traders from the coast of what is now Tanzania in exchange for beads from Europe and copper from Katanga 1,000 miles away. One explorer even reported that a piece of cloth labeled "Wachusetts Mills" that had come all the way from New England, hung in the Kabaka's palace. But the most coveted Arab imports were guns, percussion caps and powder.

Mutesa had no standing army, but his war drums could summon 250,000 men and hundreds of war canoes. Military

might was all. Cowards were ostracized or killed. Even today,
Ugandans have an inordinate respect for their military heroes.
It's hard to imagine an American rap musician trying to seem
cool by calling himself Colonel and performing in uniform
alongside a CIA director or member of the Joint Chiefs of Staff,
but such things happen in Uganda, where it's also normal for
army officers to turn up at fashionable discos or appear on TV
opining about religion, love, and romance.

In his memoirs, the nineteenth-century explorer Henry
Morton Stanley boasts of his special relationship with Mutesa,
but it was not Stanley's charm alone that attracted the Kabaka.
Mutesa was worried about Egyptian garrisons to the north,
and pleaded with his Welsh visitor for weapons with which to
defend himself. Instead, the explorer sent missionaries. Mutesa
grudgingly allowed them to teach reading and writing to his
young pages, the 400 or so teenaged boys who ran errands for
the royal family and guarded the palace. Catholic missionaries
arrived from France two years after the Anglicans, and Arab holy
men also vied for the Kabaka's favor.

The newcomers were impressed by the Buganda court,
but also shocked by its cruelty. Sometimes the Kabaka seemed
to kill his subjects just for sport. During the 1840s, an Arab
trader named Ahmed bin Abraham bravely told Mutesa's father
Kabaka Suna that his victims were Allah's creatures, and it was
wrong to destroy them. Suna replied that he knew of no other
way of preventing conspiracies and keeping his subjects in awe
of him.

Mutesa died in 1884 and his hemp-smoking 18-year-old
son Mwanga ascended the throne. Mwanga saw the emerging
religious movements in his kingdom politically, and was deeply
concerned about the growing power of the Christians. He chafed
at his Bible-reading pages, who exchanged their white kanzus

46   for more elaborate dress, sneaked out of the palace at night and gossiped about Mwanga behind his back. The Arabs stoked the young Kabaka's fears. The missionaries were an advance guard, they said, and were turning his pages against him; the orphans they cared for were a secret army; reinforcements would soon come from the coast to annex Buganda, force everyone to marry only one wife, and free their slaves.

Between 1885 and 1887, Mwanga had 45 Christian pages put to death. First, their arms were severed and then they were slowly burned alive, singing Christian hymns as they died. Some were accused of spying for the missionaries; others, having learned that sodomy was a sin, were killed for refusing to perform this act upon the bisexual Mwanga. Their abstinence seems to have enraged the young Kabaka less than the thought that their new religious faith was stronger than his own mystique.

A shrine to the Uganda Martyrs now stands at Namugongo, a village just east of Kampala. In 2014, the Ugandan government passed a law imposing harsh penalties on homosexuals. The law was born out of an internecine power struggle among Ugandan politicians not worth explaining here, but fear of homosexuals remains widespread in the country, where there has been little modern sex education and where the idea of homosexuality evokes historical memories of a mad young king at the dawn of modern times, whose territory swirled with rumors of approaching armies.

After the Martyrs' execution, a series of ferocious battles among Catholics, Protestants, and Muslims rocked Buganda. The causes remain poorly understood, but everything began to settle down after the arrival in 1890 of British Captain Frederick Lugard who armed the Protestants against the others, planted the British flag, and exiled Kabaka Mwanga to the Seychelles, where he died in 1903.

The British, using the Baganda as a sub-Imperial force, eventually conquered four smaller kingdoms within the borders of what became the Ugandan Protectorate: Toro, Busoga, Bunyoro, and Ankole—along with numerous smaller tribes and clans that did not have kings such as the Acholi and Langi of northern Uganda and the Teso in the east. The locals did not yield without a struggle. Historian Ogenga Otunnu has detailed how the British, their Baganda troops, and Sudanese mercenaries committed numerous atrocities including mass rape, the torching of entire villages, the herding of people into concentration camps, the theft of cattle and the humiliation of local leaders. In Acholiland, Acting Commissioner J.R.P. Postlethwaite, nicknamed "chicken thief" by the Acholi, publicly strung up a rebellious chief and lowered him head first into a pit latrine until he died. In a British-backed operation against the Bavuma people, "such was the enormity of the slaughter," wrote historian Michael Twaddle, "that, not only were sections of Lake Victoria 'all blood', there were so many dead bodies bobbing up and down in the water that their heads resembled a multitude of upturned cooking pots."

The colony was overseen by a British governor, who was soon joined by British teachers, doctors and others. There were few settlers so race relations, though hardly smooth, were not as bad as those in colonies like Kenya and Rhodesia where large numbers of Africans were thrown off their land to make way for white-owned farms. However, the British did introduce a tribal caste system, the legacy of which still divides the nation today.

Although the Baganda had helped them conquer Uganda, by World War II, the army comprised mainly northerners such as the Acholi and Langi, who made up 70 percent of all Africans enlisted for the Allies.

Meanwhile, the Baganda and other southern tribes, deemed by the British to be more civilized, received more education,

48   grew crops for export, staffed the civil service and considered themselves superior to the northerners.

As soon as Lugard's gunpowder cleared, Baganda elites began building brick houses, learning to ride horses, wearing shoes, carrying umbrellas, eating with knives and forks, serving tea to visitors, writing on typewriters, marrying one wife with a ring, and giving their children Christian names like Benedicto, Boniface and Polycarp—or at least western sounding ones like Yusufu, Yacobo and Yokosofati.Outward appearances were one thing, however; inner attitudes, beliefs, and behaviors another. The Baganda, and the people of Uganda's other ethnic groups thereafter existed in multiple worlds. They looked up to their betters, but mocked them in proverbs and songs; they professed the ideal of monogamy, but didn't always practice it; they respected truthfulness, but their folk hero was the hare, the eternal role model of the oppressed, who outwits his more powerful adversaries with charm, cunning, and deceit.

If Uganda's post-independence whirlpools of revenge have a source, it lies not in Uganda but at Lancaster House, a solemn Georgian mansion near London's Green Park. There, in early October 1961, Britain's Secretary of State for the Colonies Ian MacLeod presided over a gathering of some 50 Ugandan delegates to discuss the fledgling nation's future constitution. The British had created the trappings of a democratic system, with a Parliament, a system of local government, and a hierarchy of courts with judges in horsehair wigs, but at that meeting, they kicked the foundation right out from under it.

Topping the agenda was the mechanism for choosing representatives to Uganda's National Assembly (the precursor of its Parliament), which would then elect the prime minister. On one side were the modernizers who favored one-person-one-vote suffrage; on the other were the traditionalists who wanted

MPs chosen by representatives of tribal kingdoms, such as
Buganda.

Underlying this technicality was a profound question that
has yet to be answered, and not only in Uganda: How should
people be governed? Whose leadership will they respect? Even
today most Ugandans rely upon tribe, clan, and family for just
about everything, from jobs, to justice, to social security from
birth to death as well as for a sense of identity and meaning in
life. Uganda was about to become a modern state, with a government that was supposed to provide many of these things, but
few Ugandans understood how this would work in practice. Nor
did they trust people they didn't know to govern fairly. Certainly
the colonial government favored some tribes over others. Their
fellow Ugandans could only be expected to do the same.

The main advocate for a tribally appointed National
Assembly was Buganda's Kabaka Edward Mutesa II, Mwanga's
37-year-old, Cambridge-educated grandson. Fearful that a
strong Kabaka could be trouble, the British had molded Mutesa
II into a weak, pampered royal like one of their own. He and his
circle had benefited enormously under the Protectorate, and
were loath to surrender their privileges. The colonial administration paid their salaries, funded the activities of the royal
administration, and built the fine white palace at Mengo from
which it operated. In England, they put the Kabaka up in the
best hotels, introduced him to Princess Margaret, and bought
him a Rolls Royce with ivory knobs fashioned from the tusks of
elephants he shot himself. There was a natural affinity between
the Baganda aristocracy and the laid-back upper class British
civil servants who arrived to administer the Protectorate. Life
at the palace during the six decades of colonial rule sometimes
seemed like an endless round of shooting parties, picnics, and
outings on Lake Victoria. When matters of policy came up,

50   they tended to be dealt with in whispers on the periphery of cocktail parties.

In 1952, Andrew Cohen, a young progressive governor, arrived to prepare Uganda for independence. When the subject of one-person-one-vote suffrage came up, Mutesa II informed Cohen that he was having none of it. He and his hand-picked Buganda legislature, known as the Lukiiko, didn't want to be represented by commoner Baganda or—perish the thought— men from other tribes. If they couldn't appoint Buganda's MPs themselves, they'd happily secede from Uganda. Cohen sent Mutesa into exile, hoping his subjects would soon forget their quisling king. But to his surprise, the Baganda staged vehement protests and boycotts. Farmers went on strike and nearly shut down the economy. The Kabaka returned, more arrogant than ever. He agreed to keep Buganda in Uganda, but insisted that he and his Lukiiko choose Uganda's future MPs.

At Lancaster House everyone knew that since roughly 25 percent of Uganda's population was Baganda, a Lukiiko "electoral college" would give Mutesa enormous power over the entire country. Opposing him was the modernizer Benedicto Kiwanuka, a commoner Muganda (singular of Baganda) and leader of the Democratic Party (or DP), which favored universal suffrage throughout the country.Hoping to free his people and the rest of Uganda from the Kabaka's "selfish political racketeers"he wanted the Kabaka out of national affairs. It was widely believed that had an election been conducted on a one-person-one-vote basis, the DP would have prevailed and Kiwanuka would have become prime minister.

But the man who won the day at Lancaster House was Milton Obote, a shrewd, hot-tempered political operator from the northern Ugandan district of Lira whose Uganda People's Congress party drew patchy support mainly from outside of

Buganda. His parents had named him Apollo, but he'd adopted
the name Milton out of admiration for the British poet and
statesman. Like Kiwanuka and his namesake John, Obote hated
hereditary privilege and favored direct, universal elections
throughout Uganda. But he also resented Kiwanuka, simply
because he was a Muganda. Like many northerners, Obote felt,
with some justification, that the British had given the Baganda
all the advantages, and he would sacrifice his democratic ideals
for a chance at power and revenge.

Lurking in the shadows of the Lancaster House conference
was Archbishop of Canterbury Geoffrey Fisher. Throughout the
empire, the British had tried to make Protestantism the established religion. Even though most Ugandans were Catholic, the
Kabaka and his circle were Protestants; Protestant bishops and
priests worked behind the scenes to smooth over political dis-
agreements between Ugandans and their British administrators;
Protestant regalia was dusted off for official state ceremonies;
Protestant students were favored for university admission and
scholarships overseas, and Protestants tended to get the best
civil service jobs and adopted the Anglicans' snobbery toward
Catholics. Archbishop Fisher wanted to keep it that way, but he
knew that Kiwanuka, a Catholic, was the most popular politician in the country.

During Mutesa II's exile, Fisher had gently counseled the
young Kabaka on his numerous extramarital affairs. These sessions had no effect on Mutesa II's sexual behavior, but they did
create a bond between the two men.

Shortly before the Lancaster House meeting, the Kabaka
created a new, chauvinistically Protestant political party
called Kabaka Yekka (or KY) meaning King Alone in Luganda.
Members of its youth wing chanted insults and brandished
spears at Catholic politicians, dressed a sheep in the costume

52   of the Catholic Archbishop, and even killed a woman during an anti-Catholic riot as the British authorities stood by and did virtually nothing.

Shortly before the Lancaster House meeting Obote and Mutesa made a deal. KY and UPC would form a coalition to block Kiwanuka's DP from power. In exchange for the Kabaka's support, Obote would allow Buganda to elect its National Assembly representatives indirectly, through Mutesa's hand-picked Lukiiko. The rest of the country would enjoy universal suffrage, but the combination of Buganda's and UPC's MPs would push Obote ahead of Kiwanuka.

Kiwanuka only learned that Colonial Secretary MacLeod approved of the compact between Mutesa II's KY and Obote's UPC on the first day of the Lancaster House meeting. He stormed out at once; then returned, and stormed out again, along with his supporters. The day after this second exit, Kiwanuka received a message from Archbishop Fisher urging him to accept the UPC-Kabaka-Yekka arrangement gracefully.

Kiwanuka shot back, "Can you, Archbishop, support these wicked moves, knowing fully their implications, and still feel quite safe in your conscience?" The deal would essentially dis-enfranchise the Baganda—a quarter of the country—he pointed out. Fisher's condescending reply stressed the need for compromise, the lack of a perfect political system anywhere in the world, and a concern for "temper of mind."

There was nothing Kiwanuka could do. Obote became prime minister and in the years that followed, Mutesa would be routed from Uganda by Obote's army and Kiwanuka would be arrested, humiliated, and eventually murdered by Obote's successor Idi Amin.

Obote began scheming against Mutesa as soon as the British departed in 1962. First, he returned part of Buganda territory to its traditional rivals, the Banyoro, from whom it had been taken after the British granted it as a reward for Buganda's help in conquering Bunyoro in 1896. Mutesa reacted in fury; his people gathered at roadsides and slaughtered goats and sheep to invoke their gods to curse the prime minister. Obote bided his time and began stacking the army with officers from his own tribe.

In 1965, Mutesa discovered that Obote and deputy army commander Idi Amin were funneling weapons to Congolese rebels. The matter was referred to Parliament where the MPs, already chafing under Obote's authoritarianism, considered ousting him.

On the morning of April 15, 1966, MPs arrived at Parliament to find a new constitution in their pigeonholes. Obote sat in the Speaker's chair and ordered them to vote on it that day, without even reading it. If the MPs required a hint as to whether or not to approve it, they need only observe the army trucks parked outside the Parliament building and the air force planes circling overhead. What later became known as the "pigeonhole constitution" gave Obote executive powers over virtually every government activity.

Obote accused Mutesa of instigating the parliamentary rebellion, stockpiling weapons, and asking his British friends to assist in a coup. On May 22, Mutesa's Lukiiko angrily ordered Obote's government out of Kampala, which happened to be Buganda territory. The following day, reconnaissance planes were seen flying over the palace and police began blocking off the roads around it. Hundreds of people, virtually all unarmed, gathered inside the palace to defend their king, or just to be near him. On May 24, the Kabaka awoke to sounds of gunfire. Idi Amin's troops had surrounded the palace. In his memoirs, Mutesa recalls the screams of a woman as she burned to death and the

54   sight of his horses galloping to and fro, mad with fear. Hundreds
      of people, perhaps more, were killed during the ensuing raid on
      the palace. It took two days to clear the bodies. Precious artifacts
      including the royal drums, hundreds of years old, were burned
      and smashed.

      Mutesa II managed to escape and eventually fled to London
      where he died in poverty three years later. Buganda had been
      conquered, but just as in John Milton's seventeenth-century
      England, this did not lead to republican utopia. In 1971, Idi Amin
      overthrew Obote, and installed his own reign of terror. In 1979,
      Ugandan rebels backed by the Tanzanian army overthrew Amin.
      After a chaotic interim during which the nation was ruled by a
      Tanzania-backed military commission and two presidents who
      were installed and toppled within months, elections were held
      in December 1980. The main candidates were Obote, back at the
      helm of the UPC, and Kiwanuka's protégé Paul Ssemogerere, the
      gentle intellectual leader of the Democratic Party.

      Voting took two days and on the morning of the second day,
      the head of the Electoral Commission called Ssemogerere to
      congratulate him. The DP was way ahead. Crowds began gath-
      ering to celebrate. Then, at 11 a.m., military commission chief
      Paulo Muwanga announced that vote counts were no longer to be
      reported at polling stations. The results would have to go through
      him, and he would announce the final tally. Transgressors faced
      a huge fine and five years in jail. The DP revelers were dispersed
      with gunfire. The 10,000 Tanzanian troops still stationed in
      the country did nothing to defend Uganda against this apparent
      coup, and Muwanga declared Obote the winner.

      In early 1982 Lawrence's father Joseph went into hiding.
      Rebel groups were operating in his area, and President Obote
      suspected that prominent Baganda like Joseph, still furious
      about the destruction of their kingdom and the rigging of the

election, were supporting them. Seven of Joseph's friends were
arrested around the same time and never seen again.

Money became tighter, but Lawrence's co-mothers worked
together to make ends meet. One day, two government officials
came to the house to collect taxes. "Our husband has gone away,"
one of the women told them, "We need what we have for the
children." The men proceeded to beat her until she collapsed.
Lawrence witnessed the attack, and resolved to join the rebels at
once. He was 14 years old.

The rebel group Lawrence joined was known as the Uganda
Freedom Movement (or UFM) led by Andrew Lutaakome
Kayiira, a Muganda former prisons officer with a Ph.D. who
had briefly taught criminal justice at a community college in
upstate New York. Kayiira had visited Joseph once or twice, and
although the boy hadn't really understood what the men talked
about so long into the night, he admired the tall, good looking
visitor, who pinched his cheeks and made his father laugh.

One of Joseph's friends knew Kayiira. At first the older man
laughed when Lawrence said he wanted to join the rebels, but
when the boy insisted, he realized that a kid in a school uniform
might make a good scout, and Lawrence soon began ferrying
messages, medicine, and other supplies back and forth between
Kayiira's base camp and his supporters in the town.

For months, Baganda soldiers had been quietly stealing weapons from government arsenals and handing them over to
Kayiira's UFM. Libyan leader Muammar Gaddafi, champion of
underdog rebels across Africa, arranged for further clandestine
arms shipments.

Shortly after Lawrence joined the UFM, some of Kayiira's
men set up rocket launchers on the grounds of Kampala's
Catholic Cathedral which stood on a hill overlooking an army

56 barracks. Obote's soldiers fled when the rebels began firing and a UFM soldier made off with a truckload of mortars, grenades, automatic rifles, and ammunition. On the way back to Kayiira's basecamp, he was ambushed. The soldiers who took the weapons weren't from Obote's army; they were from another rebel group, known as the National Resistance Army, or NRA. Their leader was Yoweri Museveni.

Kayiira and Museveni should have been allies, but Museveni seemed as intent on fighting him as Obote. Soon after the barracks raid, government reinforcements stormed Kayiira's forest base camp. Both UFM and government soldiers suffered casualties, but the rebels suffered far more. Kayiira's men fled into the bush. The UFM disbanded soon after, and Kayiira left for the U.S., where he hoped to raise money to regroup. Veteran NRA sources told me the location of Kayiira's camp was no secret, but Kayiira suspected that Obote's soldiers were tipped off by Museveni, who wanted to rid Uganda of a rival.

Lawrence was in his village when the raid occurred, but one of Kayiira's operatives ordered him back to the forest to help the stranded rebels. On the way, he was stopped by soldiers conducting a mop-up operation.

"Where are you going?" one of them asked.

"To school," replied Lawrence, who was wearing his uniform.

"But all the schools are closed because of insecurity," the soldier said, and with that, they arrested him. Lawrence was questioned for hours in the local police station. When he insisted he knew nothing about the rebels, he was taken to a larger police station, asked more questions, beaten with a stick by several officers, and thrown in a cell where he remained for several days.

Eventually, a kindly warden, wondering what such a young boy was doing behind bars, gave him some cookies. When the warden returned later, he found Lawrence unconscious. He took him to a hospital in Kampala were he recovered and was discharged to the care of Ojok Mulozi, then publicity secretary for the Democratic Party, and a friend of his father's.

"I was not in a strange land," Lawrence remembers of his new life in the city. Early on, Ojok brought him to the national DP headquarters on Johnstone Street downtown. Everyone there knew Joseph and Lawrence was soon introduced to the editor of *The Citizen*, the DP's newspaper. Lawrence volunteered to serve as a scout, just as he had for Kayiira. He traveled around southern Uganda in his school uniform collecting information which *Citizen* journalists would then turn into stories. One of Lawrence's scoops concerned an attack on a mosque in a village called Kamwoya. A band of rebels, believing some of the worshippers to be Obote spies, stormed the building, killing dozens of worshippers. Lawrence couldn't confirm whether the rebels were NRA or FEDEMU—a new rebel group formed from the remnants of Kayiira's UFM, but the brutality of the attack shocked him, and he tried writing the story himself. The editor was impressed and soon the now-15-year-old Lawrence was writing regularly for the paper.

The Citizen wasn't a polished publication. Galleys were prepared on an ordinary typewriter, and if someone made a mistake or breaking news came through at press time, the typist would have to redo the whole page. Last-minute corrections were made by pen. Lines of type were sometimes crooked and malapropisms like "Detainees Brutally Buttered in Central Police Post," and "dust to down curfew" were common. Ads were arranged by errant cabinet ministers and civil servants willing to do favors or pay outright to keep their peccadillos—sexual

58   and otherwise—out of the news. Because *The Citizen* was an opposition paper, it could be dangerous for companies' names to appear in it. For years, an ad for a tiny Forex Bureau that didn't actually exist appeared in each issue. The ad cost the equivalent of a two-page spread and was paid for by a bank manager who risked ruin if government operatives discovered his opposition sympathies.

Before long, Obote banned *The Citizen* along with several other newspapers. Soldiers ransacked the office and destroyed the printing press. But *The Citizen* had a Luganda version called *Munannsi* (which means citizen), and the editors quickly launched an English version of that. When Obote tried to ban *Munannsi* (English version), the editors devised a mobile printing press by hiding a mimeograph machine in the back of a van. As the van drove around the city, Lawrence ran off copies and dropped bundles of them at secret locations where street hawkers—many of them former UFM rebels happy to find employment—knew where to find them. *Munannsi* (English version) soon became the most widely read newspaper in Uganda.

The war raged on after Kayiira's defeat, but Museveni was a very different type of adversary. Where Kayiira was a jovial bon vivant, Museveni was a shrewd, enigmatic tactician. Kayiira's base camp was like "a picnic site" according to one observer, well supplied with both imported Johnny Walker whiskey and locally brewed alcohol, as well as young women, some of whom were later revealed to be Obote's spies. Museveni didn't drink, and expected his men to abstain as well.

Unlike Kayiira's bleary-eyed drunks and Obote's poorly educated thugs who might beat a person just for speaking good English or wearing a necktie, Museveni's troops seldom brawled, stole, or harassed women. Their camp was well-organized, and

indiscipline was punished. Museveni taught his recruits revolutionary lore from Mao's *Little Red Book* and Sun Tzu's *The
Art of War,* and lectured them about the goals of revolution. For
young men aspiring to the radical intellectualism fashionable
across Africa in those days, he was a hero. "One cannot really
describe the awe in which we held these handsome young men,"
wrote one NRA soldier many years later.

Museveni was born, he thinks, in 1944. Few births were
registered in those days, and his parents were nomads from the
Western Uganda Bahima subgroup of the Banyankole people,
closely related to the Tutsis of Rwanda and Burundi. He grew up
around cattle, but developed a fascination with warfare early on.
He'd been a teenager in the 1950s when the British were leaving
and was beguiled by their guns and uniforms. One of his teachers remembers the boy marching around pretending to be a field
marshal. The only books that seemed to interest him concerned
weapons and military strategy. At Tanzania's University of Dar
es Salaam in the late 1960s, he led a radical student group which
organized demonstrations against Apartheid, screened docu-
mentaries on socialist topics, and held weekly seminars at which
Museveni and the others railed against the colonial, the settler,
and the insidious imperialist mentality of their professors.

Museveni's senior thesis explored Frantz Fanon's theory
that violence could be a cleansing force when committed in the
name of revolution. For fieldwork, he traveled to Mozambique
during the independence war and wrote of the alleged empow-
ering effect on peasants of gazing upon the severed heads of
Portuguese soldiers.

After university, Museveni worked briefly for Obote as an
intelligence officer before Obote was overthrown by Amin. He
then launched a rebel group, The Front for National Salvation
or FRONASA, which joined forces with Obote's exiles and the

60   Tanzanian army to oust Amin. During the chaotic interregnum after Amin's overthrow, Museveni served as vice chairman of Paulo Muwanga's military commission and then ran for president in 1980 as flagbearer of his own party, the Uganda Patriotic Movement. Like many brilliant military commanders, he was a poor politician and would have lost heavily, even if Obote hadn't rigged the vote.

In *From Obote to Obote*, a history of Uganda in verse, Obote's cousin Akena Adoko, who'd worked briefly with Museveni in Obote's spy agency, describes him as follows:

It was easier to describe him
By negatives....
He sneered at almost everybody.
I would say, "But surely
The Vice President is doing everything
With obvious successes,
To increase the population
Of exotic cattle
In the hands of the farmers...."
Answer: "He is a snake."
Question: "And what about Onama...."
Answer: "That is a CIA."
....
In the case of Museveni
The passion developed
To morbid degree
Is one for political power.
The monomania to rule over others.

* * *

Museveni based the NRA's military strategy on Mao Zedong's
concept of a "protracted people's war," —or what author Robert
Taber called "the war of the flea"—that had enabled the Chinese
and North Vietnamese communists to prevail over much larger,
state-backed armies. Museveni had seen a protracted people's
war in action in Mozambique, where FRELIMO rebels used the
method successfully against the Portuguese. The aim wasn't to
achieve victory immediately, but to establish bases in remote
areas, draw the enemy deep into the interior, and then confuse and
exhaust it and deplete its morale by moving unpredictably from
place to place. The rebels also launched occasional hit-and-run
attacks on army barracks and other targets, knowing they'd provoke brutal and disproportionate responses, which would alienate
both the local population and the international community.

Obote fell right into the trap. His security forces, which
rarely engaged in torture during his first administration in
the 1960s, unleashed a reign of terror. People were robbed and
killed by drunken soldiers at ubiquitous military checkpoints;
suspected rebels were rounded up at soccer matches and markets and detained for months in crowded underground cells,
subsisting on maggot-infested corn meal. To elicit information, detainees were beaten, crippled, and rendered impotent
by having weights suspended from their testicles; molten plastic was dripped onto bare flesh and in one case, according to a
Commission of Inquiry established after the war, friends were
forced to bite off each other's noses. Dead bodies appeared in
forests and on roadsides and beaches. "We beat the truth out
of him," one of Obote's officers told a priest who had come to
collect the body of a victim and noticed an eye hanging from its
socket, "But he died of natural causes."

At first, reports of these abuses failed to elicit condemnation from Uganda's main international aid donors, the British

62   government and the largely U.S.-controlled World Bank. Then in May 1984, news reached Washington that "hundreds of thousands" of Ugandans had been killed in government offensives against NRA rebels in the Luwero triangle—a huge bushy rural area of Buganda where Museveni's troops were camped. At a congressional hearing in June, President Reagan's Undersecretary of State for Human Rights Elliott Abrams called for a review of America's Uganda policy.

It's important to note that the NRA also committed atrocities, although they were far less brutal and numerous than those committed by Obote's army. Some killings were reprisals against suspected traitors; others were "false flags"—attacks made to look as though they were committed by the government army, but were actually the work of the NRA.

In 2013, Paul Lubwana, a villager who lost his entire family in the war told *The Monitor* newspaper that Museveni's "rebels began camouflaging in government army uniforms, stormed villages, and acted any way they desired to tarnish the government's image." Several NRA veterans confirmed to me and other reporters that the NRA sometimes burst into people's houses at night, dragged them into the forest, interrogated and then killed them.

According to historian Michael Twaddle, apportioning blame for atrocities was difficult because of "the propensity of guerrillas to dress like soldiers, and for soldiers to dress like guerrillas . . . no reasonable person can easily decide these days who is a soldier, who is a guerrilla and who is just an armed thug."

In his 2011 memoir, NRA Major John Kazoora describes an NRA massacre of Obote-loyalists belonging to the Alur tribe. "They would dig a shallow grave," he writes, "tie you [up] and lie you facing the ground and crack your skull using an old hoe called Kafuni."

In some cases, the NRA may even have killed its own. At
first Museveni mainly recruited from his own Banyankole tribe
and Buganda, but after Obote brutally forced the Tutsi refugees
into camps where many starved and died, some of them joined
the rebellion as well. They grew close to Museveni, whose Hima
people are closely related to the Tutsis, and soon began to
dominate the force. Toward the end of the war, Muganda NRA
soldiers began dying mysteriously and some suspected foul
play. "We were fighting tribalism," one Muganda NRA veteran
told *The Monitor* newspaper, "but it was growing in the bush."

In 1983, Museveni warned all Westerners, including aid
workers and diplomats, to leave Uganda at once. "We don't
possess the power to prevent accidents," he wrote in a signed
letter issued by his representatives in Kenya. Three weeks
later, a Canadian engineer was gunned down on his doorstep
in Kampala; four other European aid workers were killed a few
months later. While the killers were never definitively identified, the NRA had kidnapped and released four other Swiss
hostages and a French doctor around the same time.

Even now, these abuses are little known outside of Luwero,
because Museveni proved to be a genius at propaganda. Abrams'
source that Obote's military had killed "hundreds of thousands"
of people in the Luwero Triangle was a report in the *Washington
Post* by a journalist who was in Washington at the time, but
cited "well-informed" U.S. sources and unnamed human rights
groups. It's likely that the *Post* reporter's source was a British
freelancer who had visited Luwero a few months earlier, when
it was briefly under Museveni's control. In London's *Observer*
newspaper, he described touring Luwero with Museveni's rebels
and being shown five mass graves with thousands of skulls. He
was then given a list of 30 other sites. In all, Museveni told him
in an interview, the army probably killed 300,000 people.

64   But when a journalist for the London *Daily Telegraph*, the *Observer's* right-leaning rival, visited one of the villages where the army was alleged to have massacred hundreds of people a year earlier, he found "nothing to support [these] claims." The army had withdrawn to allow the *Telegraph* reporter to freely interview the chief and villagers. "The surprise these people showed when asked about a massacre could not have been an act," he wrote. However, they did mention that Museveni's rebels had recently killed three men and four children. Some of the rebels came from the area and locals recognized them. "They were dressed halfway," the chief said. "I mean they were in army and civilian clothes, all mixed up."

The truth of what really happened in Luwero probably lies between the accounts in the *Telegraph* and the *Observer*. As the army advanced, Obote's special forces led a ruthless counter-insurgency campaign in which many rebel sympathizers, real and alleged, were killed. Hundreds of thousands of others fled to makeshift camps where epidemics of measles and malaria swept through the starving crowds—in part because the Red Cross and other groups, fearing rebel ambushes, couldn't reach them. Horrible as conditions were, the total number of deaths was likely in the tens, not hundreds of thousands. As in most wars, responsibility lay on both sides.

Whatever the reality, Abrams' testimony contributed to a change of heart about Obote, and the donors soon began pulling out.

In July 1985, Obote's troops, under the command of Brigadier Basilio Okello, mutinied. The NRA was in retreat at the time, and Museveni was with his family in Sweden where they had been given sanctuary by the UN Refugee Agency. He returned to Uganda at once, and Okello's men offered the NRA weapons if it would join forces against Obote, who was ousted the same month. Kayiira also returned to Uganda and he, Museveni, and Okello met for peace talks in Nairobi, Kenya. But Museveni displayed little interest in negotiation. He referred to Okello's men as "primitives" and "criminals" who didn't understand the "art of revolution"; he agreed to items on the agenda only after lengthy, painstaking discussion and then changed his mind; he left the venue for days on end without notice and at one point his commanders even shredded an agreement before the mediators' eyes. Meanwhile, NRA rebels, now armed with weapons given them by Okello, kept advancing, and the war raged on.

In late January 1986, Okello's and Obote's soldiers fled the capital. Museveni was sworn in as Uganda's new leader on January 29. At the ceremony, he spoke eloquently of a new Africa: democratic, peaceful, and free of the tribal and religious competition that had torn the continent apart since independence. Ugandans deserved democracy, he said, and a fundamental change in the politics of the country. In a gesture of reconciliation, he appointed Kayiira Energy Minister, and Paul Ssemogerere—the Democratic Party leader who had been rigged out of the 1980 election by Obote—Interior Minister.

During the war, London's *Observer* newspaper had published the harshest criticism of Obote. Now a series of glowing tributes to Museveni appeared in its pages. "Polite Guerrillas End Fourteen Years of Torture and Killing," read one headline; "The Pearl of Africa Shines Again," read another. According to his admirers, Museveni was Robin Hood, Che Guevara, and Field Marshal Montgomery all rolled into one.

The *Observer* had been taken over in 1983 by Tiny Rowland, the mysterious tycoon and former Hitler Youth member who left Germany for Britain in the 1930s, changed his name, and joined the powerful British business elite known as the "Mayfair

66   Set." Rowland was one of the few entrepreneurs to move into Africa after the old colonials left in the 1960s. The holdings of his vast Lonrho Company included mines, factories, and newspapers and had members of Britain's intelligence agency MI6 on its board. Rowland was close to those African leaders such as Zambia's Kenneth Kaunda and Zimbabwe's Robert Mugabe in whose countries Lonrho had major stakes. He provided them with behind the scenes diplomatic support, favorable media coverage in his newspapers and free room and board in his fashionable Metropole Hotel, which became a home away from home for various African potentates in the 1980s. Where leaders seemed less cooperative, Rowland lavished similar benefits on rebels fighting to overthrow them. He once bragged to journalist Deborah Scroggins that he'd put "150 million pounds into national liberation movements" in Africa including Angola's UNITA, Mozambique's RENAMO and the Sudan People's Liberation Army. In 1983, Obote reportedly rebuffed Rowland's request to take over Uganda's cotton trade and construct an oil pipeline. Rowland began assisting Museveni financially during the fraught Nairobi negotiations, after Obote's government fell.

While outsiders lavished praise on Museveni, many Ugandans feared him. His powers of deception were the stuff of myth. People whispered that he could read minds to identify traitors in his ranks, disappear into thin air, and turn into a cat and walk through roadblocks.

Ugandans also quickly saw through Museveni's professed commitment to human rights. In two damning reports published in 1989 and 1992, Amnesty International acknowledged that Museveni's regime was a marked improvement over Idi Amin's and Obote's, but that wasn't saying much. The NRA detained suspects without charge for months and years and ignored habeas corpus demands to produce them in court. In

secret prisons, suspects were beaten with iron rods, had nails
drilled into their heads, and their genitals electrocuted, stapled,
and crushed with pliers. Although such cases were less common
than they had been under Obote, they were common enough.
The most prevalent torture method was the "three-piece-tie,"
in which the arms of the victim are tied tightly behind the back
above the elbows so that the chest protrudes outward, produc-
ing searing pain. Sometimes the legs were also bound to the
hands and the victim was hung from a tree or a rafter, "suitcase style." Many of these abuses were also covered by *Citizen*
reporters.

The worst abuses were meted out in northern and eastern
Uganda. Most of Obote's and Okello's troops had come from
those areas, and the population was most worried that the predominantly southern army of Baganda, Ankole, and Rwandan
Tutsi soldiers would want revenge. While Museveni claims that
"there was total peace in the north between March and August
1986," political scientist Adam Branch notes that "stories of
harassment and abuse of civilians by the NRA began circulating
in mid-April, 1986." Museveni's soldiers looted farms and raped
civilians while on "operations for hidden guns," supposedly
in the hands of former Obote or Okello soldiers. When some
Acholi fought back, indiscriminate army abuses worsened and
the violence escalated. Hundreds were detained and killed.

In early August 1986, the NRA's 35th battalion brutally
attacked suspected Okello loyalists who were believed to be hiding weapons in Namokora sub-county, Kitgum District. "Many
victims were tied up 'three-piece' with ropes," a survivor named
Ventorino Okidi told Uganda *Monitor* journalist Jimmy Kwo
in 2014. About 80 villagers were rounded up that day, including a woman whom Okidi saw emerging from a grass-thatched
hut in the company of soldiers who had clearly just raped her.

68   That night, Okidi himself was raped by two soldiers. The next morning, he and the others were piled into the back of a military truck destined for Namokora town, about an hour away. As they neared the town, some captives jumped off and dashed into the bush. The soldiers chased them, and most were shot as they ran. Those who remained in the truck were killed too. Okidi was one of the few survivors.

The 35th Battalion comprised mainly soldiers from the UFM, Kayiira's former rebel group, and FEDEMU who had joined the NRA as part of the peace deal. Lawrence was with Kayiira in Kampala when he learned what his former troops had done. Shocked and angry, the former UFM leader sent orders for the 35th Battalion to stop the abuses.

A few days later, a group of Obote's former soldiers launched a reprisal attack against the 35th Battalion at Namokora. This time, the soldiers simply retreated and the ex-Obote men made off with weapons and other supplies. Senior NRA commanders accused the 35th Battalion of cowardice, but Lawrence believed they were simply confused; Museveni was claiming the people of Namokora should be shown no mercy; but their former commander Kayiira was telling them to hold their guns.

Lawrence published part one of a story about the Namokora incident in *The Citizen* in October 1986. Part two would have described how one of Museveni's commanders rushed up to Namokora, herded hundreds of members of the 35th Battalion into an empty goods container, locked the door, and allowed them to stew under the hot equatorial sun until nearly all of them were dead. Lawrence believes the soldiers of the 35th were punished not for brutalizing the people of Namokora, but for obeying their former commander Kayiira and refusing to fight back against the rebels.

The truth of what really happened may never be known,   69
because *The Citizen* offices were ransacked before part two
of Lawrence's account could be published. Everything was
destroyed and notes and documents that might have shed light
on the matter were stolen. In his memoir Pecos Kutesa, who
was NRA commander in the area at the time, claims the 35th
Battalion was simply disbanded.

On October 3, 1986, NRA troops stormed a meeting in a
hotel in Mukono, a provincial town near Kampala, and arrested
six former UFM officers. Andrew Kayiira was arrested the same
day. Lawrence's editor at *The Citizen*, Anthony Ssekweyama,
was also arrested, along with about 40 other members of the
Democratic Party. All were charged with plotting a coup.

While their trial was underway, Museveni met with U.S.
Ambassador Robert Houdek, who was concerned that the NRA's
favored torture method sometimes left its victims paralyzed or
caused gangrene, necessitating amputation.

"Why should the three-piece-tie be America's concern?"
asked Museveni.

"Because it is a form of torture," replied the ambassador,
"and a violation of human rights."

"If you just use verbal interrogation, you won't get anywhere," explained Museveni.

Houdek sympathized, but hinted that World Bank loans and
a visit to the White House were contingent upon an improved
human rights record.

Houdek also said he hoped that Kayiira and the other treason suspects would receive a fair trial.

Museveni assured the ambassador that if the evidence was
insufficient, they'd be freed.

In February, Kayiira was acquitted by Uganda's High Court.
Two days later, Museveni told the Uganda Law Society that he

70   still thought the ex-UFM leader was guilty. Three weeks later, men in NRA uniforms stormed a dinner party in the garden of the house where Kayiira was staying. The former UFM commander leaped from the table and was chased into the house, where he was gunned down in one of the bathrooms. According to the government's version of events, Kayiira was killed by former UFM rebels who were angry because he'd bought a New York penthouse with $2 million meant for them. This is unlikely, as a news story in a Westchester newspaper indicates Kayiira's wife Betty was living on welfare in Poughkeepsie, New York at the time.

Angry Baganda called for an independent investigation of Kayiira's murder. To quell tensions, Museveni asked Scotland Yard to investigate. Two British detectives flew to Uganda and produced a report which has yet to be released, 30 years later. Ugandans have submitted numerous Freedom of Information Act requests to obtain it, but all have been denied because, according to Scotland Yard, releasing it would damage UK–Uganda relations.

The death of Kayiira was a crucial turning point. The U.S., Britain, and Uganda's other donors could have cut off aid and diplomatic ties to Uganda until Museveni's human rights record improved and elections were held. Around this time, the donors did suspend, or threaten to suspend, aid to Kenya, Malawi, Ghana, Zambia, and of course South Africa on human rights grounds. This pressure resulted in momentous reforms and an improved, although still not perfect, human rights environment in all of these countries. But the donors lavished more and more aid on Museveni, even as his human rights performance continued to deteriorate. This "blind-eye-diplomacy" puzzled Lawrence and many other Ugandans.

In October 1987, Museveni traveled to Washington where he met with President Ronald Reagan and Vice President George H. W. Bush and was greeted with full honors on Capitol Hill. Museveni hired a public relations firm owned by Reagan's son-in-law Dennis Revell to buff up his image. The firm was based in California, not Washington, and wasn't high-powered, but the relationship would likely have given the novice African leader occasional access to Reagan himself, or at least the Great Communicator's second-hand opinions, as well as an intimate perspective on how the foreign aid system works, how military alliances are forged and how to use his personal charisma to charm decision-makers in the U.S. and abroad.

Soon Museveni's government was receiving generous loans and grants from the World Bank and other donors. Museveni returned to Washington in 1988, and again in 1989, when he detoured to California to spend time at Reagan's ranch. I could find no record of what Reagan and Museveni discussed, but the end of the Cold War was by then in sight, and the political map of Africa was shifting. As America drew closer to its old adversaries in Eastern Europe, it came to see many of its Cold War allies in the Islamic world as enemies. Eastern and central Africa, just south of Egypt and Sudan and across the Red Sea from Yemen and Saudi Arabia, must have posed a conundrum to American policy makers. I can only imagine their thoughts as they pondered this supposedly lawless region of savage tribes with strange gods and witchcraft potions and child soldiers and warlord politicians. There was a huge pot of gold in the center of it, and the world's richest uranium deposits as well. How was America going to keep all this—especially the raw material for atom bombs—out of Islam's hands?

72   During the Cold War, the U.S. had been able to rely on Apartheid South Africa and a few CIA-backed dictators to protect its interests on the African continent. But the Apartheid regime was on the way out, and Cold War dictators like Zaire's Mobutu Sese Seko were growing old and their abuses were by now embarrassingly well known. Washington needed a new African partner, preferably someone young, who spoke the language of guns that Washington security officials understood. Museveni's human rights record was not promising, but he was a shrewd military strategist and controlled one of the best armies in Africa. With little outside support, he'd risen to power through sheer cunning. His demeanor was unvarnished, even slightly unhinged. In the years to come, Museveni would publicly proclaim his critics "those stupid ones," Members of Uganda's Parliament "fools and idiots," and the International Criminal Court, which tries cases involving crimes against humanity, "a bunch of useless people." But during Museveni's visit, Reagan and Bush may have concluded that they'd found their man in Africa, a cattleman like themselves, who knew how strong men tame wild things.

Warlords in
Northern Uganda

*The cult of Hitler's personality set up a fake opposition between
leader and party. . . .After Kristallnacht, as after other outrages,
many Germans . . . commented that "the Führer surely did not
intend this."*

—Neal Ascherson, "Hopping in His Matchbox"

Civil service salaries in Uganda were extremely low in the late
1980s, so to get stories, Lawrence sometimes paid ministers'
secretaries to type official letters on carbon paper and give one
copy to him. When he traveled in war zones, he hid his notes in
the tires of his bicycle. In order to interview political prisoners
and torture victims, he'd write stories he knew would get him
arrested. Most journalists in Uganda follow what they call the
"three-to-one" approach. They'd produce three articles praising the president and then one critical one. When Museveni
complained, the editors would simply apologize. The reporter

74   got the story, after all, and there was no way to explain to him why it shouldn't be published. Lawrence didn't obey the three-to-one rule, and once found himself tied by the wrists to an overhead beam in a military prison.

A soldier came by with a pair of pliers and crushed the testicles of the man hanging next to him. Lawrence panicked and kicked the soldier, who spat at him in return. Then, for reasons he doesn't know, he was released a few hours later.

Visitors from around the country were always turning up at *The Citizen* offices with news. It was here that Lawrence first learned that thousands of cattle were being stolen in massive raids throughout northern and eastern Uganda. By the mid-1990s, the Acholi people had lost some 300,000 animals, nearly all they owned. Cattle were far more than a source of food for these people. They knew each animal by name, and slaughtered them only on special occasions. Cows were exchanged as bride-price and to secure friendships and political alliances, or sold to pay for medicine or school fees. Large herds conferred political power and a man without cattle was almost without identity.

During the raids, houses and huts were reduced to ashes and crops and grain stores were destroyed. People fled into the rocky hills, only to return and find all their animals gone. People throughout northern and eastern Uganda still speak of relatives killed, of schooling and careers cut short, of children left to die because even the cheapest medicine was no longer affordable. In a moving article in *The Citizen* in March 1989, journalist Norah Tamale recounts how an elderly Teso man told of passing an abattoir in Kampala and seeing in the enclosure his favorite bull, who had been stolen in a raid. He called out to it by name, and as it turned to look at him, security men chased the man away.

Officially, the cattle raids were blamed on the Karamojong,
a pastoralist ethnic group known for ornamental scars and
elaborate beaded necklaces, but eyewitnesses say Museveni's
soldiers also took their share. The Karamojong had been raid-
ing the herds of neighboring tribes for as long as anyone can
remember. But until the 1980s, they'd been armed only with
spears, traveled on foot, and made lightning strikes on villages.
Now they carried machine guns, decimated entire villages, and
drove the animals away on trucks. To the victims, these seemed
more like military operations than cattle raids. After all, why
were the rustlers wearing gumboots, rather than going barefoot
or wearing traditional Karamojong sandals? And why were the
trucks with the animals heading south, toward Kampala, rather
than north or east, where the Karamojong live? And since when
did the Karamojong acquire helicopter gunships, which were
reportedly seen during some of the raids?

Why did the NRA disarm the Teso and Acholi militias
that had in the past defended against Karamojong raids, while
allowing the Karamojong to keep their weapons? And why did
the NRA always withdraw when the raiders attacked, instead of
fighting? When 18 Acholi politicians demanded the NRA stop
the raids, they were beaten, arrested, and charged with treason.

The Acholi, Teso and other ethnic groups from which
Obote and Okello's armies were drawn suffered most. To some,
it seemed as though Museveni was punishing entire tribes—
millions of people—for the crimes of the relatively modest
number of soldiers responsible for the worst abuses in Luwero.

The suspicion that the NRA was behind some of the cattle
thefts sparked the creation of new rebel groups. In May 1986, a
30-year-old fish vendor named Alice Auma, claiming to be pos-
sessed by a dead Italian World War I soldier, renamed herself

76 Lakwena (meaning *messenger* in Acholi) and camped out in a game park in northern Uganda for 40 days. When she asked the hippos, giraffes, and crocodiles whom they blamed for the troubles in Acholiland, they showed her their wounds and broken limbs and said, "those with two legs." Lakwena returned to her village, set up a temple near a railway station, and began performing healing rituals on former Obote/Okello soldiers.

From these sessions, she raised her own army to take up the battle where the Obote/Okello men had failed. Armed only with a few rifles, some Bibles, and various magical objects, her 10,000 fighters marched right through the country chanting Christian songs. At first astonished NRA soldiers fled in their path, but as her movement gained strength on the ground, her spiritual powers waned. In the summer of 1987, her forces were defeated a mere 80 miles from Kampala. She fled to Kenya and died in a refugee camp 20 years later. In 1988, the NRA cordoned off most of Kitgum and Gulu districts where the Acholi live and conducted house-to-house searches for any remaining Obote/Okello/Lakwena rebels. Journalists were banned from the area, but Amnesty International later reported that villagers thought to be rebel sympathizers were shot, tortured, raped, and burned alive in their huts.

Lawrence wanted to see for himself what was going on, so with the help of a network of Catholic priests, he crossed into northern Uganda from Sudan in November 1988. He traveled around by bicycle, taking down the names of victims and then published them in *The Citizen* when he returned to Kampala. He then wrote a follow-up article criticizing religious leaders for ignoring the suffering in northern Uganda. Uganda's bishops responded a week later with a joint statement calling for peace. "There are thousands of displaced people who are shelterless, living in pathetic conditions with no food and lacking essential

commodities like salt, soap, sugar, and medical services," the
bishops wrote. "Women and children have been caught up in
the crossfire." They appealed to all Ugandans to contribute food,
clothing, and other essentials which the diocese would distrib-
ute to the needy.

As donations poured in, Museveni's army commanders
scrambled to arrange a press tour to convince other journalists
that *The Citizen's* stories were not true. About a dozen reporters,
including Lawrence, were flown up to the war zone by airplane
and meetings were arranged with army commanders and locals.
Everyone said they were unaware of any abuses committed by
the army. On the contrary, the Acholis were happy that the NRA
was pacifying the area.

Lawrence was skeptical about what seemed to him a staged
public relations exercise, so he contacted a source from his previous trip, who suggested he visit Kalongo Hospital, near the
Sudan border. A new rebel group had recently emerged which
would eventually come to be known as the Lord's Resistance
Army, or LRA. It was led by a mystical former choirboy named
Joseph Kony who, like Alice Lakwena, also claimed to be inspired
by God to fight Museveni. Kony targeted anyone thought to be a
civilian collaborator of the NRA, as if he were fighting not only
the army, but also the spirit that supported it. He became notorious for abducting thousands of children and forcing them to
mutilate and kill their own relatives.

By early 1989, Kony's troops had reached Kalongo, and hundreds of refugees from his attacks were now camped out under
the trees outside the hospital.

"We've seen terrible things here," a nurse told Lawrence.
She introduced him to a teenage girl whose ears and lower lip
had been cut off with a knife. Her head was covered in ban-
dages, and she could barely speak. Although she was Acholi, she

78   had spent some time in southern Uganda and knew enough Luganda so that she and Lawrence could communicate without a translator.

The chopping off of ears and lips would become one of the LRA's signature forms of torture, but the girl said two things about the men who attacked her that puzzled Lawrence. First, unlike Kony's ragtag rebels, these men weren't shabbily dressed, she said. Second, they didn't speak Acholi, the language of the LRA, but a southern language similar to Luganda that she didn't recognize. Lawrence didn't need to ask her to whom she was referring. Most NRA soldiers in the area spoke Runyankole or Kinyarwanda, which are far more similar to Luganda than to Acholi. Lawrence wondered whether the assault on the girl, like some of the cattle raids, might have been committed not by Kony's troops, but by Museveni's soldiers in disguise, in order to terrorize the local population and win support for their brutal counterinsurgency.

Lawrence's hunch might have been wrong. Amnesty International reports make no mention of NRA "false flag" attacks involving facial mutilations, nor do any other independent sources. However, the NRA false flag attacks in Luwero and eyewitness reports that NRA soldiers dressed up like rebels and attacked civilians later in the LRA war suggest the story about the girl isn't entirely implausible.

Lawrence told the girl he would return the next day with a camera and tape recorder. Back with his press tour colleagues that evening, he mentioned her to three other journalists, one of whom would soon be appointed Museveni's press secretary. When Lawrence returned to the hospital the next day, the girl was gone. The nurses said she'd been taken away for further treatment, but they didn't know where. She remains on his conscience to this day.

Joseph Kony's LRA would continue to terrorize the people of northern and eastern Uganda for another 17 years. But his army comprised only a few thousand soldiers at its peak, and most of those were children whom he'd kidnapped. Many observers wondered why Uganda's much larger army, trained and equipped by the Americans and Israelis, was unable to defeat them for so long.

Some suspected Museveni wanted the LRA war to continue. According to NRA commander David Sejusa, Kony was severely wounded in 1992 and offered to surrender. Sejusa was about to send a unit to pick the warlord up from a village called Opit when Museveni, without explanation, ordered him stop the operation. Kony was evacuated to Sudan, from where he returned with more recruits and firepower the following year.

Museveni sabotaged another chance for peace in 1994. Betty Bigombe, then Minister for Acholi Affairs, had contacted Kony through a group of Acholi elders in the hope of negotiating a ceasefire. Once she courageously met him in a deserted forest without military protection because he said he didn't trust the army. Peace talks began in January 1994, but then on February 6 Museveni suddenly gave Kony an ultimatum: Disarm within a week, or the ceasefire is off. With that, Bigombe's delicate negotiations over the terms of an armistice were destroyed. Kony, fearing a trap, fled back to Sudan, only to return to wreak havoc again later that year.

Ms. Bigombe, now a senior World Bank official, has always insisted that Kony wanted to make peace with the government, but whenever she tried to contact him, the army would track her phone or radio signals and attack his camp. Throughout the 20-year Kony war, Ugandan army soldiers bombed peace talk venues, killed women and children whom Kony had kidnapped along with his soldiers, and arrived at besieged villages only

80 after the LRA had done its dirty work, even when given advance
    warnings of attacks.

    In 2002, a group of Catholic priests successfully negoti-
    ated the release of dozens of children who had been kidnapped
    by the LRA. Encouraged, three of the priests—two Italians
    and a Spaniard named Carlos Rodriquez, arranged to meet
    with Kony's commanders to discuss peace. They notified local
    Ugandan army officers where the meeting would take place and
    received written permission to travel there.

    During the meeting, one of Kony's commanders, a stam-
    merer, told the priests, "We-e wa-nt pe-eace . . . but if
    Mu-useveni does not wa-ant pe-eace, we-e shall no-ot leave
    any-ybo-ody a-li-ive. . . ."

    Suddenly gunshots rang out. Ugandan army soldiers
    attacked the village and the priests were almost burned alive
    when the hut they were hiding in burst into flames. The troops
    captured and beat the child soldiers, and forced the priests—
    one suffering from kidney stones and another who'd recently
    had heart surgery—to the ground, kicked them, and stole their
    watches. The priests were then driven to a military barracks and
    held in a tiny metal container without food, water, or sanitary
    facilities for 24 hours.

    The priests had brought along a few boxes of medicine as
    a standard peace offering for the rebels. The officer in charge
    of the barracks informed them that these would be used as
    evidence of collaboration if they did not sign a confession.
    Fearing worse abuse, the priests signed and were released,
    only to be humiliated in the pages of the government-owned
    New Vision newspaper a few days later. The priests had been
    carrying, "an amazingly huge amount of drugs," a government
    spokesman said.

In his memoir, Father Rodriquez insists that the fault lay
not with Museveni, but with his corrupt and ruthless army
commanders, "who were trying to make us fail." Over the years,
I've been struck by how many members of the local intelligentsia—Ugandan and expatriate alike—including newspaper
editors, businessmen, diplomats, NGO officials, clergy, and even
respected lawyers and professors, have told me that Uganda's
human rights problems are not Museveni's fault. The President
is simply overwhelmed with the responsibility of governing a
poor, chaotic nation to rein in his freewheeling army and police
commanders, they say.

Eventually, it became impossible for serious scholars to
deny that Museveni himself was complicit in prolonging the
LRA war. But why would a leader want to waste time and money
on a war that made his own army look inept? Some analysts
have suggested that the LRA war allowed Museveni to inflate
his defense budget, with little objection from donors; inflict
revenge on the Acholi people, whom he felt were disloyal; and
placate his senior officers by allowing them to plunder the
Acholi and skim off the salaries of non-existent "ghost soldiers."

But as discussed in the next chapter, there is another reason
why the international community overlooked the suffering of
the people of northern Uganda for so long.

A Visit from the U.S. Department of Agriculture

Not too much pressure was exerted; no great demands were made on anyone ... arrests ... were carried out quietly .... The catchwords were freedom and democracy.

—Czeslaw Milosz, *The Captive Mind*

According to a story—perhaps true, perhaps not—told in Ugandan security circles, a pair of American agronomists visited Museveni at State House in 1989 and presented him with a small pot of hybrid maize seedlings developed by U.S. government scientists. Museveni and his team noticed the plants were in fact sorghum, not maize, but curious to see how the meeting would proceed, said nothing. According to the story, the seedlings were then placed on a sunny balcony, and the men sat down to talk. Pleased to find that the president was more interested in security matters than agriculture, the Americans introduced the subject of Sudan, the vast, troubled nation on Uganda's northern border. A radical Islamist regime had just taken over there, and it threatened the stability of Egypt, and perhaps the whole of north Africa and the Middle East.

Sudan had been in turmoil since colonial times. The country straddled the edge of the Sahara, bounding together two very different peoples who did not get along. In the north, Arabs had long ago united diverse African tribes under Islam and created a central form of government; in the south, myriad African clans lived independently, each with its own customs, gods, and leaders. When Sudan was granted independence in 1956, the southerners chafed at the dominance of the northerners in government and the perceived erosion of their culture and autonomy. A rebel group known as the Anya-Nya emerged in the 1960s and declared war on the government. Hostilities were suspended in 1972 when Khartoum allowed the southerners to govern themselves in a quasi-federal arrangement, but tensions resumed later in the decade when U.S. energy giant Chevron brokered a series of secret oil deals with Sudan's President Gaafar Nimeiry.

Southern Sudanese leaders, already bitter about ethnic discrimination and the concentration of development projects in the north, took umbrage and Nimeiry found himself short of allies. Formerly a secularist, he teamed up with hardline Islamists. Sharia law was imposed throughout the country. Forced confessions were televised to humiliate and terrify potential dissidents. Adulterers faced hanging and thieves, amputation. Young ex-convicts lined the main thoroughfares in the capital Khartoum displaying the stumps of their former hands and feet as a macabre tourist attraction for Western journalists. In 1983, John Garang, then a colonel in Sudan's army, created the Sudan People's Liberation Army (or SPLA) and declared war on Nimeiry.

84   Nimeiry was overthrown in 1985 and elections held the same year brought Prime Minister Sadiq al-Mahdi to power. He was toppled four years later by a murky coalition of army officers and hardline Islamists. The front man was Colonel Omar Al-Bashir, but the real power lay with Hassan Al-Turabi, a Sorbonne-trained lawyer, self-styled philosopher-politician, and founder of the National Islamic Front, the Sudanese branch of the Egypt-based Muslim Brotherhood. For years Turabi had been holding rallies around Khartoum calling for a "real Islamic revolution," an end to the military dictatorship of Egyptian strongman Hosni Mubarak, and the breaking of the Egypt–Israel peace deal.

After the coup, Turabi declared the U.S. an enemy of Sudan and sponsored semi-annual conferences for terrorist organizations interested in planning a future global caliphate. Delegates included Palestine's Hamas, Lebanon's Hezbollah, and Osama bin Laden's Al Qaeda. Turabi's National Islamic Front was not only turning Sudan into a "Holiday Inn" for terrorists, as one diplomat put it, it also pledged support for Saddam Hussein during the first Gulf War.

Turabi's ascent alarmed the Americans, not to mention the Egyptians, whose treaty with Israel depended upon keeping the Egyptian Muslim Brotherhood under control. This may be what occasioned the visit of the American "agronomists." Museveni had known John Garang, the leader of the SPLA, since the 1960s, where they belonged to the same radical student revolutionary group at the University of Dar es Salaam. Museveni's troops were already involved in border skirmishes with Sudan where remnants of Obote and Okello's armies had fled the marauding NRA. Museveni, therefore, had a potential interest in delivering clandestine military support to Garang's SPLA for its war against Khartoum.

In 1991 Garang, a grizzly bearded 44-year-old revolutionary with a University of Iowa Ph.D. in agricultural economics, was hanging around Kampala drinking too much. The SPLA's patron, Ethiopia's Marxist dictator Mengistu Haile Mariam, was preoccupied with Ethiopia's own civil war. The Soviet Union, which supported Mengistu, had disappeared. Weapons were drying up and Garang's fellow SPLA commanders were feuding with him, and among themselves.

During the Cold War, President Reagan had backed Nimeiry, whose government was the largest recipient of U.S. foreign aid in sub-Saharan Africa, even as his war against Garang's SPLA claimed thousands of mainly southern Sudanese lives. But Turabi's growing power in Sudan turned out to be Garang's lucky break, because it meant that his former American adversaries were about to become his friends.

State Department officials met with Garang in 1990, and in 1992, U.S. Customs agents in Orlando, Florida caught Ugandan diplomats in the process of smuggling 400 anti-tank missiles out of the U.S. The missiles, along with 34 launchers, were hidden in a container under refrigeration equipment destined for Entebbe, via Cyprus, and were reportedly to be delivered to the SPLA by road. A year later, the Customs Department quietly dropped the smuggling case against the Ugandans after a U.S. judge determined that the U.S. had in fact approved this mysterious deal.

Two years later, another shipment of U.S. weapons, also reportedly destined for the SPLA via Uganda, was discovered at the airport in Cyprus.

As the 1990s wore on, reports surfaced that SPLA troops were training inside Uganda which supplied them with heat-seeking chaparral missiles, Hawk ground-to-air missiles, howitzers, TOW anti-tank missiles, Vulcan cannons, and even

86   canned beans and corned beef. Although Assistant Secretary Cohen insists that the U.S. didn't support the SPLA in the early 1990s, U.S. military assistance to Uganda soared during this period, despite Museveni's poor human rights record.

The Sudanese military, aware of what Museveni was doing and suspecting that America was quietly behind him, began arming various anti-Museveni rebel groups, including Joseph Kony's notorious Lord's Resistance Army, greatly escalating the war in northern Uganda.

Some of the Acholi who had been victimized by the NRA sympathized with Kony. Perhaps sensing this, Museveni ordered the entire Acholi population—some two million people—into internment camps, supposedly for their own protection. Soldiers bombed villages to get people out. For years, more than a thousand Acholis died from hunger and disease each week in the squalid, barren, overcrowded camps. There were outbreaks of Ebola, cholera, and nodding disease, a strange form of brain damage that no one had ever seen before and whose cause remains unknown. Starving women exchanged sex with the soldiers in order to feed their children; sometimes the soldiers simply raped them.

For ten years, the international community all but ignored this living hell. When UN Undersecretary General for Humanitarian Affairs Jan Egeland finally visited northern Uganda in November 2003, he told reporters that the LRA war was "the biggest forgotten, neglected humanitarian emergency in the world today."

It's worth asking what took the international community so long to realize what was going on. Perhaps this is an example of America's successful obfuscation of the crimes of its allies, as described by Yale economist Nancy Qian in the Introduction to this book. Just as the State Department and the U.S. media downplayed atrocities committed by our allies during the Cold War, the international community overlooked the suffering of Museveni's many victims during the 1990s.

Prelude to Apocalypse

"Oh" Christmas said. "They might have done that? Dug them up after they were already killed dead? Just when do men that have different blood in them stop hating one another?"
— William Faulkner, *Light in August*

One afternoon in early 1988 when the news was slow, Lawrence stopped by to see his old friend the Deputy Minister of Transport. Two senior army officers whom Lawrence also knew happened to be in the waiting room when he arrived. Like many NRA officers, they were Rwandan Tutsi refugees.

After some polite preliminaries, Lawrence asked the men what they were doing there.

"We want some of our people to be in Rwanda," one of them replied.

Lawrence shuddered. He knew Rwanda was a powder keg of Tutsi/Hutu ethnic tension. He'd grown up among Hutus

who'd fled Tutsi oppression in Rwanda before independence, as
well as Tutsis who'd fled the Hutu-led pogroms that followed
it. Lawrence's childhood catechist had been a Tutsi; the Hutus
who worked in his family's gardens wouldn't attend his lessons. Instead, they swapped fantastic tales about how Tutsis
once used their Hutu slaves as spittoons, expectorating in their
mouths, instead of on the ground. During the 1960s, Tutsi refugees had launched periodic attacks on Rwanda from Uganda.
Most were easily quashed by Rwanda's army, but they sent shock
waves through fearful Hutu populations. Reprisals against those
Tutsis who remained in Rwanda were brutal. Then in 1972, some
75,000 Hutus—virtually all who could read—were massacred in
Tutsi-ruled Burundi, a small country neighboring Rwanda with
a similar ethnic makeup. In both countries, ethnic anger and fear
hung over every barroom altercation, every office dispute and
every church sermon, notes historian Andre Guichaoua.

Rwanda's Hutu President Juvenal Habyarimana was under
intense pressure to allow the Tutsi refugees in Uganda and other
countries to return, but he continued to refuse, citing land shortages. "Where will I fix them?" Habyarimana told *The Citizen,* "I
cannot fix them in the air!" Lawrence suspected overpopula-
tion wasn't the Rwandan president's only concern. Everyone
suspected that if the refugees returned to Rwanda, they would
not be content with a plot of land and a hoe. They wanted power,
and Museveni had taught them how to fight for it. The officers
in the Deputy Minister's waiting room were members of a newly
created refugee pressure group known as the Rwandan Patriotic
Front—or RPF, whose aim was already an open secret around
Kampala: to overthrow Habyarimana's government and take
over Rwanda by force.

90   The officers went in to speak to the Deputy Transport Minister first, and when Lawrence's turn came, he asked his friend what had transpired. The Deputy Minister was elated. The Rwandans had come to express their support for a new open borders program, he said. Soon Rwandans living in Uganda would be allowed to cross over and visit their relatives visa-free. This would help solve the vexing refugee issue, he explained.

Lawrence was less sanguine. A few days later, he dropped in on a Rwandan Tutsi NRA colonel he knew named Stephen Ndugute.

"We are going back to Rwanda," he said. When the RPF eventually took over Rwanda in 1994, Ndugute would be second in command.

Many Ugandans were eager to see the Rwandan Tutsi NRA men depart. The Rwandans were not only occupying senior army positions many Ugandans felt should be held by Ugandans, they were also becoming notorious for their brutality. Paul Kagame, who went on to lead the RPF takeover of Rwanda and is now Rwanda's president, was acting Chief of Military Intelligence, headquartered at Basima House, where Lawrence and others were tortured. Some of the worst attacks in northern and eastern Uganda had been carried out by Rwandan Tutsi NRA officers including the massacre of suspected rebels in an area of northern Uganda known as Corner Kilak where some 600 unarmed men were rounded up and killed in cold blood. In 1989, soldiers under the command of NRA Captain Chris Bunyenyezi, also an RPF leader, herded scores of suspected rebels in the Teso village of Mukura into an empty railway wagon, locked the doors, and allowed them to die of suffocation.

"These Rwandans use the most unacceptable counter-insurgency strategies," Italian priest Vittorino Colla told historian Ogenga Otunnu in 1988:

They herd women, children and old people into houses and set the houses on fire. They rape women in the presence of their male relatives, and at times they force the male relatives to sleep with the women after they [the soldiers] have exhausted their sexual desire. . . . These people are determined to spread slim [AIDS] to the Acholi. I also witnessed them mutilate unarmed people, including school children, from the Holy Rosary primary school. . . . The surviving victims are often paraded by the soldiers or government functionaries before a group of reporters and told to expose those who mutilated them. Naturally, they say the rebels did it. . . .

Lawrence suspected the Rwandans might use the open borders program to conduct surveillance for an invasion and perhaps carry out attacks. He had little doubt that if war broke out in Rwanda, it was going to be very, very bloody. He decided to warn Rwanda's president.

Juvenal Habyarimana agreed to meet Lawrence during a state visit to Tanzania. At a hotel in Dar es Salaam, the 20-year-old journalist warned the Rwandan leader about the dangers of the open border program. "Don't worry," Lawrence says Habyarimana told him. "Museveni is my friend and would never allow the RPF to invade."

Habyarimana was bluffing. He too was worried. Museveni had informed him that the Tutsi exiles might invade if he didn't allow them to return to Rwanda, and Habyarimana told U.S. State Department officials that he feared an invasion from Uganda.

The open border program was actually part of Habyarimana's own ruthless counter-strategy. Every person inside Rwanda visited by a Tutsi refugee would be followed by state

92   agents and automatically branded an RPF sympathizer; many were arrested, tortured, and killed by Rwandan government operatives. The Tutsis inside Rwanda thus became pawns in a power struggle between the RPF exiles and Habyarimana's government. Five years later, they would be crushed altogether in one of most brutal genocides in human history.

A New World Order

It is the clear, common sense of the African situation that while these precious regions remain divided up between a number of competitive European imperialisms, each resolutely set upon the exploitation of its "possessions" to its own advantage and to the disadvantage of the others, there can be no permanent peace in the world. It is impossible.

—H.G. Wells, *In the Fourth Year*

Despite a nationwide crime wave and a stock market crash, George H. W. Bush was in an upbeat mood when he assumed the U.S. presidency on a blustery January 20, 1989. In foreign policy everything seemed to be going America's way. The Soviet Empire was crumbling and we'd driven the communists off the Caribbean island of Grenada and the drug dealing thug Manuel Noriega out of Panama.

94   "A new breeze is blowing," the new president said in his inaugural speech. "For in man's heart, if not in fact, the day of the dictator is over. The totalitarian era is passing. . . . Great nations of the world are moving toward democracy through the door to freedom." Billy Graham read a homily that day, and the Mormon Tabernacle Choir sang a hymn, underscoring the missionary spirit of the occasion.

The Cold War had been harrowing for the people of Africa, with coups and civil wars in Uganda, Mozambique, Angola, Somalia, Namibia, Nigeria, South Africa, Burkina Faso, Congo/ Zaire, and Liberia. President Bush himself, as head of the CIA during the 1970s, had funneled cash to some of Africa's most brutal dictators. But now he spoke of a New World Order, in which "the rule of law, not the rule of the jungle, would govern the conduct of nations." Under Bush Sr., American money would go to pro-democracy think tanks, NGOs and election observer missions. Countries that received U.S. foreign aid would be pressured to democratize. As a result, some African countries—including Zambia, Malawi, Kenya, and Ghana allowed political parties to compete in elections for the first time. Nelson Mandela would soon be South Africa's first black president.

But these positive developments were desultory, limited to a few countries and overshadowed by a much darker global trend. A New World Order was emerging, but it wasn't the peaceful, democratic Shangri-La envisioned in Bush Sr.'s inauguration speech. It was a living hell, torn by extremist religious ideology, primitive violence, and authoritarian takeovers from Afghanistan to Zaire. Museveni, with America's help, was already preparing the African theater for this complex disaster.

Although Museveni had promised his people democracy when he took over the country in 1986, he never intended to follow through. Instead, he constructed a façade of emancipation, while keeping most of the brutality and repression offstage. He allowed political parties like the Democratic Party and the remnants of Obote's Uganda People's Congress to exist, but forbade them from holding rallies, fundraisers, or radio campaigns He allowed independent newspapers to operate, but shut them down and jailed their editors when they became too critical. He often allowed the courts to hand down independent judgments, but if a case had the smallest political wrinkle, the ruling was governed by "orders from above."

Museveni justified the ban on political parties with a theory. As he explains in his memoir *Sowing the Mustard Seed*, political parties only emerged in wealthy countries during industrialization when workers began doing specialized jobs and developed genuine class interests. In peasant societies like Uganda, people do everything themselves. Each homestead is responsible for its own food production, shelter construction, education of the young, care of the sick, and so on. The only external allegiances are to clan and tribe, and thus political parties are inevitably tribal and sectarian. Voters don't internalize democratic values and accept the results of elections. Instead, they rebel when their tribal representatives don't win. Only a mass movement like his own National Resistance Movement—the political wing of the NRA—could focus the mind of the peasant on the challenges of development and guarantee stability.

Lawrence and many other Ugandans had another theory: Tribal violence resulted not from peasant economics, they said, but from political repression and human rights abuses. Time has proved them right. The most peaceful nations in Africa are those that were forced to democratize in the early 1990s, such as Malawi, Ghana, Zambia, and Namibia. Problems remain in all of these countries, but they are nothing like as serious as those afflicting the eastern African autocracies Rwanda, Uganda, Ethiopia, and Eritrea.

Lawrence hoped that Uganda's foreign aid donors would see it his way. The U.S., Britain, and other European countries contributed vast sums to Uganda's budget each year and paid over 50 percent of the government's bills, giving them enormous leverage. Museveni certainly needed the money. When he took over in 1986, his treasury contained roughly $24 million in foreign exchange, barely enough to pay for three weeks' worth of oil and other imports. At first he initiated a barter trade program with North Korea, Yugoslavia, and other socialist-leaning countries, in which oil, weapons, and other imports would be exchanged for Uganda's cotton, coffee, tea, corn, beans, and fish, but this proved a fiasco. Crates of farm implements imported from India were found to contain only stones; electrical transformers and bicycles supposedly manufactured in North Korea turned out to be useless secondhand castoffs from China.

Within a year, Museveni requested help from the World Bank, and by the early 1990s, hundreds of millions of foreign aid dollars were flowing into Uganda. But the donors did not pressure Museveni to implement democratic reforms, and the crackdown on the opposition continued. Some pro-democracy activists were imprisoned and tortured; others disappeared completely. In May 1992, Robert Wasswa-Lule, a courageous deputy in the office of the Inspector General of Government publicly announced that most political detainees' police files were empty—meaning there was no evidence against them. Three months later he was fired.

In June, arsonists broke into the Democratic Party office shortly after the guards left at 6 a.m. They gathered all the files, papers, T-shirts, and other flammable objects into a heap, doused them with kerosene, and set them ablaze. Lawrence and others suspected the government's hand, but there was no police investigation.

Around this time, the U.S. Embassy began sponsoring public discussions about democracy. At one seminar entitled, "The Future of Africa in the New Global Context," Deputy Prime Minister Eriya Kategaya attacked pro-democracy activists for "parading around the embassies in Uganda" asking for support. The donors should butt out of Uganda's internal affairs, he declared. After all, it was the Russians not the Americans who supplied the guns that defeated the hated Obote regime.

Sitting next to Kategaeya on the podium was U.S. Ambassador Johnnie Carson, a grizzly bearded African-American career diplomat with much experience in Africa. "The people who gave you those guns" wanted power, not democracy, Carson said. Many countries claim to be democratic when they are not, he continued, but that is not the way forward, and such countries would be left behind. "Political parties are part and parcel of the process which brings forward an element of internal stability. They shape a democratic society, and we in the U.S. hold them dear. . . . Identify for me any democratic society in the world that operates without political parties."

The audience roared with applause.

By 1993, elections were underway across the country for representatives to a Constituent Assembly which would draft Uganda's new constitution. The greatest bone of contention was the legalization of political party activity. The U.S. embassy's democracy fund provided $500,000 for the campaigns, but virtually all of it went to Museveni's NRM, which used it to organize "voter education" meetings around the country at which NRM leaders discussed the virtues of the one-party system and the tribalist and sectarian nature of the other political parties.

At one of these voter education meetings Lawrence stood up after an NRM candidate had spoken and shared his concerns about human rights abuses in northern and eastern Uganda, torture in military installations, and the harassment of journalists and political activists. "I'm not allowed to say I'm DP," he said, "And I can't tell you I'm Catholic. . . ." The supervisor of the meeting cut him off. Lawrence walked out of the venue, but when he reached the main road, he heard a crowd of people singing DP party songs and turned around. Virtually everyone had followed him out of the meeting. After that he had some posters printed and began campaigning for a seat on the Constituent Assembly.

Three months before the elections, the Americans funded a group of lawyers, journalists, human rights activists, and religious leaders to report on preparations for the Constituent Assembly election. Noting widespread problems with voter registration, interference by security forces and misuse of donor funds by the ruling party, they declared the election rigged in advance and warned the Americans that if they continued shoring up Museveni's regime, they risked "grooming a dictatorship." Some UN diplomats agreed.

On the morning of election day, Lawrence voted and was arrested on the way home from the polling station. He spent the day behind bars without charge while a man on a motorcycle went from one polling station to another in his constituency telling people they shouldn't waste their vote on him because he'd soon be charged with treason. He was released that evening, but in an area where Lawrence was especially popular, the polling officer allowed voting to continue after the official closing time. When the Electoral Commission disqualified all the votes from that polling station, Lawrence petitioned a judge to have the votes counted. The judge ruled in his favor but the night before the scheduled count, a High Court judge, who happened to be the sister of one of Museveni's cabinet ministers, reversed the decision. Despite these shenanigans, Lawrence lost by only 62 votes.

After the election, a donor report pronounced it "transparent," "open," and "a legitimate expression of the will of the people."

A month after the elections, Lawrence decided to organize a Democratic Party rally in City Square, a grassy open space in the center of Kampala. There was no Facebook or Twitter then, and because the rally was illegal, the party couldn't issue announcements on the radio. So teams of organizers traversed the country notifying supporters. A sympathetic station manager ran a story about the government's ban on the rally again and again, day after day, so just about everyone soon knew about it, including the diplomats. The Europeans were enthusiastic that Ugandans were mobilizing to redress their grievances peacefully. Some diplomats said they'd attend and even offered support from their democracy promotion funds.

On the morning of the planned rally, Lawrence set out on foot from the DP office on Johnstone Street. But as he approached City Square, he noticed it was surrounded by armored vehicles and police in riot gear.

"Look behind you," a Ugandan officer with a machine gun told him. Bullets were whizzing in all directions and the crowd was fleeing into the nearby streets. "Please turn and run. I don't want to have to shoot you."

A few days after the aborted rally, Ambassador Carson appeared at another U.S.-sponsored democracy seminar. An audience member pointed out that the more money the West poured into Uganda, the more blatant the government's abuses became. Why was America using sanctions and foreign aid cuts to pressure other African leaders into holding multi-party elections, but not Museveni?

Ambassador Carson replied by comparing President Museveni to a five-gear car. "You cannot apply full-blooded democracy on Museveni all at once," he reportedly said. When climbing a hill, a strong gear is applied; when going down a slope, a different gear is applied. On level ground another gear is used. The journalist interpreted these mysterious words to mean that "the donors were prepared to close their eyes to Museveni's dictatorship and undemocratic approach."

Between 2011 and 2015, I wrote to Ambassador Carson several times requesting an interview about America's support for Museveni's regime. He never replied and I don't really blame him. He seems to have been assigned a contradictory policy, to support democracy in Uganda rhetorically, even as the government he served shored up Museveni's dictatorship.

Invasion

Then Abram bound the youth with belts and straps,
and builded parapets and trenches there,
And stretchèd forth the knife to slay his son.
When lo! an angel called him out of heaven,
Saying, Lay not thy hand upon the lad,
Neither do anything to him. Behold,
A ram, caught in a thicket by its horns;
Offer the Ram of Pride instead of him.
But the old man would not so, but slew his son,
And half the seed of Europe, one by one.

—Wilfred Owen,

"The Parable of the Old Man and the Young"

In September 1990, a large order of gumboots arrived at Bata, Kampala's largest shoe store. Later that month, a convoy of trucks loaded with heavy machine guns, mortars, multiple

102   rocket launchers, rifles, Russian-made light cannon, and radio communications equipment, all taken from NRA arsenals assembled on a disused airstrip near Kampala's city center. It then set out for the Rwandan border.

On the morning of October 1, thousands of RPF fighters gathered in a football stadium about 20 miles from the border. Some were NRA deserters from army barracks around the country; others were volunteers from the refugee camps. Two nearby hospitals were readied for casualties. When locals asked what was going on, Fred Rwigyema, who was both an NRA commander and the leader of the RPF, said they were preparing for Uganda's upcoming Independence Day celebrations, but some excited rebels let the true purpose of the mobilization slip out. The RPF then crossed into Rwanda that afternoon. The Rwandan army, with help from French and Zairean commandos, stopped their advance and they retreated back into Uganda. They then invaded once again, and eventually established bases in the Virunga Mountains of northern Rwanda. The Rwandan civil war between the government and RPF rebels would continue until the 1994 assassination of President Habyarimana, the genocide that followed and the RPF takeover in July of that year.

The RPF's strategy was similar to the NRA's protracted people's war. But whereas the NRA could rely for food on Ugandan villagers, many of whom hated Obote, the RPF could not do the same in Rwanda. Most Hutu peasants were terrified of the Tutsi refugee warriors, and many of Rwanda's internal Tutsis were wary of them too, fearing, correctly, that RPF aggression would provoke Hutu reprisals against all Tutsis. The RPF therefore needed to bring their provisions with them. This was provided, unknowingly, unwillingly, and at gunpoint, by innocent Ugandans.

By 1989, Uganda's cattle raid problem had spread to the ranches of the southern cattle corridor, a giant sash of grassland running right across the country from the arid northeast to the bushy, lush southwest. For centuries pastoralists had moved their animals back and forth along the cattle corridor following the rains, but during the 1960s and '70s, the southern section was broken up into individual ranches as part of a U.S. Agency for International Development program to encourage large-scale ranchers to provide meat for local and export markets. In 1987, Museveni accused the beneficiaries of the USAID program of being "telephone ranchers"—absentee landlords who exploited their workers, many of them Rwandese Tutsi pastoralists. He then launched a project known as the Ranch Restructuring Scheme to break these ranches up and hand them over to the Tutsi pastoralists. The ranchers protested; some had invested in their farms and at the very least wanted compensation for the fences, barns, and dams they'd built.

Museveni refused the ranchers any compensation and the Rwandan pastoralists moved in by force, cutting fences, smashing in windows and doors, pulling out pumps, and stealing animals. When the ranchers armed themselves, Museveni sent hundreds of soldiers to set up roadblocks in the area.

Joseph Mulwanyamuli Ssemogerere was Special District Administrator in Masaka, the heart of the Ranch Restructuring Scheme, when the invasions occurred. Special District Administrators had quasi-military status and carried weapons. Mulwanyamuli had heard that armed men were stealing cattle in the area—his own uncle had been robbed—so he set out with a couple of deputies to investigate. Mulwanyamuli was an old friend of Museveni's, and had obtained a letter from the president authorizing him to tour the area. Most of the guards at the roadblocks allowed him through, but at one checkpoint he dove under his vehicle and exchanged fire with soldiers who tried to block his way. They had not expected him to shoot back, but when he did, they let him pass.

Eventually Mulwanyamuli arrived in the cordoned off area. New villages, populated entirely by Tutsi refugees, had arisen almost overnight. Most of the men were occupied in slaughtering animals and smoking the meat in giant outdoor ovens.

At the time, Mulwanyamuli had no idea what was going on, but now he suspects the meat was used to supply the RPF. "They were preparing for the invasion of Rwanda," he told me in 2016.

Presidents Museveni and Habyarimana were in New York attending UNICEF's World Summit for Children when the RPF invaded Rwanda in 1990. They were staying in the same hotel and Museveni rang Habyarimana's room at 5 a.m. to say he'd just learned that 14 of his officers had deserted and crossed into Rwanda. "I would like to make it very clear that we did not know about the desertion of these boys nor do we support it," he reportedly said.

In Washington a few days later, Museveni told the State Department's Africa chief Herman Cohen that he'd court martial the Rwandan NRA/RPF deserters if they attempted to cross back into Uganda. But a few days after that, he quietly requested France and Belgium not to assist the Rwandan government in repelling the invasion. Cohen writes that he now believes Museveni must have been lying, feigning shock when he knew what was going on all along. Indeed, thousands of Tutsis had left their refugee camps in the weeks before the invasion. Thousands of cattle in the Ranch Restructuring areas had been stolen and slaughtered by Rwandans under the protection of Museveni's army. RPF operatives had removed munitions, including heavy weapons, from Ugandan arsenals.

If Museveni had admitted that he'd supported the invasion, it would have constituted a breach of the United Nations Charter and Organization of African Union rules. When Museveni returned to Uganda, Robert Gribbin, then Deputy Chief of Mission at the U.S. embassy in Kampala, had some "stiff talking points" for him. Stop the invasion, the American said, and ensure no support flowed to the RPF from Ugandan soil.

Museveni had already issued a statement promising to seal all Uganda–Rwanda border-crossings, provide no assistance to the RPF, and arrest any rebels who tried to return to Uganda. But he proceeded to do none of those things and the Americans appear to have made no objection. When the invasion occurred, Paul Kagame, then a senior officer in both the NRA and the RPF, was attending a course at the United States Army Command and General Staff College at Fort Leavenworth, Kansas on field tactics and "psyops" (or psychological operations), propaganda techniques to win the hearts and minds of foreign audiences, sometimes deceptively. In early October, he told his American commanders that he was dropping out to join the invasion of Rwanda. They apparently supported this decision and Kagame flew in to Entebbe Airport, traveled to the Rwanda border by road, and crossed over to join the rebels without incident.

For the next three and a half years, the Ugandan army continued to supply the RPF with provisions and weapons, and to allow its soldiers free passage back and forth across the border. In 1991, Habyarimana accused Museveni of allowing the RPF to attack Rwanda from sanctuaries on Ugandan territory. Then a Ugandan journalist published an article on these very bases in the government-owned *New Vision* newspaper. Museveni

106   threatened to charge the journalist and his editor with sedition, and the entire border area was cordoned off. Even a French and Italian military inspection team was denied access.

The U.S. government was not ignorant of what was going on. U.S. officials met quietly with RPF leaders in Kampala in 1990 and 1991, so obviously the Americans knew that Museveni was not honoring his promise to court martial them.

According to Gribbin, the U.S. began monitoring Ugandan weapons shipments to the RPF in 1992. But instead of punishing Museveni, Western donors doubled aid to his government and allowed his defense spending to balloon to 48 percent of Uganda's recurrent budget, compared to 13 percent for education and 5 percent for health—even as AIDS was ravaging the country.

The invasion was all the more disturbing because Habyarimana had actually acceded to many of the RPF's demands, including the return of refugees and multiparty competition, shortly before it occurred. So it wasn't clear what the RPF was fighting for. Certainly negotiations over refugee repatriation would have dragged on and might not have been resolved to the RPF's satisfaction, or at all. But abandoning negotiations before they'd even begun in favor of war probably cost hundreds of thousands of Rwandan lives.

At least one American was concerned about this. U.S. ambassador to Rwanda Robert Flaten saw with his own eyes that the RPF invasion had sent shock waves through Rwanda, where the majority Hutu population had long feared a Tutsi onslaught from Uganda. Flaten urged the Bush Sr. administration to impose sanctions on Uganda, noting that Saddam Hussein had invaded Kuwait only two months earlier and been met with near-universal condemnation, a UN Security Council demand that he withdrew, and the imminent threat of war from the U.S., which in due course occurred.

But when the RPF invaded Rwanda, Museveni received no more than Ambassador Gribbin's "stiff questions." "In short," Gribbin writes, "We said that the cat was out of the bag, and neither the United States nor Uganda was going to rebag it." Sanctioning Museveni might harm America's interests in Uganda, he explains. "We sought a stable nation after years of violence and uncertainty. We encouraged nascent democratic initiatives. We supported a full range of economic reforms."

But of course, the U.S. wasn't fostering nascent democratic initiatives; it was allowing Museveni to crush them with impunity. Far from seeking stability, the U.S., by allowing Uganda to arm the RPF, was setting the stage for what would turn out to be the worst outbreak of violence ever recorded on the African continent.

Years later, Assistant Secretary of State for Africa Herman Cohen expressed regret for failing to pressure Uganda to stop supporting the RPF, but by then it was far too late.

This was America's second point of no return on the road to pandemonium in central Africa. The first was in 1987 when, despite evidence that Museveni's army was involved in torture and possible war crimes in northern Uganda, and the apparent extra-judicial killing of Andrew Kayiira, the Reagan administration embraced the Ugandan dictator anyway. Now the Bush Sr. and Clinton administrations, faced with the Rwandan refugee crisis, once again chose the path of violence over the possibility of sanctions, pressure, and negotiation to persuade the RPF and their Ugandan patrons to renounce violence and Habyarimana to allow the refugees to go home peacefully.

For Habyarimana and his circle of Hutu elites, the RPF

108   invasion had a silver lining. At the time, Hutu/Tutsi tensions
inside Rwanda were actually at an all-time low. Habyarimana
had sought reconciliation with the Tutsis still living in Rwanda
by reserving civil service jobs and university places for them in
proportion to their share of the population. Though desultory,
this program was modestly successful, and the greatest tensions in the country now lay along class, not ethnic lines. A
tiny educated Hutu clique linked to Habyarimina's family who
called themselves "evoluees"—the evolved ones—was living
off the labor of millions of impoverished rural Hutus, whom
they exploited just as brutally as the Tutsi overlords of bygone
days. The evoluees subjected the peasants to forced labor and
fattened themselves on World Bank "anti-poverty" projects
that provided jobs and other perks for evoluees, but did little
to alleviate poverty.

As the Soviet threat waned, Rwanda's donors began pres-
suring Habyarimina to allow opposition political parties to
operate. Many of these new parties were ethnically mixed,
with both Hutu and Tutsi leaders, but they were united in
criticizing Habyarimana's autocratic behavior and nepotism
and the vast economic inequalities in the country. When
Rwanda's ethnic bonfires roared back to life in the days after
the RPF invasion, Habyarimina and his circle seem to have
sensed a political opportunity: now they could distract the
disaffected Hutu masses from their own abuses by reawaken-
ing fears of the "demon Tutsis." Right after the RPF invasion,
a small group of Hutu elites began planning a genocidal propaganda campaign that would bear hideous fruit three and a
half years later. Scores of non-RPF Tutsis were rounded up and
tortured, and chauvinist Hutu newspapers, magazines, and
radio programs reminded readers that Hutus were the original occupants of the Great Lakes region and that Tutsis were

Nilotics—supposedly warlike pastoralists from Ethiopia who had conquered and enslaved them in the seventeenth century. The RPF invasion was nothing more than a plot by Museveni, Kagame, and their Tutsi co-conspirators to reestablish this evil Nilotic empire. Cartoons of Tutsis killing Hutus began appearing in magazines, along with warnings that all Tutsis were RPF spies bent on dragging the country back to the days when the Tutsi queen supposedly rose from her seat supported by swords driven between the shoulders of Hutu children. In December 1993, a picture of a machete appeared on the front page of one Hutu-chauvinist publication under the headline, "What to do about the Tutsis?"

Three years after the RPF invasion and just six months before the genocide, the UN Security Council finally authorized a peacekeeping force to ensure no weapons crossed the border between Uganda and Rwanda. The United Nations Observer Mission Uganda–Rwanda, or UNOMUR, was under the command of Canadian Lieutenant-General Roméo Dallaire, who was also commander of the more well known UN Mission to Rwanda, or UNAMIR. Dallaire spent most of his time inside Rwanda, but in October 1993, he visited the Ugandan border town of Kabale, where a Ugandan officer told him that his peacekeepers would have to provide the NRA twelve hours' notice so that escorts could be arranged to accompany them on their border patrols. Dallaire protested. After all, the element of surprise is crucial for such monitoring missions. But the Ugandans insisted and eventually Dallaire, who was much more concerned about developments inside Rwanda, gave in.

"The border was a sieve" in any case, Dallaire writes in *Shake Hands with the Devil,* his memoir of the Rwanda genocide. There were five official crossing sites and countless unmapped

110   mountain trails. It was impossible to monitor, especially without a surveillance helicopter that would allow the peace-keepers to see what was going on at night.

Dallaire had also heard that an arsenal in Mbarara, a Ugandan town about 80 miles from the Rwanda border, was being used to supply the RPF. The Security Council had included Mbarara in UNOMUR's inspection mandate, but the NRA refused to allow the peacekeepers there either.

Dallaire does not say whether he brought Uganda's obstruction to the attention of the Security Council. However, in 2004, he told a U.S. congressional hearing that Museveni laughed in his face when they met at a gathering to commemo-rate the tenth anniversary of the genocide. "I remember that UN mission on the border," Dallaire says Museveni told him. "We maneuvered ways to get around it, and of course we did support the [RPF invasion]."

Habyarimana knew the RPF was better armed, trained, and disciplined than his own army. Under immense international pressure, he agreed in August 1993 to grant the RPF seats in a transitional government and nearly half of all posts in the army.

Even Tutsis inside Rwanda were against giving the RPF so much power because they knew it would provoke the angry, fear-ful Hutus to rebel, and they were right. Hutu mayors and other local officials were already stockpiling rifles, and government-linked anti-Tutsi militia groups (including the notorious Interahamwe) were distributing machetes and kerosene to prospective genocidaires. In January 1994, four months before the genocide, the CIA predicted that if tensions were not somehow defused, hundreds of thousands of people might die in ethnic violence. The powder keg awaited a spark to set it off.

That spark arrived at around 8 p.m. on April 6, 1994 when operatives positioned rocket launchers near the airport in

Kigali and shot down President Habyarimana's plane as it was preparing to land. The next morning, frantic Hutu militia groups, convinced that the Nilotic apocalypse was at hand, launched a three-month genocide against the Tutsi people, the vast majority of whom had nothing to do with the RPF.

Few subjects are more polarizing than the modern history of Rwanda. Questions such as "Has the RPF committed human rights abuses?" or "Who shot down President Habyarimana's plane?" have been known to trigger riots at academic conferences. The Rwandan government bans and expels critical scholars from the country, labeling them "enemies of Rwanda" and "genocide deniers," and President Kagame has stated that he doesn't think "anyone in the media, UN, human rights organizations has any moral right whatsoever to level any accusations against me or Rwanda."

Be that as it may, several lines of evidence suggest RPF responsibility for the downing of Habyarimana's plane. The missiles used to shoot down president Habyarimana's plane were recovered shortly after the crash and found to be Russian-made SAM-16s. The Rwandan army was not known to possess these weapons, but the RPF did. On May 18, 1991, the RPF had fired a similar missile at a Rwandan army aircraft. It failed to explode and Rwandan soldiers carefully transferred the dud to their barracks, recorded the serial number, and shared this with the French military attache in Kigali. After the genocide, Belgian historian Filip Reyntjens determined that the serial number of the dud was in the same series as the missiles fired at Habyarimana's plane, strongly implicating the RPF in the president's assassination. About three weeks after the plane crash, local peasants found two SAM-16 single-use launchers in a valley near Masaka Hill, an area within range of the airport that was accessible to the RPF. According to the Russian military prosecutor's office, the launchers had been sold to Uganda by the USSR in 1987.

Since 1997, five additional investigations of the crash have been carried out, including one by a UN-appointed team, and one each by French and Spanish judges working independently. These three concluded that the RPF was responsible. Two Rwandan government investigations concluded that Hutu elites and members of Habyarimana's own army were responsible. More details of these investigations can be found in the footnote on page 244.

In 2012, news outlets around the world claimed that a report on the Habyarimana plane crash commissioned by two French judges supposedly exonerated the RPF. The authors of the report used ballistic and acoustic evidence to argue that the missiles were probably fired by the Rwandan army from Kanombe military barracks. However, the authors admit that their technical findings had a margin of error and couldn't exclude the possibility that the missiles were fired from Masaka Hill, where the launchers were actually found. The report also fails to explain how the Rwandan army, which did not possess SAM-16s, could have shot down the plane using such weapons.

As soon as the plane hit the ground, the RPF began advancing. But its troop movements puzzled UNAMIR's General Dallaire. Rather than heading south, where most of the killings were taking place, the RPF circled around Kigali. By the time it reached the capital weeks later, most of the Tutsis there were dead.

When Dallaire met RPF commander Kagame during the genocide, he asked about the delay. "He knew full well that every day of fighting on the periphery meant certain death

for Tutsis still behind [Rwanda Government Forces] lines,"
Dallaire writes in *Shake Hands with the Devil.* "[Kagame]
ignored the implications of my question."

In the years that followed, President Bill Clinton apologized numerous times for America's shocking inaction during
the genocide. "If we'd gone in sooner, I believe we could have
saved at least a third of the lives that were lost," he told journalist Tania Bryer in 2013. Instead, Europeans and Americans
extracted their own citizens and the UN peacekeepers quietly withdrew. But Dallaire indicates that the RPF would
have rejected Clinton's help in any case. "The international
community is looking at sending an intervention force on
humanitarian grounds," Dallaire says Kagame told him, "But
for what reason? If an intervention force is sent to Rwanda, we
will fight it."

As the RPF advanced, Hutu refugees fled into neighboring countries. In late April, television stations around the
world broadcast images of thousands upon thousands of them
crossing the Rusumo Bridge from Rwanda into Tanzania, as
the bloated corpses of Rwandans who had not been so lucky
floated down the Kagera River beneath them. Most viewers
assumed that all the corpses were Tutsis killed by the Hutu
genocidaires. But the river drains mainly from areas then held
by the RPF, and Mark Prutsalis, a UN official working in the
Tanzanian refugee camps maintains that at least some of the
bodies were probably Hutu victims of reprisal killings by the
RPF. One refugee after another told him that RPF soldiers had
gone house to house in Hutu areas, dragging people out, tying
them up, and throwing them in the river. The UN estimated
later that the RPF killed some 10,000 civilians each month
during the genocide.

114   Lawrence was among the journalists on Rusumo Bridge
that day. As the bodies floated by, he noticed something
strange. Many of them were tied "three-piece," the infamous
torture method used by Uganda's NRA that had so troubled
U.S. Ambassador Houdek seven years earlier.

In June 1994, while the genocide was still underway, President
Museveni traveled to Minneapolis, where he received a Hubert
H. Humphrey public service medal and honorary doctorate from
the University of Minnesota. The dean, a former World Bank
official, praised Museveni for ending human rights abuses in
Uganda and preparing his country for multiparty democracy.

Western journalists and academics, also seemingly ignorant of the reality, showered Museveni with praise. "Uganda [is]
one of the few flickers of hope for the future of black Africa . . ."
wrote one. *The New York Times* compared the Ugandan tyrant
to Nelson Mandela, and *Time* magazine hailed him as a "herdsman philosopher" and "Central Africa's intellectual compass."
The World Bank continued to shower Museveni with cash,
while the diplomats and captains of industry at Davos said they
found Museveni charming.

Museveni also visited Washington on that trip, where he
met with President Clinton and National Security Advisor
Anthony Lake. I could find no record of what the men discussed, but I can imagine the Americans lamenting the tragedy
in Rwanda, and the Ugandan explaining that this disaster only
confirmed his long-held theory that Africans were too attached
to clan loyalties for multi-party democracy. The continent's
ignorant peasants belonged under the control of autocrats like
himself.

The Old Leopard

When will they ever learn?

—Pete Seeger

Old men dream in one world and act in another. When the Berlin Wall finally collapsed in 1989, the real world of Marshal Mobutu Sese Seko, Zaire's notorious Cold War dictator, fell with it. As a 35-year-old army commander, Mobutu had taken over the former Belgian colony known as Congo in the 1960s, renamed it Zaire, and created a model kleptocracy—a government based on theft. During his heyday, the CIA gave him $15 million each year to spend as he wished, and Western donors filled his treasury with roughly $10 billion more, to which he liberally helped himself. The money kept flowing, even when Mobutu nationalized foreign companies worth $16 billion and handed them over to inexperienced cronies who ruined them; the money kept flowing even as Mobutu siphoned $100 million a year from the state

116   mining company; it kept flowing even after Mobutu's thuggish security men assaulted a diplomat who'd offended him, and raped the man's wife and daughter for good measure; and it kept flowing when Belgian politicians, civil servants, and lobbyists were discovered on Mobutu's payroll.

Mobutu's obligation to his Western benefactors had been to keep his nation's vast mineral wealth, estimated to be worth some $24 trillion in today's dollars, out of Soviet hands. He was also expected to funnel weapons to right-wing rebels such as Angola's UNITA, and to avoid assisting left wing ones such as South Africa's African National Congress.

Mobutu built himself a giant complex of palaces in Gbadolite, the rural village where he grew up, finished with Italian marble, 20-foot doors, and Murano glass chandeliers. There was a golden pagoda, a private zoo, a 10,000-bottle wine cellar, and an airport that could land the Concorde, which Mobutu frequently chartered for visits to the French Riviera.

Mobutu also splurged on some unusual development schemes, including a very short-lived space program and a rather scary one-megawatt nuclear reactor. But most of the money went to sycophants in the army, cabinet, and Zaire's vast but ineffectual civil service that filtered the cash down to the masses to keep it from rebelling. "Go ahead and steal," he once told his people on national TV, and so they did.

As soon as the Cold War was over, the World Bank and IMF cut Mobutu off and pressured him into allowing multi-party democracy. Four hundred fractious opposition parties emerged virtually overnight. All needed to be coopted or otherwise placated, but all the looting had knocked the economy back to its 1950s level, so Mobutu had fewer resources at his disposal. The army went unpaid and rioted in protest. Amid the

pandemonium, the nation's impoverished doctors and nurses
were powerless to stop epidemics of cholera, AIDS, and bubonic
plague from ravaging the cities and the countryside.

By April 1994, Mobutu had been avoiding the capital
Kinshasa for months, skipping cabinet meetings and army
inductions and barely even reading newspapers. But when the
Old Leopard, as the Zairean was nicknamed, learned that his
friend Juvenal Habyarimana had been killed in a plane crash in
Kigali, he roused himself for one last fight.

By the time the genocide was over and the RPF had taken
control of Rwanda, more than a million Hutu refugees had settled in vast refugee camps, just a few miles inside Zaire. Most
were ordinary women and children who were terrified of the
RPF. But at least 30,000 were so-called "genocidaires"—former
government officials, ex-Rwandan army soldiers, and members
of the vicious Interahamwe militia that had orchestrated the
massacres of Tutsis inside Rwanda.

The camps seethed with anti-Tutsi hate speeches and radio
broadcasts. Everyone knew the genocidaires were arming themselves with the intention of attacking Rwanda, ousting the RPF,
and retaking their country. Weapons deliveries took place right
in front of aid workers.

Throughout 1995 and into 1996, Hutu militants from the
camps launched deadly hit and run attacks into Rwanda, killing hundreds, perhaps thousands of Tutsis both within Rwanda
and in the areas around the camps where many Zairean Tutsis
happened to live. Reprisals against Hutus inside Rwanda were
swift, cruel, and indiscriminate. During the genocide, RPF
officers would invite local Hutus to "peace and reconciliation"
meetings and then slaughter everyone who turned up. Millions
of frightened Hutus fled—some to Zaire and some to a camp

called Kibeho inside Rwanda near the Zairean border. The RPF attempted to close Kibeho in April 1995, but when thousands of terrified Hutus refused to go home, Kagame's soldiers launched a massacre. UN medics had counted four thousand bodies when RPA officers ordered them to stop counting.

In Kigali and elsewhere soldiers went house-to-house murdering Hutus, especially returned refugees. No attempt was made to determine whether the victims had been involved either in the genocide against the Tutsis or the cross-border attacks.

You'd think Mobutu and Museveni would see eye to eye on the Rwanda conundrum. After all, they had much in common. Museveni's taste was more rustic, Mobutu's more cosmopolitan, but both had the common touch with their citizens; both had enough charisma to warm up the stiffest Western diplomat with pointless banter; both easily persuaded said diplomats that democracy led to disaster in Africa, and that no other leader could conceivably rule their counties besides themselves; both made liberal use of the torture chamber and brown envelope to placate domestic critics; both stacked their armies with officers from their own tribe and clan and played other tribes off each other with a skill that would impress an anthropologist.

Nevertheless, the two men despised each other. Museveni saw Mobutu as a Cold War relic and wanted him out of the way; Mobutu saw Museveni as a violent closet Tutsi bent on subjugating all of Africa to Nilotic domination. Mobutu had even sent troops into Uganda in 1985 in a last-ditch attempt to prevent Museveni's NRA from taking over. When that failed, he reportedly tried to kill his Ugandan counterpart.

The evening after Museveni's swearing-in in January 1986, Museveni and Kizza Besigye, his new political commissar, had flown to Goma, a small city in northeastern Zaire for a meeting with Mobutu. Presidents Habyarimana of Rwanda and Daniel Arap Moi of Kenya were also there. All three countries border Uganda, and the leaders were worried that Obote's ouster might set a precedent. They wanted to ensure that Museveni wasn't planning any mischief with rebels who might threaten their own countries. Of course, this is precisely what Museveni was planning, but at the meeting, he and the others all played diplomat. The Ugandans were greeted at the airport by acrobats and a Zairean singing and dancing troupe. In the meeting, Museveni expressed eagerness to be guided by the other leaders' wisdom and experience. When Mobutu bade his visitors farewell, he presented Museveni with a wrapped gift. It turned out to be a bomb, set to detonate on Museveni's return flight. Museveni's aides discovered it in time, and everyone made it home without incident, but relations between the two leaders remained frosty.

The Hutu militants in the Zairean refugee camps not only wanted to retake Rwanda; they also had their sights on Museveni, whom they saw as the mastermind of the RPF conquest of their country. Zaire's corrupt generals quietly provided them with weapons. Museveni and Kagame resolved to cross the border and shut the camps down by force, and get rid of Mobutu once and for all.

But in order to do this they had to make the operation look like an indigenous Zairean uprising. For decades, beleaguered Zairean anti-Mobutu rebels had been languishing in various eastern African capitals, but the Old Leopard's Cold War benefactors ensured they were always outgunned. Now the tables were turning and in November 1994, Museveni convened a meeting in Kampala of Congolese exile groups interested in overthrowing Mobutu. Numerous candidates were considered to lead this rebellion, but Museveni and Kagame eventually

120   settled on an aging, overweight Marxist named Laurent Kabila, known for scooting around on a motorbike wearing sandals, and for having fathered nearly 30 children. Kabila had been commander of an ill-fated anti-Mobutu rebellion in the 1960s. His Conseil National de Libération even received assistance from Che Guevara, who blamed Kabila's sloppiness, drunkenness, womanizing, and "lack of revolutionary seriousness" for its failure. In the years that followed, Kabila earned money trading, sometimes illegally, and once kidnapped four university students from primatologist Jane Goodall's chimpanzee observation camp in Tanzania's Gombe Stream National Park. They were released after their families paid nearly $500,000 in ransom.

When Congo expert Jason Stearns asked Rwanda's intelligence chief Patrick Karegeya why Kabila, of all people, was chosen to lead the struggle for a better Zaire, Stearns reports that the Rwandan told him, "We just needed someone to make the whole operation look Congolese."

The Rwandan army, along with Kabila's rebels (now known as the Alliance of Democratic Forces for the Liberation of Congo, or AFDL), invaded the Zaire camps in October 1996. The refugees were ordered to march back to Rwanda, but hundreds of thousands either refused to go or fled deeper into Zaire and on to other countries. Kagame's troops tracked them down and massacred them. Fugitive refugees were strangled, shot, bayonetted, hacked to death, and had their skulls bashed in. No effort was made to determine whether they were genocidaires or simply refugees too frightened to go home. Roughly 260,000 remain unaccounted for.

Then the Ugandan army joined the Rwandans and the AFDL for the march to Kinshasa to topple Mobutu.

A Sudden Departure

In this world, we walk on the roof of Hell, gazing at flowers.
—Kobayashi Issa

In February 1995, Lawrence was thriving. Now 27, he was married and had several small businesses including a hardware store and a taxi service. His articles in *The Citizen* continued to poke thorns into the hide of Museveni's regime.

It was another slow day in the office when he received a visitor from the External Security Organization—or ESO—Uganda's CIA. A group of ESO spies had written a letter to Museveni concerning Uganda's interference in the affairs of other countries, and they wanted *The Citizen* to publish it.

"We members of ESO," the spies began, "are writing to Your Excellency to express our disappointment with the continued foreigners (sic) who are working in ESO." The agency was infiltrated by Rwandan operatives, they explained, who had not

122   only planned and executed the takeover of Rwanda, they were now training Kenyans and "Zairos" (meaning Zaireans), as well. "All these are to be used in destabilizing our neighbors. Mr. President, don't we have enough problems to work on?"

"Mr. President, we have chosen to write an open letter to you because the times we have tried to write to you all our letters have been removed and thrown in the dustbin. We hope one day you will have time to come and talk to us and we shall have the opportunity to tell you more."

No doubt the spies who wrote the ESO letter knew Museveni knew what ESO was doing, but the operative told Lawrence that they were worried that if France discovered Uganda was backing the Zairean rebels, President Mitterand, already furious about the killing of France's longstanding friend President Habyarimana, might bomb Kampala.

After all, the spies continued,

> [In the RPF war] every planning (sic) was done here, even the top security personnel were all aware, and they were directly involved. . . . This is not good, for as you know, Rwanda was a foreign state. The good loving (sic) people of the world will never like this. If you are not aware, when the [RPF] war was at its climax, 850 NRA soldiers were taken to beef up the RPA.

The letter's most startling claim was that the Americans were secretly involved in the mission to topple Mobutu. This slipped out in an aside about the high cost of hiring Cubans, who were also involved in training the foreign rebel groups.

"The Cuban trainers, unlike their CIA counterparts," the ESO operatives wrote, "extort a lot of money from the Ugandan government while the latter were doing it for free."

Excerpts of the ESO letter appeared in an unsigned article in the March 16, 1995 issue of *The Citizen*. A few days later, Lawrence received an invitation to meet the president. Museveni informed him that the ESO article had angered many people; some wanted Lawrence dead. But Museveni said he had known Lawrence's father Joseph and wanted to protect him. Money was discussed. Lawrence thanked the president, but did not accept the money and refused to name the operative who leaked the letter to him.

On April 13, the police burst into Lawrence's house at midnight, just as he was emerging from the shower. He was ordered to dress and then bundled into a pickup truck with civilian plates. For the next week, Lawrence was shuttled from one detention center to another while his colleagues frantically searched for him.

They eventually found him at Kampala's Central Police Station, but the officer in charge didn't know what the charges were or when he'd be produced in court. While Lawrence's wife wept in the hallway and his father Joseph paced back and forth, the officer phoned headquarters and asked his superiors what he should tell the irate reporters in his office. "Please be patient," he said finally.

Lawrence appeared in court the next day, where he was charged with sedition for printing the ESO letter. The bail amount was very high, but friends and relatives quickly collected the cash and delivered it to the bail clerk in a large plastic bag.

While Lawrence was awaiting trial, a security operative from his home village approached him in a Kampala grocery store, gave him $400 in U.S. notes, and said, "Take this and leave the country. If I see you again, I'll have to kill you."

Three days later Lawrence turned up on the doorstep of the Catholic Maryknoll Fathers in Nairobi, Kenya. Ugandan spies were tracking his every move and he was terrified. In June, the

124   Kenyan police arrested an undercover Ugandan police officer named Paul Nsubuga who confessed that he was on a mission to try to assassinate Lawrence.

A Ugandan delegation, including the director of ESO and the foreign minister, arrived in Nairobi for talks with Kenya's president Daniel Arap Moi two days after Nsubuuga was apprehended. It is not known if Lawrence's case was discussed, but he was by then under the protection of the UN High Commissioner for Refugees, so there was little Moi could do, even if he had wanted to extradite him. Back in Uganda, Lawrence's father Joseph was brutally beaten by unknown thugs on his way home from his shop. He was permanently paralyzed and died two years later.

Lawrence isn't sure how he ended up in the United States, but shortly after he arrived in Nairobi, one of the priests received a phone call from an official at the U.S. embassy in Nairobi, asking about him. "They seem to know you," the priest said.

Lawrence and the priest met two American Embassy officials at a hotel in Nairobi's fashionable Ngong Hills the following day. The brief interview mainly concerned the ESO letter. "They were interested in the allegation that Americans were training Congolese to attack Zaire," he told me in 2015. Again, Lawrence refused to identify who had leaked the document.

"He's a tough nut to crack," Lawrence remembers one of the Americans telling the priest. It was an expression he had not heard before.

When Lawrence arrived at JFK airport in New York, two men were waiting for him. They drove him to La Guardia airport, and put him on a plane to Boston, where he transferred to a flight to Newburgh, New York. There he was met by another man who drove him to Poughkeepsie. He spent a few weeks with his host and was eventually settled in an apartment of his own.

For months Lawrence was afraid to approach the police, even to ask directions, for fear they'd rob, beat, or arrest him. When William Safire called First Lady Hillary Clinton a "congenital liar" in print Lawrence was sure *The New York Times* columnist was going straight to jail. During his first American autumn, he wondered why Americans drove for miles just to look at leaves. When winter arrived, he left his car in a lot for a few days and panicked when he returned and couldn't find it. Then he noticed an antenna poking out of a massive snowdrift. By spring, he was enrolled at a local community college. Two years later he transferred to Vassar and graduated in 2001. But Uganda never left him, and from his new American home he continued to work for democracy in his country of origin.

Meanwhile, all hell was breaking loose in Zaire.

A Leopard in Winter

Oh, my piglets, we are the origins of war: not history's forces, nor the times, nor justice, nor the lack of it, nor causes, nor religions, nor ideas, nor kinds of government, nor any other thing. We are the killers. We breed wars. We carry it like syphilis inside. Dead bodies rot in field and stream because the living ones are rotten.

—*The Lion in Winter*

Depressed, lethargic, and suffering from terminal prostate cancer, Mobutu Sese Seko could barely walk when Clinton's UN ambassador Bill Richardson met him in Kinshasa in April 1997.

"We told Mobutu that his army was going to lose," recalled ambassador to Zaire Daniel Simpson, who was present at the meeting. "If you refuse to withdraw peacefully, your body could be dragged through the streets of Kinshasa."

As Kabila's AFDL and its Rwandan and Ugandan backers advanced across the country, Mobutu's impoverished army melted away, looting and raping as it went. At first Museveni and Kagame denied they had anything to do with the invasion, claiming the AFDL was an entirely indigenous Congolese force. Museveni even had the nerve to play the diplomat, urging Mobutu to negotiate. But the Old Leopard refused to talk unless Rwanda and Uganda pulled their troops out of Zaire. U.S. diplomats accused Mobutu of stubbornness, but Mobutu knew that negotiating with Museveni was a fool's errand. The wily Ugandan had extended a hand to Andrew Kayiira, Tito Okello, Juvenal Habyarimana, and Joseph Kony (via Betty Bigombe) and then betrayed every one of them. Now Museveni was pretending to plead for peace, even as his troops were already on the battlefield, and Uganda's airports were being used to ship equipment and supplies into the war zone.

Mobutu hung on for another month after Richardson left, and then departed for Morocco, where he died in exile shortly thereafter.

Laurent Kabila—ex-kidnapper, smuggler, comrade of Che Guevara, and leader of the AFDL—became Zaire's new president in May 1997. He changed the country's name to Democratic Republic of Congo and was greeted warmly by the Americans and Europeans, at first. In December, U.S. Secretary of State Madeleine Albright praised him for making a "strong start" toward transforming his country into an "engine of regional growth." When the Americans whom Kabila had kidnapped from Jane Goodall's chimpanzee camp realized their former tormenter was Congo's new leader, they asked Ambassador Simpson to denounce him. "I was amazed at how we were rebuffed," one ex-hostage told a reporter from the Stanford alumni magazine. "I just made this plea—here I am, an American citizen, asking my government to do one thing for me—and [Simpson] flat-out refused."

128   "To administration officials, the 'one thing' [the ex-hostage]
wants is no small request," surmised journalist Brian Aronstam.
"The U.S. government has decided to support Kabila, not
embarrass him."

But Kabila would soon blow it with the Americans—and
with his Ugandan and Rwandan backers as well. By August
1998, a new and even bloodier phase of the war was underway,
as Uganda and Rwanda, along with roughly a dozen Congolese
militia groups, tried to overthrow Kabila, and Angola, Zimbabwe
and other countries tried to prop him up. Millions would die in
massacres or from hunger and disease.

Uganda's role was particularly notorious. Between 1999 and
2003, Uganda and its proxy militias controlled Congo's Ituri
region, home to some of the richest gold and diamond deposits on earth, as well as coltan—sales of which were set to soar
in the years to come. During this period, some 50,000 Iturians
were killed and half a million displaced while the Ugandans and
their allies looted property, committed murders, and grabbed
land. Villagers were raped, herded into churches, and burned
alive.

Just as in northern Uganda, Museveni's military stoked ethnic conflict deliberately by supporting at one time or another
10 different militant groups in Ituri, and then standing by as
they massacred each other, along with civilians they suspected
of collaboration with their opponents. The Ugandans also
recruited hundreds of child soldiers and took them to Uganda
for indoctrination and training.

Throughout the conflict, Ugandan military planes ferried gold, diamonds, and coltan out of the occupied areas, and
brought consumer goods in. Most of the diamond shipments
were arranged by the Victoria Group, a company not listed in

Uganda's official Companies Registry but whose owners include Museveni's half-brother Salim Saleh. Viktor Bout, the notorious Russian arms trafficker now serving a 25-year prison sentence in Marion, Illinois for conspiracy and aiding terrorists was also part of this operation.

Most of the gold came from small mines maintained by local Congolese artisanal miners. The Ugandans forced the artisanals to use dangerous methods involving explosives that ultimately destroyed several mines. One collapsed in 1999, killing a hundred miners. When their colleagues protested, the Ugandans murdered them.

Uganda and Rwanda also looted timber, elephant tusks, and other natural resources from eastern Congo, and turned it into the "rape capital of the world." Congolese rebels raped local women so they'd produce future child soldiers to attack the Tutsi invaders, and Rwanda-backed Tutsi rebels mutilated the same women by ramming them with guns and other objects to prevent them from ever becoming pregnant. Roughly one woman in five in the war zone was raped at least once. As one survivor told journalist Paul Ndiho, "I've been violated so many times I feel part of me is not my body."

In 2005, Congo sued Uganda in the UN's International Court of Justice for crimes committed by its army during the war. The justices concluded that Uganda owed Congo $10 billion in reparations. The debt remains outstanding and Uganda continued to back Congolese proxy armies including M23, which the UN has accused of mass rape, looting, summary execution and other crimes. According to a UN investigation, 900kg of gold arrived in Dubai from Uganda in 2014, but the Ugandan government reported only 14 kg of gold exports. Most of the unreported 886 kg almost certainly came from Congo. In March

2012, poachers killed 22 elephants in a Congolese national park, the largest mass killing in recent memory. The adults had clustered around the babies, as elephants typically do when they feel threatened. Most had been shot from above with AK-47s and their tusks and the male genitalia had been removed. Shortly afterwards, park authorities chased away a Ugandan military helicopter that was flying low over the park. No helicopter attacks on elephants have since occurred.

Uganda and Rwanda received diplomatic and material support from the U.S., even as the mayhem in Zaire unfolded. After the RPF took over Rwanda in July 1994, a small group of Americans based at the embassy in Kigali developed a warm relationship with several RPF commanders. According to Roessler and Verhoeven, Rick Orth of the Defense Intelligence Agency, Robert Gribbin, now in harness as U.S. ambassador to Rwanda, Gribbin's deputy Peter Whaley, and the embassy's military attache Thomas Odom spent their leisure hours socializing on the tennis court and drinking beer with Paul Kagame and other RPF leaders. When a new International Criminal Tribunal for Rwanda was established to investigate the genocide, the U.S. pressured it to overlook crimes committed by the RPF and focus only on the genocidaires.

Also according to Roessler and Verhoeven, in July 1994, 200 U.S. Special Forces troops began training the RPA in marksmanship, navigation, small unit management, and other techniques that would later be used to track down and kill the genocidaires, as well as thousands of innocent, frightened refugees in Zaire and elsewhere.

The U.S. also gave Rwanda aerial reconnaissance and radio intelligence which helped the RPA assess the strength and positions of Mobutu's feeble army. Rwanda was then under an arms embargo, but in 1995, the Clinton administration began transferring military vehicles and other equipment to Uganda, Eritrea, and Ethiopia. In theory, these transfers were to help the three nations defend themselves against terrorist incursions from Sudan, but tanks, grenades, and other light weapons were donated by these countries to the Rwandan army shortly before it invaded Zaire. According to a European defense analyst quoted by Cambridge University political scientist Adam Branch, weapons given to Uganda to fight the LRA would have been useless in northern Uganda—where the LRA was—and were almost certainly diverted to Congo, with U.S. approval.

Pentagon officials were seen on the ground in eastern Zaire during the invasion. Old CIA hands were also seen around Kigali. Throughout the AFDL's march to Kinshasa, Laurent Kabila was in regular contact with Peter Whaley at the U.S. embassy in Kigali, and would sometimes call him in the middle of the night. Their meetings in the field were so frequent the conflict became known as "Whaley's War" in some diplomatic circles.

While the Clinton administration was overlooking the stifling of democracy in Uganda, reprisals against Hutus inside Rwanda, and the storming of refugee camps in Zaire, it was also sidelining the peaceful Zairean opposition. During the late 1980s and early '90s, Presidents Reagan and Bush had supported an increasingly emboldened Zairean pro-democracy movement. Church groups, NGOs, journalists, and others courageously denounced the corruption of Mobutu's government and marched into prisons and paid lawyers to defend dissidents. Civil society groups supported by U.S. funds created draft laws and a new constitution and elected their own prime minister, opposition leader Etienne Tshisekedi. These programs so energized Zairean society that market women began refusing money from soldiers involved in looting.

But as soon as Clinton took office, U.S. funds for democratization activities dried up; the embassy in Kinshasa remained without an ambassador for months, and the U.S. Cultural Center, which had once hosted numerous civil society activities closed, as did the USAID office. Throughout the Clinton administration, "the disengagement from Zairean civil society and the opposition was profound," observed Congo specialist Peter Rosenblum in 2016. Just as in Rwanda, the Americans clearly supported a military, rather than a political solution to Zaire's problems.

As attacks on Rwanda from the refugee camps grew bloodier, and reprisals against Hutus within Rwanda more indiscriminate, humanitarian aid workers tried to draw attention to the crisis. The UN sensibly proposed to separate the genocidaires from the other refugees and confine them to military camps further from the border, but the U.S. government did not support this plan, choosing instead to let the Rwandans and Ugandans handle it their way.

When Susan Rice, Clinton's senior advisor on Africa at the National Security Council, returned from her first trip to eastern Africa shortly before the invasion, she told her staff, "Museveni and Kagame agree that the basic problem . . . is a danger of a resurgence of genocide and they know how to deal with that," according to a lawyer who was present when she said it. "The only thing we"—meaning the U.S.—"have to do is look the other way."

During the early 1990s, Mobutu began making overtures to Sudan's Bashir in the hope of joining forces against their shared enemy Museveni. Numerous Sudan-backed anti-Museveni rebel groups found sanctuary in the weakly governed eastern provinces of Mobutu's Zaire, and after the Rwanda genocide, they were reportedly teaming up with the Rwandan Hutu militants in the refugee camps. With help from Mobutu and Bashir, they might have posed a considerable threat to Museveni and Kagame.

By then U.S. security officials were seriously concerned about terrorist activities in Sudan. In 1993, American law enforcement officials linked two Sudanese consular officials in New York to the first World Trade Center bombing, as well as to a shadowy plot to blow up four other New York City landmarks including the UN and the Holland Tunnel. Scant evidence linked the bombing to the Sudanese government—the culprits hailed from Egypt, Kuwait, Pakistan, and Palestine—but Sudan was nevertheless placed on America's list of state sponsors of terror.

U.S. intelligence agents then began linking Sudanese operatives to scores of other outlandish terror plots, including a conspiracy to assassinate then National Security Adviser Anthony Lake and bomb a children's party at a diplomatic residence in Khartoum. These turned out to be false, but were believed at the time.

Then in 1995, assassins linked to the Egyptian terrorist group Jamaat al-Islamiyya fired on the limousine of Egypt's President Hosni Mubarak during a state visit to Ethiopia. Mubarak survived, but when he discovered that the assassins were among those headquartered in Sudan, he lashed out publicly at the "pygmy despot" Bashir. Keeping Mubarak in power was central to U.S. Middle East policy. Little would have alarmed Washington more than an Iran-like Islamic fundamentalist uprising on Israel's doorstep.

134   Both Bashir and Mobutu were by then supporting Zaire-based anti-Museveni and anti-Kagame rebels. Museveni and Kagame were in turn supporting anti-Mobutu rebels. Throw in Bashir and Garang's armies battling it out in Sudan and President Daniel Arap Moi of Kenya, who sympathized with the Mobutu/Bashir axis, President Pierre Buyoya of Burundi, who sided with Museveni and Kagame, and Presidents Robert Mugabe of Zimbabwe and Jose Eduardo Dos Santos of Angola, who sided with Museveni and Kagame during the first Congo war, and against them in the second, and you have a truly fine mess indeed.

By early 1998, some U.S. legislators were becoming concerned that America's new military allies—Uganda and Rwanda, as well as Ethiopia and Eritrea (who were about to go to war against each other)—were trampling on the rights of their citizens. In all four countries, elections, if held at all, were rigged, the media faced repression, law courts were manipulated, and military units served as the rulers' private armies. Secretary of State Madeleine Albright had recently praised the leaders of these countries as a "new generation" bringing "a new spirit of hope and accomplishment to their countries." She singled out Museveni in particular as a "beacon in the Central African region." When a journalist pointed out to her that Museveni and the others were not paragons of democracy, she shrugged, "Every country's human rights record can be improved."

Republican Senator John Ashcroft of Missouri was having none of it. "It is tyranny and oppression that have been responsible for violence and bloodshed in Africa," he told the Foreign Relations Committee. "When implemented prudently, I think democracy in Africa has been a stabilizing force that has eased social tension and has given disparate groups a voice in governance . . . each missed opportunity [to promote democracy] sends a chill up and down our spines and leads us to suspect that Africa is heading down the road of oppression."

In reply, Susan Rice conceded that America's new African friends were "on the path to democracy"—having not reached that destination, but they were all emerging from conflicts rooted in tribal competition and a weak sense of national identity. An overnight transition to democracy in countries accustomed to strongman rule risked further bloodshed, she claimed—ignoring the fact that this had not happened in Ghana, Zambia, Malawi, and even South Africa when these countries democratized.

Human rights experts also addressed the committee. What Africa needed, according to American University Professor George Ayittey, were strong institutions: politically neutral armies and independent media and courts of law, not another generation of military dictators. But he too was ignored.

Two weeks after the hearing, president Clinton commenced a 12-day Africa tour. He visited six countries, including Uganda, where he announced further increases in foreign aid and declined an invitation to meet with opposition leaders. Instead, he sent special envoy Jesse Jackson who bought the opposition leaders lunch but addressed none of their human rights concerns.

On that trip, Clinton stood before a group of Ugandan schoolchildren in a rural hamlet and apologized for slavery. The children and their teachers must have been baffled. Virtually all American slaves came from West Africa; none are known to have come from Uganda, which was unknown to Western explorers until after the Atlantic slave trade had ceased. Clinton

136   also told the students that during the Cold War, America often "dealt with countries in Africa and in other parts of the world based more on how they stood in the struggle between the United States and the Soviet Union than how they stood in the struggle for their own people's aspirations to live up to the fullest of their God-given abilities."

The enemies may have changed from the Soviets to the Islamists, but for millions of Africans, America's pursuit of what it saw as its strategic interests had not.

Breeding Ground

My intention is to work for my people but not for me. That is the reason why if you check all the banks all over the world . . . you will never find account belong to me because I work for the people of Uganda.

—Idi Amin, 1980

Interviewer: Do you wake up sometimes and feel, you know what, this is too much for me? Listen, this is too much! You don't feel appreciated enough.

Yoweri Museveni: It doesn't matter, because . . . I am working for myself. I am not working for other people. I am working for my grandchildren; my children.

—May 2011

I was first drawn to Uganda by its remarkable medical history. Well before colonial times, the people of this region had their

138   own gods to distinguish plague from smallpox, and performed Caesarian sections, operations considered too difficult and dangerous by Europeans at the time. In 1878, a British missionary doctor named Robert Felkin witnessed a Muganda traditional surgeon perform one on a woman who had been in labor for two days and would almost certainly have died without intervention. After smearing her belly with banana wine and ensuring she was quite drunk on the same substance, the Muganda surgeon sliced her open with a sharp knife, extracted the baby and afterbirth, and closed the wound with iron nails tied around with reeds. When Felkin visited mother and baby a week later, both were well.

Ugandans were similarly fascinated by Western medicine. When Albert Cook, founder of Uganda's first hospital in 1897, restored the sight of a man with cataracts, the ecstatic patient declared that Cook must be God himself. The first medical school opened in British colonial Uganda in the 1920s, and competition for a place was so tough that "to get in you had to be a genius," according to one young aspirant. Ugandan scientists helped pioneer treatment for childhood cancers and malnutrition and the mass immunization campaigns that UNICEF would later promote throughout the developing world. When Singapore was looking to reform its own health care system in the 1960s, it sent a delegation to Uganda.

Today, this system is a shambles. Bats, snakes, and other wildlife have taken up residence in once-functioning rural clinics. I have seen fecal material rain down from the crumbling ceilings of operating theaters. Power cuts and water shortages in hospitals kill thousands of patients each year, and emergency operations on pregnant women are sometimes carried out by the light of torches made from burning grass.

The salaries of government doctors, a mere $350 per month, are a third or less of those of their counterparts in much poorer neighboring countries such as Rwanda and even South Sudan. As a result, only half of Uganda's health workers show up to work on any given day, and nearly half of those are so ill-qualified they can't diagnose pneumonia. Some steal medicines from public pharmacies and refuse to treat patients without a bribe, even in emergencies. Court testimony and newspaper reports describe doctors standing around chatting and watching soccer games while women under their care die in childbirth, screaming for help.

In 2012, women were seven times more likely to die in childbirth at Mulago Hospital than when Idi Amin was president 40 years earlier. Uganda was losing one child to malaria every seven minutes, the highest death rate from that disease in the world. Since 2013, scores, perhaps hundreds of people have died of famine in this lush, fertile country, not because of food shortages, but because the government fails to send food where it is needed. During a drought in 2017, poor people in one rural area were sleeping next to boreholes, so they wouldn't miss a trickle of water, if and when it came. Meanwhile, Museveni's State House alone consumed more of the government budget than agriculture, which employs 80 percent of the population, and spent $150 million a year flying the president and his cronies to Kenya, India and Europe for health care.

Only a third of Uganda's children complete primary school. Eighty percent of their teachers can't read English, the official language of government. Two-thirds of the population still survive on subsistence agriculture, fewer than 20 percent have electricity, and roughly half live at least a ten minute walk from the nearest water source.

Corruption, combined with callous indifference to the plight of ordinary people on the part of Uganda's leaders are the main causes of these problems. Soon after Uganda began receiving generous amounts of foreign aid, it became the subject of a series of enormous corruption scandals. In 1995, the World Bank recapitalized the defunct Uganda Commercial Bank with a loan of $72 million. Museveni then sold it to a consortium that included his own brother for $11 million. The same brother procured Belorussian junk helicopters for the army, pocketing $800,000 from the deal even though they couldn't fly. Then the World Bank provided Uganda with a multimillion-dollar loan to construct 15 irrigation dams. A few weeks after Museveni's agriculture minister reported to Parliament that the dams were nearly complete, an investigative team confirmed that they did not exist. When elders from the area where the dams were supposed to be protested, the Agriculture Minister reportedly replied, "The valley dams they are complaining about do exist. The problem with Ugandans is they will stand on the dams and then ask you where they are."

When donor funding increased in the 2000s, so did the number of scandals. A million dollars donated by the Global Alliance for Vaccines and Immunization intended for children's health programs ended up in the First Lady's office; millions more intended for forestry projects, road building, and assistance to victims of the notorious warlord Joseph Kony turned up under ministers' beds, in flowerpots in the prime minister's office, in Las Vegas casinos, in personal bank accounts, and in heaps on the floor in President Museveni's official residence. Millions more disappeared into the accounts of nonexistent schools and hospitals and pensioners, and such initiatives as the "Rabbit Multiplication" project that performed no activities at all.

During the early 2000s, an internal investigation found that two thirds of soldiers on the military payroll did not exist, although someone was receiving their salaries. Those soldiers who did exist were so poorly equipped they didn't have a chance. Many testified to investigators that they were in worse shape than the LRA and other groups they were supposed to be fighting.

In 2009, Museveni spent $50 million of a UK government grant intended for the reconstruction of war-torn northern Uganda on a new private jet, described by its manufacturers as "the world's most versatile and stylish." The following year, he drained the treasury of $741 million, and—without parliamentary approval, or even its knowledge—purchased four Russian fighter jets. Hundreds of millions more is looted from the treasury before each election and handed out to voters as bribes.

While Museveni was in New York lecturing the Council on Foreign Relations about the wonders of the free market for African development, his relatives were trying to loot Uganda's workers' pension fund of five million dollars each month, according to the minister who oversaw the fund.

When the World Bank launched an anti-corruption initiative in the late 1990s, Museveni created a dozen or so government anticorruption agencies and NGOs, which had no powers to seriously prosecute the real graft-masters in Uganda, and which were subject to repeated break-ins and computer thefts.

And yet Western diplomats unfailingly tout Museveni as a brilliant leader. When British political scientist Jonathan Fisher was conducting Ph.D. research on Uganda in the mid-2000s, he was struck by how many British and American officials described the Ugandan tyrant as "jovial," "intelligent," "thoughtful," and "smart." Meetings with Museveni were "like opening a bottle of champagne" said one.

While UK Minister of Overseas Development Lynda Chalker was threatening to cut off aid to Kenya over corruption and political repression during the 1990s, she was spending so much time at Museveni's side in Kampala that Ugandan journalists referred to her as "Auntie Lynda."

Chalker's successor Clare Short told Fisher that bilateral talks with Museveni were like getting together with "old friends."

Short acknowledged being "disappointed" by atrocities perpetrated by the Ugandan army in Congo, but hadn't cut off aid to Museveni's government because she didn't want "politics" to interfere with poverty reduction, an odd statement, since Museveni was using so much of Britain's funding for "poverty reduction" to further impoverish Ugandans.

Even in 2016, the World Bank touted the country as an economic success story, with a 19 percent poverty rate, one of Africa's lowest. But the text of the same report indicates that the poverty rate is actually twice as high because Uganda's poverty line is artificially low. The report also indicates that 70 percent of Ugandans think they are poor. Mere observation would tend to support the Ugandans' view over the Bank's: the remains of long-shuttered factories, empty, nonfunctional health centers, schools under trees, dirt roads even on major routes.

Unlike the World Bank, multinational companies take real investment risks and they are pulling out of Uganda. British Airways, Barclays Bank, several cell phone companies, and Uchumi, a large Kenyan supermarket chain, closed shop in 2015, and others will soon follow.

Meanwhile, Uganda's population is soaring, putting huge pressure on the nation's fragile social services. In 2016, Ugandan
women bore six children each on average, among the highest
birthrates in the world. As a result, the population had more
than doubled during Museveni's 30-year reign.

I once asked a Ugandan Health Ministry official why the
government didn't do more to promote family planning, considering the enormous demand from women exhausted by near
annual pregnancies.

The official told me that Museveni had forbidden the ministry from carrying out family planning programs, even if paid
for by donors. Family planning NGOs reached a tiny fraction of
the women who wanted contraception; condoms were available
at many roadside kiosks, but he acknowledged that few men
used them.

"What's Museveni's beef with family planning?" I
wondered.

We were sitting at an outdoor café, and he looked stealthily
around before answering.

"Please don't write my name," he whispered, "but the truth
is, it's the army. The president wants a big army."

Now I understood. Museveni had turned his beautiful country into a poorly maintained breeding colony for soldiers, whom
he deployed in monstrous and unnecessary wars, often at the
behest of American generals and politicians who rattled their
sabers at Afro-Islamic terrorists, but wouldn't dream of sending Americans—let alone their own children—to fight them.

A Good Man in Africa

"Don't forget, we have enemies. We have many enemies across the ocean," my editor told me again threateningly. And that is why we only have good things, nothing bad.

> —Journalist Anatoly Shimanskiy, explaining why
> the dangers of the Chernobyl nuclear accident were
> not accurately reported, in Svetlana Alexievich's
> *Voices from Chernobyl: The Oral History of a Nuclear Disaster*

Ambassador Jimmy Kolker, an affable Missourian who speaks four languages, arrived in Uganda for the second time in 2002. Fresh out of college in the early 1970s, he'd spent four months at Makerere University studying popular perceptions of Idi Amin, the fat, smiling dictator who had just toppled Milton Obote. Many people liked Amin at first. Students made fun of his buffoonish ways, but they also saw him as a man of the people and a welcome relief from the pompous elitists in Obote's administration. Only later did they realize how profound Amin's contempt for their nation's institutions really was.

Like Amin, Museveni also charmed Ugandans with jokes, anecdotes, and African proverbs. But while Amin dispensed with democracy altogether, Museveni shrewdly held sham elections that he and his cronies always seemed to win. In 2001, Kizza Besigye, a retired army colonel who had been Museveni's doctor during the war against Obote ran against Museveni as the flag-bearer of the Reform Agenda, an NRM breakaway group.

Besigye, gravel-voiced and taciturn, had authored a dossier on the erosion of Uganda's justice system, security sector, and other organs of government under Museveni. His rallies proved remarkably popular with an electorate that had increasingly come to see Museveni as yet another tribalist tyrant and wanted a more serious leader.

In the months leading up to polling day, Museveni's hacks spread rumors that Besigye had AIDS, was stockpiling machetes for a massacre and had ignored his dying toddler son—who was in fact alive and well. When this failed to staunch Besigye's soaring popularity, Museveni's personal guards, the Presidential Protection Unit, and a state funded militia called the Kalangala Action Plan invaded opposition strongholds and beat people with sticks and iron bars. Several of Besigye's agents were kidnapped, tortured, and killed.

After Museveni was declared the winner, Besigye challenged the results in court, alleging that 2.5 million ghost votes had been cast in Museveni's favor. The Supreme Court decided 3–2, to uphold the election, and Museveni was sworn in to another presidential term. However, according to prominent Ugandan journalist Charles Onyango-Obbo and retired Supreme Court judge George Kanyeihamba, the Court originally decided 4-1 to annul the election, but Museveni informed two of the judges that he would call in the army if they did not revise their opinions in his favor.

146   By the time Ambassador Kolker arrived, Museveni was already preparing to rig the 2006 election. But back in Washington, the tables were turning. Sudan's president Bashir had managed to push aside the Islamic fundamentalist fanatic Hassan Al-Turabi, and agreed to share intelligence about terrorism with the Bush administration. Museveni's prospects seemed to darken further after the 9/11 attacks, when Bush launched his short-lived Freedom Agenda.

Echoing his father's words a decade earlier, George W. Bush declared that

> Successful societies limit the power of the state ... so that governments respond to the will of the people, and not the will of an elite. . . . Sixty years of Western nations excusing and accommodating the lack of freedom in the Middle East did nothing to make us safe—because in the long run, stability cannot be purchased at the expense of liberty.

"The freedom prize is not for us alone," Bush said. "It is the right and capacity of all mankind . . . liberty is the design of nature."

In Uganda, Ambassador Kolker was determined to implement this inspiring new policy.

After the 2001 election, Besigye was followed everywhere by security men. They disrupted his meetings, blocked his vehicle when he attempted to travel around the country, and dragged him off airplanes when he tried to fly abroad.

Then Museveni accused Besigye of masterminding a series of mysterious grenade attacks in Kampala. No evidence has ever linked the opposition candidate to the explosions, but in August 2001, Besigye fled to South Africa, fearing for his life.

Shortly before he left, U.S. Secretary of State Colin Powell visited Uganda and listened to Besigye's complaints, most of which had to do with Museveni's corruption, repression, and assaults on the rule of law.

Powell pocketed a copy of Besigye's speech as he was leaving and then called upon Museveni. The American reportedly read the Ugandan president the riot act: Get your troops out of Congo, Powell said, and implement real democracy in the next three years, or else.

In June 2003, Museveni flew to Washington and met President George W. Bush at the White House. There's no public record of what they discussed, but Museveni had been among the first to join Bush's Coalition of the Willing against Iraq, and Uganda would soon be sending private contractor guards to serve in that country.

"What should I tell this guy?" Bush asked Ambassador Kolker before the meeting.

Kolker suggested Bush urge Museveni to respect Uganda's constitution and not run again.

"I know how much you like your cattle," Kolker says Bush ended up telling Museveni. "I don't know if I'm going to be re-elected even once. But I know I won't be re-elected twice. That's our system. And after my terms are up, I'm going to be happy to get back to my ranch. Isn't that what you want too? To get back to your cattle?"

Museveni just stared straight ahead. "It was like there were daggers coming out of his eyes," Kolker recalls.

Uganda's 1995 constitution limited each president to two five-year terms and Museveni was therefore supposed to retire in 2006, but it was well known that he was planning to ram through a constitutional amendment to lift the two-term clause and run again.

Museveni's strategy for removing term limits was known as the Kisanja Project—Kisanja meaning both "banana leaves" and "term" in Luganda. First, he appointed a Constitutional Review Commission and then bribed its members to support scrapping term limits. Then, he fired anti-Kisanja cabinet ministers and replaced anti-Kisanja Parliamentary Speaker Francis Ayume with the more accommodating Edward Ssekandi.

Ayume, reshuffled to the post of attorney general, continued to oppose Kisanja. In what some maintain was a stage-managed assassination, Ayume then died in a car crash. He'd been playing golf in the northern town of Arua when Museveni ordered him back to Kampala for an early morning meeting. It was late afternoon and Ayume's friends told him the eight hour drive was dangerous at night. The government-run *New Vision* newspaper claimed he'd died after his vehicle hit a pothole; the Public Works Minister presented a photograph to Parliament showing there was no pothole near where the crash occurred. The *New Vision* then claimed the pothole had been miraculously filled in just hours after the accident.

After Ayume's death, Museveni went for the soft underbelly of Parliament. Pro-Kisanja agents approached women Parliamentarians, who tended to be more persuadable, as well as the spouses, siblings, and adult children of others. In a bizarre pro-Kisanja song and dance fest in a provincial town, a loyal cabinet minister sang that Museveni should rule forever like Fidel Castro, Muammar Gaddafi, and Teodoro Obiang of Equatorial Guinea (who is alleged to have eaten an opposition politician).

The coup de grace for term limits was a $2,500 bribe for each MP who voted for the Kisanja amendment. No one would have known about this had one pro-Kisanja MP, told to wait for his payout, not revealed the scam in Parliament. The news made no difference. Anti-Kisanja MPs were sent out of the country on study tours on the day of the vote, and the amendment passed in June 2005, opening the way for Museveni to run again in 2006.

One of Kolker's main responsibilities was administering multi-million-dollar grants to Uganda from George W. Bush's new international AIDS program known as PEPFAR. Uganda also received about $45 million from the Global Fund for AIDS, TB, and Malaria, a Geneva-based program that, like PEPFAR, procured medicine and supported health promotion activities. The two programs were supposed to collaborate, but early on Kolker noticed that the Global Fund programs weren't performing. Life-saving medicines weren't being delivered and planned community-based activities were not taking place. Kolker found evidence to support rumors that Museveni's health minister Jim Muhwezi and two of his deputies had created scores of fake NGOs, into which they were funneling millions of dollars of Global Fund money intended to benefit Uganda's impoverished AIDS, tuberculosis, and malaria victims. Kolker and others believe some of the money was used to enrich the minister and his deputies, but most was diverted to the war chest for Kisanja's and Museveni's 2006 campaign. Muhwezi also happened to be Museveni's campaign manager.

Kolker informed Global Fund Executive Director Richard Feachem, but the problems persisted. After Feachem stepped down, the Global Fund suspended support to Uganda for several

150   years, and HIV, TB and malaria incidence increased. Ugandan taxpayers refunded the money, but Muhwezi and the others were never punished.

Under U.S. law, foreign officials who benefit from diversion of public funds are denied U.S. travel visas. In the wake of scandal after scandal, Museveni would typically appoint a blue-ribbon commission, identify high-level thieves and then fail to prosecute them. A lawyer on Kolker's embassy staff vetted these commission reports, compiled a list of verifiably guilty Ugandans and placed them on a visa ban list. President Museveni's brother Salim Saleh and Saleh's wife were on it.

In 2005, Kolker and UK High Commissioner Adam Wood visited Museveni at the president's rural retreat in western Uganda and offered him a deal: Retire from office in 2006, and we'll help you find you lucrative work as a UN negotiator. The ambassadors also offered to help arrange a deal so that Museveni would not be prosecuted for acts committed in office. In 2003, the international community had established an International Criminal Court (or ICC). Unlike the International Court of Justice, which deals only with disputes between states, the ICC tries individuals, including sitting presidents. Its Chief Prosecutor Luis Moreno-Ocampo had announced that an investigation into atrocities committed in Congo would be among his first priorities. By April 2004, Congo's President Joseph Kabila had already referred a case against domestic parties to the conflict, but it seemed possible that Ocampo's investigation might go further, possibly implicating senior Ugandan officials, including Museveni or members of his family.

Museveni looked distracted as the ambassadors presented their offer. One of his tactics with foreign visitors was to distract them with digressions about African history—the Great

Rift Valley, the interesting customs of its varied ethnic groups, his own tribe's affection for cattle and so on. American generals and Pentagon officials "ate this up," Kolker told me. "He'd leave their questions about Uganda's troops marauding in Congo for the last minute. Museveni did not attempt such distractions with Kolker and Wood, and the meeting ended without resolution. "He didn't kick us out," Kolker reflected when we met in October 2015, "He just dismissed us like flies."

What Museveni knew, but Kolker and Wood did not, is that Museveni had been working behind the scenes with a Washington lobbyist to secure a deal with the Bush administration that would embroil Uganda in yet another bloodbath, this time in Somalia. More about that in the next chapter.

Kolker's tour of duty in Uganda ended in September 2005. By then the Freedom Agenda had been drowned out by the War on Terror and he returned to the State Department to find that his boss, Assistant Secretary of State for African Affairs Jendayi Frazer, had reversed the travel bans he'd placed on Museveni's family and other corrupt Ugandans and the IMF, World Bank, and ICC, which are supposed to be apolitical, also appear to have gone soft on the Ugandan ruler.

In 2004, Joel Barkan, a World Bank consultant had drafted an explosive report accusing Uganda's donors of creating a brutal autocracy responsible for grand corruption involving Museveni's family, stacking the army and civil service with members of the president's ethnic group and the sabotaging of peace negotiations with Joseph Kony's LRA. It also noted that Museveni had diverted 23 percent of all discretionary ministry budgets—Health, Education, Transport, and so on—to a classified military fund, which was "thence used for managing dissent and election expenditures." The World Bank sat on the report for nearly two years. In the interim, the IMF granted

152   Uganda $4 billion in debt relief. A watered-down version of
        Barkan's report was eventually released. It omitted mention of
        the involvement of Museveni's family in corruption, the diver-
        sion of the discretionary ministry budgets, and the sabotaging
        of LRA peace negotiations.

        For good measure, Scribe, a U.S. public relations firm,
        organized a Congressional Uganda Caucus which opposed leg-
        islators who criticized Museveni. Six Uganda Caucus members
        received donations from Scribe, including Ken Calvert ($500),
        Jeff Fortenberry ($100), David Hobson ($1,000), Dan Burton
        ($2,000), Robert Simmons ($300), and Edolphus Towns ($500).

        Meanwhile the ICC also appears to have given Museveni a pass.
        Since 2005, the ICC has charged several Congolese warlords
        with crimes against humanity, including Thomas Lubanga and
        Jean-Pierre Bemba who were convicted and Bosco Ntaganda
        who remains on trial. All three led rebel groups that were cre-
        ated and/or heavily supported at one time or another by Uganda,
        and yet no officials have yet been indicted. Uganda's support for
        these groups largely predated the Rome Statute which created
        the ICC, and thus Uganda's crimes in Congo might be out of the
        Court's jurisdiction. Still, it seemed odd to let the true archi-
        tects of the mayhem in Ituri off the hook.

        In 2012, Obama's National Security Advisor Susan Rice
        attempted to prevent the UN Security Council from men-
        tioning Uganda and Rwanda's links to M23, a Congolese rebel
        group accused of mass rapes, killings and other crimes. The
        ICC declined to investigate, even after the reports describing
        the relationship between the rebels and the two countries were
        made public.

        In November 2016, Museveni ordered his security force to
        storm the royal palace of the Rwenzururu, a traditional kingdom

in western Uganda. More than a hundred unarmed people were
killed point blank, including children, women, and men who were
tied up at the time, according to Human Rights Watch. And yet
the ICC appears to have taken no interest in this either.

The selective nature of the ICC prosecutions sends a message to the people of Uganda that the international community is
only interested in one side of the story and helps perpetuate the
myth that Museveni is a regional peace-maker and a trustworthy
interpreter of the eastern and central African security situation.

Museveni Finds a New Terror Trove

And when there is the possibility of peace, a new fight erupts, based on an old complaint, and which some people call justice and others madness.

—Nuruddin Farah

Few tourists miss a visit to Nairobi's fashionable Westgate Mall, with its fine restaurants and shops selling elegant furnishings, iPhones and jewelry and its upbeat, pleasant atmosphere, promising a chic vision of a new, rising Africa. But when terrorists stormed the building on Saturday, September 21 2013, they dragged it back into the horror of the War on Terror. At 12:25pm, just as lunch crowds were assembling, four men wearing black scarves around their faces drove up in a silver Mitsubishi SUV, threw a pair of hand-grenades at the main building and began shooting their way in with assault rifles. At first some employees and customers thought it was a robbery; then one of the

gunmen strolled over to some tents that had been set up near
the entrance for a cooking contest and tossed a hand-grenade at
dozens of would-be contestants and spectators huddled nearby.
Four hours later, 67 people were dead, including a nephew of
Kenyan president Uhuru Kenyatta and Ghanaian Kofi Awoonor,
one of Africa's finest poets.

The attackers were soon identified to be members of
Somalia's Islamist terrorist group Al-Shabaab, but their story,
or a big part of it, can be traced to Uganda.

For nearly two decades, Museveni had relied on America's
fear of Sudan to secure virtually unlimited impunity from the
West. But after Sudan's president Bashir began sharing intelligence about terrorists in the wake of 9/11, it briefly seemed
as though Washington might abandon their Ugandan partner.
Unfortunately, this did not happen. Even as Ambassador Kolker
was trying to marshal diplomatic pressure to force Museveni
into retirement, the Ugandan trickster was searching the bleak
sands of Somalia for a new group of African bogeymen to dangle
before the Americans and distract them from his own crimes.
After Kolker and Wood left Uganda, diplomatic pressure on
Museveni to democratize largely disappeared, the World Bank
and IMF ploughed more money into Museveni's treasury and
a new and deadly chapter in eastern Africa's troubled history
commenced.

During the 1970s and '80s, Somalia's erratic dictator, Siad
Barre, blew with the winds of the Cold War, siding sometimes
with the Soviets and sometimes with the West, depending upon
who was willing to sell him more weapons. Widely hated for his
repression and human rights abuses, Barre was deposed in 1991
by a warlord named Mohamed Aideed, whose Somali National
Alliance and other groups then began fighting among themselves. Agricultural production all but ceased and people began

156   to starve. Food aid poured in from the West, but 80 percent of
it was stolen by combatants and sold in exchange for guns. In
1992, the UN authorized Operation Restore Hope, a peacekeeping mission led by the U.S. military, whose mandate was
to ensure food reached hungry Somalis. But U.S. servicemen
soon became embroiled in the conflict. After Aideed's militia killed 25 Pakistani peacekeepers, the Americans bombed a
house where they believed the warlord was hiding, killing scores
of civilians; then in September 1993 they tried to arrest two of
Aideed's lieutenants in Mogadishu. Local militias fought back,
downing two U.S. Black Hawk helicopters. Eighteen American
soldiers were killed and their charred bodies were dragged
through the streets of Mogadishu by angry mobs.

During the 1990s, evidence emerged that Al Qaeda operatives may have advised the militants who shot down the
helicopters. Three other Al Qaeda fighters alleged to have been
involved in the 1998 embassy bombings in Nairobi and Dar
es Salaam were also believed to be hiding there. Increasingly,
this lawless territory, with its long unpatrolled coastline,
hundreds of unmonitored airstrips, extreme poverty, Sharia
courts, and numerous madrassas funded by Persian Gulf
tycoons, seemed, from Washington's point of view, another
African mire threatening to unleash radical Islamic pandemonium upon the free world.

Shortly after the 9/11 attacks, Museveni hired Rosa
Whitaker, a shrewd Bible-quoting African-American lobbyist and former assistant trade representative in the Clinton
and George W. Bush administrations to promote his image in
Washington as an expert on the Somalia situation. Newspaper
articles and a WikiLeaks cable suggested Whitaker may have
encouraged the Uganda government to make financially unfa-
vorable choices involving a defunct textile firm and a railway

contract in which a Chinese contractor attempted to overcharge
the Uganda government by $450 million.

But all that was in the future. In 2003, Whitaker arranged Museveni's White House visit and sent letters reminding State Department officials that Museveni was "strongly supporting the U.S. in the global war against terrorism." Soon Bush and Museveni were speaking frequently by telephone.

By 2004, Somalia's numerous clan leaders and warlords had split into two factions, one secular and the other Islamic. After painstaking peace negotiations they formed a government. This rapprochement worried the leaders of neighboring Ethiopia. In 1946, Britain handed over the Ogaden region, home to millions of pastoralists who considered themselves Somali, to Ethiopia, and they had been fighting ever since to secede and rejoin Somalia. The Ethiopians feared that the Somali Islamists might team up with Ogaden separatists, so they bribed and co-opted the secular warlords. This further weakened the already divided Somali government, which collapsed entirely after a chair-throwing brawl erupted Parliament.

In 2005, the CIA also began funding and arming the secular warlords in the hope that they'd help track down Al Qaeda operatives responsible for the 1998 U.S. embassy bombings, who the CIA claimed were hiding in Somalia. The warlords optimistically named their new coalition the Alliance for the Restoration of Peace and Counterterrorism—or ARPC, but soon began fighting both against the Islamists and among themselves, while failing to pursue the alleged embassy bombers.

Finally in June 2006, the Somali Islamists, who called themselves the Islamic Courts Union (or ICU), took over the capital Mogadishu from the unruly Ethiopia/U.S.-backed ARPC. Suddenly the country actually began to function for the first time in a generation. Bandits and roadblocks disappeared,

158   garbage that had been piling up in the streets for a decade was cleared, and air and seaports opened. The ICU imposed a moderate form of Sharia law; girls were permitted to attend school and ICU courts eschewed harsh punishments like stoning and the slicing off of hands. Instead, they began dealing with the enormous backlog of contract and land disputes.

Not everyone was happy. Women had to wear the veil, public video halls were banned, and people were forbidden to chew the amphetamine-like substance quat, to which many were addicted. But at last there was order and peace and the streets were safe, even at night.

Six months later, Ethiopia, with clandestine U.S. support, launched a disastrous mission to topple the ICU. Ugandan troops were then enlisted to shore up the U.S./Ethiopia-backed secular warlords while they attempted to create their own army. These plans did not go smoothly. Uganda—with U.S. and European backing—soon became bogged down in a deadly quagmire that killed thousands, flattened cities, generated a huge refugee crisis, and provoked the rise of Al-Shabaab, a terrifying radical Islamic militant group that has attacked bars, schools and shopping malls throughout eastern Africa, including the Westgate Mall.

When the ICU first took over, the George W. Bush administration seemed to behave diplomatically, urging it to work with the beleaguered Ethiopia-backed secular warlords then camped out in the provincial city of Baidoa. However, behind the scenes, Uganda, Ethiopia and the U.S. had been cooking up war plans for more than a year. In 2005, three senior Ugandan army officers visited the secular warlords—who would eventually call themselves the Transitional Federal Government, or TFG—to study the security and political situation. Then, as soon as the ICU came to power in June 2006, Museveni briefed his army high command on a plan to deploy Ugandan troops in Somalia. Two months later, Museveni's lobbyist Rosa Whitaker penned a letter to Bush's National Security Council team. "President Museveni shares President Bush's particular concern about Somalia and its potential as a writhing hotbed of terrorism," she wrote. The Ugandan president "would like to talk to [Bush] about . . . a policy aimed at keeping Somalia out of terrorist hands."

In an October meeting with Museveni, Frazer brooded that the ICU's real agenda was to create a radical Islamic expansionist state just like Sudan's, and at a December press conference, she claimed the ICU, whom she'd called "moderates" only months earlier, were "extremists to the core." She then accused the group of declaring war on the U.S.—which was not true, and urged the UN to lift an arms embargo, effectively giving Ethiopia a green light to invade Somalia, overthrow the ICU, and install the weak, disorganized TFG.

Ethiopian tanks entered Mogadishu on Christmas Eve 2006 and proceeded to flatten entire neighborhoods in the city. The Pentagon assisted this operation with special forces, armed drones, and Tomahawk cruise missiles from Navy ships. More than two-thirds of the population fled the city over the next two years.

Al-Shabaab had begun as the armed youth wing of the ICU. Before the Islamists took over in 2006, its militants had assassinated several secularist officials and supporters. These killings ceased while the ICU held power, but the brutal Ethiopian and American assault engendered great sympathy for the group in the Persian Gulf and donations soon began pouring in. Before long, Al-Shabaab controlled much of the country, where it forcibly conscripted young men into its ranks, raised local taxes,

160   and imposed a much harsher form of Sharia law than the ICU did. The group bans movies, dancing, soccer, musical cellphone ringtones, and the wearing of brassieres—on the grounds that they aren't "natural." Stonings, hangings, and amputations became routine.

A month after the joint Ethiopian/U.S. invasion, the UN Security Council authorized the African Union to send peace-keepers to support the TFG while it trained its own army. Few African leaders were willing to support what appeared to be Ethiopia's (and America's) unprovoked assault on Somalia, but the U.S. and its European allies had already been preparing Museveni's troops for months. In November 2006, two months before the invasion, American, French, and British instructors were in Uganda training Museveni's troops in urban combat techniques in preparation for deployment to Somalia. In December, a trainload of food, tents, tanks, rockets, and assorted artillery began making its way from Uganda to Somalia at U.S. government expense. Thousands of Ugandan soldiers followed within days of the Security Council resolution. Their mission, known as AMISOM, would earn Museveni's regime roughly $20 million a year, and continues more than ten years later.

For the first three years of AMISOM's mission, Al-Shabaab grew stronger by the day, and the Ugandan peacekeepers were sitting ducks. The terrorists regularly detonated bombs outside the peacekeepers' camps and then set traps for them when they went out on patrol to investigate.

In September 2009, Al-Shabaab suicide bombers posing as UN workers killed 17 AMISOM soldiers, including the Burundian Deputy Force Commander. After that disaster, Museveni held a series of meetings with U.S. officials in Entebbe and on the sidelines of the UN Security Council. Joining him

were Obama's ambassador to the UN Susan Rice, U.S. ambassador to Uganda Jerry Lanier, and Johnnie Carson, now in charge
of African Affairs at State.

Give me more weapons, more money, more troops and a
mandate to fight Al-Shabaab, Museveni told the Americans,
or I'll pull my men out of Somalia. The Americans were still
mulling over this ultimatum on July 11, 2010, when suicide bombers blew themselves up at a Kampala restaurant
and a nearby rugby stadium where crowds were watching the
World Cup soccer final. Seventy people were injured and 74
died, including an American aid worker. Al-Shabaab claimed
responsibility, saying the bombing had been retaliation for
indiscriminate shelling of civilians by Ugandan peacekeepers
in Somalia.

The Americans and Europeans ponied up. Funding for
AMISOM greatly increased and its mandate changed from
"peacekeeping" to "peace enforcement."

Over the next year, Ugandan and Burundian AMISOM
"peace enforcers" engaged in fierce and ingenious operations
to secure strategic areas of Somalia. They took over Mogadishu
building by building using what they called "the creep
method." While rooftop snipers pinned Al-Shabaab fighters
hiding out in buildings from above, troops inside neighboring
buildings drilled holes in the walls and shot at the militants
from all sides. When Al-Shabaab destroyed staircases to
thwart the "creep" strategy, the Ugandans and Burundians
scaled the buildings with makeshift wooden ladders. In 2011,
AMISOM captured Bakara market, a major source of revenue
for Al-Shabaab, which extorted income from traders.

AMISOM managed to take control of Mogadishu and
much of southwest Somalia, but the war remains far from
over in early 2017. At first, even Osama bin Laden considered

162 Al-Shabaab's brutality excessive, but after after he was killed, the group was officially admitted to the Al Qaeda network in 2012.

Meanwhile, many Ugandan AMISOM troops complain that they live in miserable conditions and sometimes aren't paid for months at a time. In 2013, Museveni's son and head of the Special Forces Command Muhoozi Kainerugaba visited Somalia and asked the AMISOM troops to share their concerns. When a soldier questioned why members of some tribes seldom received promotions, whereas members of the President's clan moved rapidly through the ranks, he was arrested. In 2017, a Ugandan soldier accused of stealing ammunition was tortured by having a 15 kilogram sack of weights tied to his penis. Photographs of this abuse and a doctor's reports indicating that he was now impotent were submitted to a judge in Kampala who dismissed the case against him. He was then whisked out of the country to Somalia, without his lawyers' knowledge, tried a second time, and sentenced to twenty years in prison.

Low morale harmed the mission. In 2012, Ugandan AMISOM troops were found to be luring Somali children out of displaced persons camps and raping them. In July 2015, Ugandan AMISOM soldiers barged into a wedding in Mogadishu and shot five male guests dead. According to a UN report, a third to a half of all weapons and ammunition delivered to AMISOM by the U.S. ended up in the hands of Al-Shabaab, presumably sold by disgruntled Ugandan soldiers. Thus, the U.S. has effectively been arming both sides of the conflict, guaranteeing its continuation.

In 2012, a single embassy bombing suspect was eventually tracked down and killed in Somalia, but this has come at the cost of countless African lives, and some European and one American one as well.

During the run-up to Uganda's 2006 election, Lawrence and two other Ugandan Americans traveled to Washington to meet with State Department officials in the Africa Bureau. The Somalia invasion had not yet occurred, and the Ugandans were unaware of President Bush's and Museveni's plans, nor did they know about Kolker's attempt to place travel bans on Museveni's relatives, or that Bush's Africa Bureau head Jendayi Frazer had scotched them; nor did they know that the ICC had abandoned plans to prosecute high-level Ugandans for crimes committed in Congo. They merely wanted to urge the George W. Bush administration to put some sort of pressure on Museveni to adhere to democratic norms.

A low-level Africa Bureau official listened sympathetically to their concerns. As the Ugandans were saying goodbye in the corridor, a senior Bush defense official happened to emerge from another office down the hall.

Lawrence recognized him and took the opportunity to ask him a question. "Don't you think it's important for America to deal with the people of Uganda and not just one individual?" he asked. "When that person goes, your contract goes with him. If you work with the people and their institutions, you know your contract will survive."

"You have a point," Lawrence recalls the defense official telling him. "But you have to understand that the U.S. government is not these walls. We are the government. And we have interests. Uganda has oil, and then there's the Arabization of Africa."

"At least he told the truth," Lawrence mused years later.

A Long Distance Relationship

The wisest among my race understand that the agitation of questions of social equality is the extremest folly, and that progress in the enjoyment of all the privileges that will come to us must be the result of severe and constant struggle rather than of artificial forcing.

—Booker T. Washington

In July 2009, Lawrence was settled in an apartment in a wooded cul de sac, just across a busy highway from Vassar College in Poughkeepsie. The apartment served as the editorial office of *The Crested Journal*, Lawrence's online Ugandan current affairs magazine, and headquarters of the Executive Committee of the Democratic Party-Uganda (U.S. chapter). Lawrence supported these activities by teaching political science at his alma mater, Dutchess County Community College.

A few nights a week, he also taught GED classes for incarcerated young people at a local church. The work was harrowing.

"You meet people without fathers, who've been abused, who are
so depressed they don't even know it. Every day you come home
worrying about someone."

He remembers one 22-year-old who'd grown up visiting his
father in jail and whose grandfather was in yet another prison
further upstate. "How do you explain to someone like that that
being in jail isn't normal?" Lawrence wondered. He told his student that in Africa, if your father isn't there, your clan cares
for you; that's why Africans have clan names, not their fathers'
names. "Take me to Africa," the young man said, "It sounds
better there."

Lawrence sometimes checked his email on a computer
in the church office. One evening he received a message from
Annet Namwanga, an old flame he'd not seen or heard from
since he left Uganda in 1995.

"You've gone quiet," she wrote.

Lawrence's wife had joined him in the U.S., but the couple
soon broke up and she moved to another state. In 2006, he'd
met a pretty young Ugandan woman who seemed to want to get
closer to him, but suspecting she was one of Museveni's spies,
he'd kept his distance.

Annet wrote that she'd been trying to phone him for weeks.
Lawrence remembered a few calls from Uganda on his cell
phone, but he didn't answer if he didn't recognize the number.
When he realized who it was, he called her as soon as morning
broke in Uganda.

Annet owned a cosmetics shop and also worked as a secretary to the head of Mulago Nursing School, the largest in the
country. She was seven years younger than Lawrence, and short
like him. She had an appealing irreverent charm and an intelligent, lively face. Her mother had served as the DP's official
cashier in the early 1990s. During the long school vacation when

166   Annet was 15, she volunteered to join the DP Mobilizers Group that was campaigning for multi-party democracy. Lawrence and the others teased her when she said she wanted to help out. "Go sit with your mother, you young girl!" they said. But soon she was traveling around the country with the Mobilizers, and that's when she got to know Lawrence.

Their relationship cooled off when he became engaged to someone else, but she remained a stalwart DP activist and never stopped thinking about him. In 2005, Museveni finally lifted the ban on political party activity so that DP candidates could openly campaign. But the smaller parties were no match for Museveni's NRM machine, funded in part by the millions looted from public coffers. NRM thugs disrupted opposition rallies and bribed opposition activists to spy on their colleagues. Many DP supporters were discouraged and Annet wondered whether Lawrence had any advice.

As they discussed the DP's fortunes, that old sense of the party as an extended family returned. Soon they were speaking about themselves. Was Lawrence in a relationship? Annet wanted to know.

"I am alone."

"You are lying," she said.

"I'm not," he assured her.

Skype and Whatsapp meant phone calls between the U.S. and Uganda were free, and soon they were speaking every day.

The previous four years had been turbulent ones for Uganda. In 2005, Kizza Besigye returned from exile to challenge Museveni for the presidency again. His defiance had made him a hero even in absentia and as he toured the country as flag-bearer of his new party, the Forum for Democratic Change (or FDC), he attracted enormous crowds.

About three weeks after he arrived, he was arrested and charged with treason and rape. Many Ugandans believed the allegations were false and riots broke out across the country.

The rape trial began first. A former live-in housekeeper claimed that the candidate had attacked her one evening in 1997. But the prosecution's case unraveled when the court learned that the accuser had been living with Museveni in State House for over a year, where, they argued, she'd almost certainly been coached as a witness. Then police investigator Elizabeth Kuteesa was forced to admit she'd falsified police records concerning the case. Then another Besigye housekeeper who at first refused to testify told the court that the police had given her a house and poultry farm in exchange for incriminating her old boss.

The treason trial, which took place after the election, similarly ended in embarrassment for the government. A key prosecution witness arrived at court wearing a large, awkward headdress. Asked to remove it, she collapsed on the floor and the headdress toppled off, revealing an earpiece through which state agents sitting in a vehicle outside the building were dictating answers to lawyers' questions, transmitted to them through an audio feed.

With only six weeks to go before polling day, Besigye was finally released from prison. His campaign went into high gear, but his rallies were again violently disrupted by Museveni's security forces and stick-wielding paramilitary thugs. In all, 23 opposition activists were killed during the campaign.

To prevent rigging, the opposition-leaning *Monitor* newspaper set up a parallel vote tally system. On polling day, *Monitor* agents observed the vote counting at polling stations and sent the results to *The Monitor*'s Kampala office, which began releasing them to the public at the same time as the government Electoral Commission released its results.

168   At first, the gap between the two leading candidates was razor thin. Then government agents ordered *The Monitor*'s editors to shut down their tally center. The newspaper's managers refused. Security operatives then sprang into action, disabling *The Monitor*'s website, jamming its radio station, and impounding all *Monitor* newspaper delivery vans at the borders of Kampala.

The Electoral Commission announced the final results the next day. Museveni had "won" with 59 percent to Besigye's 37 percent. Besigye again petitioned the Uganda Supreme Court to annul the election. During the deliberations, Supreme Court Justice George Kanyeihamba received a call from Joseph Mulenga, a colleague on the bench, urging him to read the affidavits carefully. "History would never forgive us if we did not allow the petition and order the holding of another presidential election," Kanyeihamba says Mulenga told him. When Kanyeihamba read Besigye's petition, he too found the evidence of electoral fraud compelling.

The judges met privately three times before issuing their decisions. At the first meeting, five judges including Mulenga and Kanyeihamba voted to annul the election and two said the results should stand. At the second meeting, one judge said he'd changed his mind. He still believed the election was a sham, but he'd been warned that Museveni would stage a coup, with attendant chaos and bloodshed, if the results were overturned. The judges met a third time just before announcing their findings to the media. The Chief Justice asked them to state, once more, their positions on the petition. All the judges gave the same verdict as before, except Justice Mulenga, who'd urged Kanyeihamba to side with Besigye in the first place. Looking chagrinned and giving no explanation he glanced over at Kanyeihamba and said, "I am sorry George, my friend. I took you down the garden path and left you there." The final tally was 4–3 in favor of Museveni, but the decisions were not published until nine months later, suggesting the majority had difficulty explaining their conclusions. Since then, two high-level security officials have confirmed that Besigye won the 2006 election. When I asked one of them how he knew this, he laughed. "Because I rigged it!" he said.

In its final report, a European Union election observer team deemed Uganda's 2006 elections "generally transparent and relatively peaceful," and Museveni was sworn in yet again.

In September 2009, riots broke out across Buganda. For four days, protestors set bonfires, pelted the police with stones, threw huge tree trunks across roads, grabbed weapons from policemen, and looted and burned shops, buses, and even a police station. In Kampala, angry Baganda youths stopped people on the street, pointed at objects such as pillows or mattresses in shop windows, and asked their captives to name them. Those who could not say the words in Luganda, the Baganda language, were beaten.

During the war against Obote, Museveni gained the support of Baganda peasants by promising to restore their Kabaka and even toured Baganda villages with Mutesa II's son, Ronald Mutebi, then working as a window salesman in London. In 1993, Museveni invited Mutebi and Uganda's other royal leaders to reclaim their kingdoms, as long as they restricted themselves to cultural activities and avoided politics.

But tensions between Museveni and Kabaka Mutebi soon emerged. Huge tracts of land seized from the kingdom by Obote were not returned, and palace elites, who included some of the wealthiest businessmen in the country, made no secret of their support for the opposition. Sometime in the early

170   2000s, Museveni seems to have developed a plan to cut the Buganda kingdom down to size.

The Buganda kingdom owns hundreds of square miles of land, and operates on the rent paid to it by thousands of tenants. This land is a source of identity for the tribe as well as income. Peasants traditionally secured the rights to property by burying their dead on it. As the bodies turned to soil, it became, literally, theirs.

In 2004, a mysterious map breaking Buganda down into "investment zones," was distributed to district officials. Although never acted upon, it sent shivers through the kingdom. Then a handful of Baganda landlords began violently evicting hundreds of tenants from their homes.

Museveni blamed the evictions on greedy Baganda elites and called for an amendment to the Land Act that would grant the Minister of Lands—rather than the Kabaka and his Lukiiko—the right to determine rents and evict defaulters. Kabaka Mutebi, mystified and angry, alleged the evictions were orchestrated by state agents to stoke tensions in his kingdom.

In 2008, a group of politicians led by Member of Parliament Betty Nambooze began warning Baganda at community meetings that Museveni's Land amendment, far from protecting tenants, would weaken the Kabaka who was their advocate. At 10 p.m. on July 18, security operatives stopped Nambooze's vehicle, smashed the windshield, and pulled her out. For the next three days, she was driven around central and western Uganda while being beaten and questioned about her alleged links to terrorists. At one point an operative tried to strangle her, she told reporters. She was eventually produced in court and charged with sedition. Three other Baganda officials experienced similar ordeals.

For years, Museveni had been employing a "divide and rule" strategy by recognizing tiny "breakaway" kingdoms within Buganda, especially in areas where many Banyankole and Rwandan people live. In 2004, a tiny Baganda subgroup known as the Banyala, claiming that other Baganda discriminated against them, declared independence. A former NRA officer named Baker Kimeze declared himself king, equal in stature to Kabaka Mutebi. Other Baganda refused to recognize him. He and the Banyala were being manipulated by Museveni, they said, in order to weaken the Kabaka. Museveni provoked the situation by calling Kimeze "Your Royal Highness," paying substantial salaries to members of his new administration, securing lucrative government jobs for Banyala youths, and giving the Banyala their own radio station to promote their language and culture as distinct from the Baganda.

In August 2009, Kabaka Mutebi announced that he would celebrate Baganda Youth Day in Kayunga District, where the Banyala comprise only 2.7 percent of the population. Kimeze, the supposed Banyala king, declared that if Mutebi wished to come to Kayunga, he must seek permission from him. Mutebi's spokesman declared that the Kabaka would not do so. Kimeze's spokesman declared Mutebi was not welcome in Kayunga.

Museveni's Internal Affairs Minister advised Mutebi not to attend the Youth Day celebration and on September 4, police fired tear gas at organizers setting up Baganda Youth Day kiosks and tents in Kayunga town.

A week later, Mutebi's Katikirro (or prime minister) Denis Walusimbi Ssengendo attempted to drive to Kayunga to check on preparations for the king's visit. A police roadblock stopped him at the border of the district and ordered him to turn around. Walusimbi refused, crowds gathered, and the police began firing

172   tear gas. When news of the standoff reached Kampala, Baganda traders shut their shops and poured out onto the streets.

Lawrence followed events closely from Poughkeepsie. By the second day this ethnic bonfire was spiraling out of control and some members of Museveni's government were said to be packing suitcases. But the uprising was poorly organized, had no leaders, alienated many non-Baganda, and soon fizzled out. By the time the security forces finally subdued the crowds four days later, at least 40 people had been killed by security forces and hundreds were in jail.

Museveni rammed the hated Land Amendment through Uganda's docile Parliament two months later.

Every couple has a matchmaker, even if they don't know it. For Lawrence and Annet, it may have been America's new president Barack Obama, who delivered a stirring speech on democracy before the Ghanaian Parliament just days before Annet wrote to Lawrence in July 2009.

"Across Africa," the president declared, "we've seen countless examples of people taking control of their destiny, and making change from the bottom up.... History is on the side of these brave Africans, not with those who use coups or change constitutions to stay in power."

The speech was music to the ears of oppressed people everywhere, and may have given two Ugandans, separated by exile, the courage to imagine a future together.

In late 2009, Lawrence and Annet spent a week together in Kenya and then met a second time in August 2010. They went shopping, toured game parks, walked on the beach, went dancing, and visited historical sites Lawrence was interested in. A few days before he was scheduled to fly back to the U.S.

they were married in a quiet civil ceremony witnessed by two
friends. Lawrence obtained a visa for Annet to come to the
U.S. and they hoped to have a larger celebration with their
families later.

The couple met in Kenya for the third and last time in
November 2010. Lawrence's flight back arrived in the afternoon and it was dark when he reached Poughkeepsie. As usual,
he went straight to the bedroom without turning on the light
and dropped his keys in a small bowl of change on his dresser.
The keys clanged against the bottom of the bowl. Was it
empty? Lawrence turned on the light and realized he'd been
robbed. Thieves had taken his computer, a watch, two suits,
and the change on the dresser.

A neighbor had witnessed the break-in and identified
another neighbor as the culprit. The man confessed, saying
two men had given him $1,000 to pick the lock and take the
computer. He'd kept the suits, watch, and money for himself.
When asked to describe the men who hired him, the culprit
said he'd never seen them before or since, but that they had
accents like Lawrence's.

Back in Uganda, campaigns for the February 2011 elections
were already underway. Kizza Besigye was running once again
as flag-bearer for the FDC, and Norbert Mao, who hailed from
northern Uganda, was leading the ticket for the Democratic
Party. As in the past, Lawrence collected money from Ugandan
Americans in the diaspora for the campaigns. Uganda's banks
keep the government informed about large deposits into
political party accounts, and so to keep out of the spotlight,
Lawrence sent smaller tranches of money to Annet and other
party agents who then distributed it to various candidates.

174   On January 18, with the election just one month away, Annet was at her desk at the nursing school when three men in plain clothes came in and asked for her by name.

"I am the one," she said.

"Please come with us," they said. "We need to ask you some questions." She was then "involuntarily dragged," according to eyewitnesses, to a waiting double cabin pickup truck with non-government plates.

"Who calls you?!" the men in the car shouted at her as they drove away. "Do you know people in America?!"

Eventually the group arrived at a three-story house surrounded by an electric fence and high perimeter wall in the fashionable Kampala neighborhood of Kololo. There must have been 80 other prisoners there. No one, not her family, co-workers, or Lawrence knew where Annett was.

For the next two and a half weeks, Annet's residence was a bathroom which some of the male guards used during the day. She was interrogated, beaten, interrogated, and then beaten again. Once she saw another torture victim miscarry, right on the floor of the bathroom.

The building was guarded by uniformed soldiers from the Joint anti-Terrorism Task Force, or JATT, a security unit comprising police, military, and intelligence officers. JATT runs numerous torture chambers—which Uganda's government calls "safe-houses"—around Kampala and probably elsewhere in Uganda. Established in 1999, JATT has no codified mandate, and none of the torture chambers are registered with the Ministry of Internal Affairs or any other public body. For years Western diplomats dismissed reports that the torture chambers even existed. Then in 2006, a captive managed to escape by jumping over the perimeter wall into the garden of the

Danish ambassador's residence next door. The ambassador's
wife watched him land right outside her window. Within minutes, soldiers stormed the ambassador's gate, overpowered the
guards, and apprehended the fugitive.

Even after this dramatic event, Museveni's ministers continued to deny the existence of torture in Uganda. "It's not
torture. It's interrogation," Uganda's then-minister for Internal
Security Ruhakana Rugunda told journalist Wendy Glauser in
2008. "We have psychosocial experts to interrogate (sic) using
acceptable international methods," echoed army spokesman,
Paddy Ankunda.

After Annet disappeared, her sisters wrote to Kale Kayihura,
Uganda's Inspector General of Police, begging him to find her.
When he did not respond, they contacted the media. "Mummy
and daddy are in such pain over her sudden disappearance,"
Annet's sister Betty told *The Monitor* newspaper.

"We also read about her in the papers," an officer told DP
leader Norbert Mao when he visited JATT headquarters asking
for Annet. Eventually a military intelligence officer admitted
she and several other DP agents were being detained, but would
not say where. The timing of these arrests—right before the
election—"is clearly intended to strike terror into the hearts of
opposition activists," Mao wrote.

During her captivity, security officers drove Annet to her house
and ordered her to surrender everything of value, including two
vehicles. They then drove her to her bank, ordered her to empty
her accounts and took the money.

Johnnie Carson—ambassador to Uganda during the Rwanda
genocide and now in charge of State's Africa Bureau—was heading to Uganda the following week. Lawrence wrote to Secretary of

State Hillary Clinton asking her to ask Carson to ask the Ugandan authorities where Annet and the other prisoners were being held.

When Ambassador Carson mentioned Annet's case to one of Museveni's cabinet ministers, he said he didn't know what Carson was talking about. When Carson pointed out that Annet's picture had been on the front pages of all the newspapers practically every day for a week, the minister agreed to look into it.

Annet was produced in court the following day. She and seven others, including Lawrence in absentia, were charged with conspiracy to commit terrorist acts. According to the charge sheet, the group was planning to acquire grenades, motorcycles, vehicles, money, and intelligence information so that one Issa Doka Laaka, a shoe-shiner from northern Uganda, could overthrow the government. Lawrence knew Issa—an old comrade from Kayiira's UFM. Issa was from a small tribe known as the Lugbara and barely spoke English or Luganda. Since Annet and the others didn't speak his language, it's unclear how he could have recruited them into his alleged plot.

Annet was eventually granted bail, but her life would never be the same. She lost her job at the nursing school. "Aren't you the one we saw on the news?" her boss asked her. "Aren't you the one fighting the government?"

During the campaign period, Museveni's agents removed some $350 million from the Ugandan treasury. Much of this was distributed to NRM candidates for parliamentary and local council seats, who in turn passed it out to voters at campaign stops. Some was stuffed into huge potato sacks and distributed by Museveni himself to youth groups and farmers' collectives during pre-election "anti-poverty" tours throughout the country. Uganda's constitution forbids voter bribery, but seedlings,

chicks, and piglets from donor-supported agricultural programs and bed nets and medicine from donor-supported
health programs were also doled out by NRM candidates. When
journalists and civil society activists launched a "Return our
Money" campaign in protest, the police warned them to stop or
they'd be charged with treason.

The electoral register was again bloated with dubious
"voters": 300 people with the same name and birthdate were
registered in one village alone, and over 200 people over 100
years of age were registered in another (Uganda's average life
expectancy is 53). "I voted fifty times in that election," a young
soldier later told me. Days before polling day, tanks, fighter jets,
and anti-riot vehicles roared through the countryside, as if to
warn voters of what would happen if the elections didn't go
Museveni's way. On election day itself, people were told to vote
NRM if they wanted to avoid a war. The Electoral Commission
announced that Museveni "won" by a landslide.

The flood of looted cash into the economy during the
elections amplified inflation, and the price of beans and
matooke—the savory bananas that are the nation's staple
food—doubled. For the first time in living memory, the people
of this fertile, rainy country faced widespread food insecurity
and the number of children hospitalized for malnutrition tripled. Even in the days of Idi Amin and Milton Obote, this had
never happened on such a scale.

Reasoning that challenging the election in court a third
time was futile, opposition leaders organized peaceful "walk-
to-work" demonstrations to protest rising prices a month after
the polls. Museveni's security forces fired on the marchers, killing at least nine, including a two-year-old. Hundreds of others
were wounded. Besigye was arrested four times and forbidden to participate in further marches. Then, after a two-hour

standoff with police on April 28, his car windows were shattered and he was sprayed in the face with several canisters of pepper spray and tear gas. As he staggered out of the vehicle, he was beaten and thrown onto the bed of a police pickup truck and driven away. Charged with "holding an unlawful demonstration" he appeared before a judge later that day, unable to see, hear, or stand unaided. The judge was so shocked by his appearance that she acquitted him at once.

Shortly before the 2011 elections, Uganda's Parliament tabled a law that would criminalize habitual homosexual behavior. Western activists staged demonstrations outside Uganda's embassies, organized petitions, sent funds to Ugandan gay rights groups, and denounced American fundamentalist Christians who were linked to the Ugandan pastors and politicians behind the bill. Western diplomats threatened to cut off aid if the anti-homosexuality bill passed. The bill died in Parliament, was briefly revived and passed in 2014, and was then overturned on a technicality. It has been buried ever since.

In 2010, shortly after the uproar over the anti-gay bill, I happened to pass a newsstand selling copies of *Bukedde*, the main Luganda-language paper. On the cover that day were two images side-by-side: one showed Obama wagging his finger; the other showed Uganda's President Museveni looking surprised and worried. "Obama Embarks on Uganda!" the headline read. The story concerned a new U.S. State Department report criticizing government corruption and urging reform of the Electoral Commission—which was stacked with officials associated with Museveni's NRM. Ugandan journalists wondered whether the Americans would impose sanctions if the elections were deemed unfair. Were Americans finally going to take all human rights abuses as seriously as they took abuses against gays?

Apparently not. After the election, Assistant Secretary of State Carson deemed it "successful" and the British government praised Museveni for his "great work" a month after the peaceful demonstrators were killed. The British then announced plans to lavish another $600 million on the Uganda government and U.S. legislators sent tens of millions of dollars in additional military aid.

This was all looking a bit familiar. During the Cold War, Western nations supported numerous African tyrants who brutalized their own people and held economic and social development back for decades. This did our international reputation no good, and helped create some of the most serious foreign policy problems we face today. Now we were doing it again.

"We're watching the situation very carefully," a State Department official told me when I asked him whether the U.S. was considering putting pressure on Uganda to implement democratic reforms. "But we aren't considering sanctions." Uganda has come a long way on the road to democracy, he explained, although he admitted there had been some "backsliding recently."

Murder in Uganda

Ugandan MP: We are all terrified. The situation is very dangerous.

Me: Why do this? Why not quit politics and work for an NGO?

Ugandan MP: And if I quit, those speaking for my people will be WHO?

                    —Anonymous interview, Kampala, August 2013

It's not clear what the British architect of Uganda's Parliament envisioned when he designed the building shortly before independence in 1962. Sitting askew on a hill in downtown Kampala, with its angular white columns it could be a modernist African Parthenon. But inside, it's a warren of hallways and balconies with AK-47-toting security guards lurking everywhere. On the wall outside the visitors' gallery looms a row of painted portraits of the thugs and generals—Idi Amin, Milton Obote, Yoweri Museveni, and others—who have ruled this country during the past 50 years, alternating with a professor and a lawyer who were ousted from power within months. "This one toppled that one, and that one toppled this one . . . ," a tour guide explained as he showed me around.

In August 2013, I spent a few days watching videos of old debates in the basement archives of Parliament. It was a quiet Saturday morning when I found the tapes I was looking for. As I watched the scratchy VHS recordings, the technician who had kindly agreed to open the studio for me on a weekend sat in the adjoining anteroom working at a computer. Most of the politicians in the videos were men in dark suits whose spectacles crept down their noses. Some spoke with passion and clarity, pounding the air with their fists; others—the scoundrels, mainly—droned on and on.

After a few hours, the speaker of Parliament, a formidable Ugandan woman in a British-style judicial wig, called on a 24-year-old MP named Cerinah Nebanda, the person I was interested in. Before I knew it, the technician was standing beside me, his eyes glued to her as she spoke. Nebanda was beautiful, in the zaftig African way, with a warm face, a powerful voice, extraordinary charisma, and, it would turn out, unusual courage. As she shook her finger and leaned over to emphasize a point, it was impossible not to watch her.

Nebanda died in December 2012, poisoned, some of her parliamentary colleagues maintain, by Ugandan government operatives. In August 2013, an online magazine published an interview with General David Sejusa, the former coordinator of Ugandan intelligence services, who had fled into exile in the UK three months earlier. The general claimed that Nebanda,

182   and many other prominent Ugandans who also died from mysterious illnesses or in sudden accidents, had been deliberately killed on "orders from on high"—meaning at the direction of President Museveni.

Since Nebanda died, I've conducted scores of interviews and read through hundreds of news articles, reports, and parliamentary transcripts to try to find out whether this was true, and if so, why the government would want this young politician dead. Those who claim that Nebanda was assassinated maintain that Museveni, concerned about a growing anti-corruption movement in Parliament wanted to intimidate anyone who threatened to challenge his grip on power. Nebanda's courage emboldened others and her death terrified them into silence and acquiescence.

After the tear gas cleared, the spirit of Kizza Besigye's Walk to Work opposition protests lingered. Car honking campaigns and lawyers' and teachers' strikes made headlines. But the most remarkable movement emerged from Uganda's legislature, where Nebanda and other MPs tried to staunch high-level corruption in Uganda's fledgling oil industry.

Since 2006, Irish, French, Italian, American, and Chinese companies had been scrambling for a foothold in what was estimated to be a $400 billion petroleum reserve in western Uganda near the Congo border. In Africa, the discovery of oil typically amplifies corruption by swelling the rivers of patronage that keep leaders in power. There was every reason to believe Uganda would be no exception.

Museveni himself, along with a handful of henchmen known as "Pioneers," negotiated all oil contracts with foreign companies. The details were entirely secret. However, newspapers,

parliamentary testimony, and a WikiLeaks cable reported that
Museveni and several of his ministers had been offered bribes
worth tens of millions of dollars by Irish firm Tullow and Italian
firm ENI in exchange for contracts and tax breaks.

The 2011 elections had brought to Parliament a group of
enlightened young MPs who were determined to introduce new
laws guaranteeing transparency, especially in the petroleum
sector. When they called for a moratorium on oil transactions,
Museveni ignored them and continued making deals.

Enraged MPs then began collecting signatures to impeach
Museveni. A nationwide campaign to inform the public about
corruption was also planned. The impeachment process bogged
down in legal technicalities, but the MPs continued to push for
passage of new transparency laws. Museveni realized he had a
problem on his hands.

Cerinah Nebanda was still a university student when she was
recruited to run for Parliament in 2009, but her political gifts
were already apparent. Uganda's Parliament has special seats
reserved for women, a policy introduced in the wake of a modest
feminist revival during the 1980s. Emmanuel Dombo, the regular MP from Butaleja district, where Nebanda spent most of her
childhood, was looking for someone to replace Dorothy Hhuya,
the unpopular incumbent woman MP.

Hhuya was a friend of Museveni's and an officer in his
National Resistance Movement party, but she had lost touch
with her constituents. For years she had been promising to
bring development projects to Butaleja—once an active trading
center on a railway line that brought in imports from the Kenyan
coast, now a wasteland of dilapidated factories and roads all
but impassable in the rainy season. Most people survived by

184   growing their own food on small plots of flood-prone land. When they managed to grow cash crops, well-connected traders manipulated the prices so they earned almost nothing. Hhuya's message—that since she was close to the president, people should vote for her if they wanted development—sounded increasingly hollow. "We felt we were being conquered, not governed," a local told me.

When Dombo met Nebanda, he knew he had found a challenger for Hhuya. During the primaries, Hhuya's supporters fought Nebanda's with sticks, and at one point, the president himself tried to persuade Nebanda to quit the race. "Let the voters decide," she told him. On primary day, turnout was huge. "People felt empowered, they were dancing around her home," a local from the area told me.

That evening, as the ballot boxes in Nebanda's district were about to be opened for counting, workers in the uniform of the national electricity company suddenly turned up in Butaleja town, the main trading center, and began turning off the electricity supply. They told a group of highly suspicious locals that they were there to do necessary repairs. The villagers suspected that the workers' intention was to plunge the entire area in darkness, so that in the confusion the real ballot boxes could be exchanged with fake ones, stuffed with votes for Nebanda's opponent. An angry crowd chased them away and Nebanda won the primary, and the election five months later, in landslide victories.

In the 22 months she spent in Parliament, Nebanda was indefatigable. She joined several committees, sometimes showing up more often than the chairmen. She sent text messages to colleagues after midnight with ideas for electrification and road projects and programs for the disabled. She built three secondary schools in her constituency, bought a boat for people

stranded in their villages during the rainy season, and helped
out countless villagers with school fees and medicine.

But her natural courage led her to take serious risks. She told the Interior Minister that the local police station in her hometown was "like a poultry house," and reported to a parliamentary delegation that she couldn't fit in the shoddy latrines constructed under one of the donor programs that had been looted. She walked out of President Museveni's speeches, called his cabinet ministers thieves, and talked back to the First Lady. When some ministers balked at moving funds for entertainment from the defense budget to the Health Ministry to pay doctors' salaries, she accused them of caring more for sausages than for people's lives.

The day before she died, Nebanda challenged her president one last time. Museveni had come to Parliament that day to address the MPs on the subject of oil. The video of this event was one of the ones I'd found in the archives that Saturday. In his speech, Museveni accused the MPs involved in the transparency law of working in the service of "parasitic" foreign interests bent on crippling Uganda's development. He assured Parliament that he had already created a special Petroleum Authority staffed with trained technocrats, so there was no need for them to worry about the details of oil contracts.

Prime Minister Amama Mbabazi, a sharply dressed man with snowy hair and a neatly groomed mustache, was in Parliament during Museveni's speech. He'd been in government since Museveni's takeover in 1986, and some of Uganda's most flamboyant corruption scandals had occurred in ministries he was heading at the time. In 2009, executives at the Irish firm Tullow had accused an Italian company of offering him a multi-million dollar bribe in exchange for the rights to a

186 Ugandan oil field that Tullow had designs on. Mbabazi denied the allegations, but he looked up when the president said he had recently signed a contract with the Chinese National Offshore Oil Corporation for the very concession Mbabazi had allegedly tried to arrange for the Italians.

"So even if Mbabazi ate that bribe," the president said beaming and waving his glasses in the air, "He ate it for nothing!" Parliament erupted in shouts.

"I'm not saying that he did!" the president called out.

"You don't seem so sure!" shouted Nebanda.

The president sighed, rolled his eyes, and twirled his index finger around his temple. "You see, my daughter, Honorable Cerinah Nebanda—that young girl, has got bad ideas in her head. She is saying that I seem not to be sure. I am sure that Right Honorable Mbabazi did not take that bribe."

Then the president turned to the subject of Uganda's beleaguered health care system, whose drug shortages, dilapidated facilities, and absentee doctors and nurses had been much in the news.

Now, facing Parliament Museveni boasted that his party cadres had solved the problems.

"You go back to your districts and find out what is happening in the health centers," he said to the MPs. "Are the drugs there or not there?"

"They are not there!" Nebanda called out.

"No, you go there," Museveni said tenderly. "I will go with Nebanda and we pay a surprise visit to one of them."

Nebanda and the president never made that trip. The following afternoon, Cerinah's mother Alice Namulwa received a phone call while she was stuck in one of Kampala's notorious Friday evening traffic jams. It was Cerinah's number, but a man whose

voice she didn't recognize was on the line. "Are you Cerinah's
mother?" he asked. "She's badly off."

Alice had spoken to Cerinah an hour earlier. She'd seemed fine. But the man insisted she was at a hospital in a neighborhood called Nsambya. Because of the traffic, Alice couldn't get there quickly, so she called Cerinah's stepfather who wove through the traffic on a hired motorcycle taxi. By the time he arrived, Cerinah was dead.

As the news spread, Uganda fell into mourning. The farms of Butaleja were abandoned as the people she represented gathered in small groups to talk about her. Newspapers and television covered the story for weeks, and in Parliament the tributes went on for two days.

Suspicions of a government sponsored assassination soon began circulating. More than a dozen of Museveni's critics had perished in mysterious car crashes or after sudden unexplained illnesses in recent years. They included senior army officers whom Museveni suspected of plotting against him, opposition party agents, and Francis Ayume, the attorney general who tried to block Museveni's campaign to lift presidential term limits. In Kampala, terrified MPs told me they avoided driving after dark or establishing routines like going to a certain bar after work in fear of poisoning. In restaurants, they ate only from buffets, and never ordered from the kitchen.

That evening, Uganda's police chief Kale Kayihura told reporters that the most likely cause of Cerinah's death was a drug overdose. She'd been dropped off at the hospital by Adam Kalungi, whom he identified as her boyfriend and a known drug dealer.

When Nebanda's family and colleagues in Parliament saw these newspaper reports, their suspicions of foul play deepened. Cerinah lived at home and none of her relatives had ever

188   seen her high on anything. Several of Nebanda's parliamentary colleagues who had traveled with her to workshop retreats and even gone dancing with her confirmed to me that they had never seen her drinking or using drugs.

Alice called a meeting of Cerinah's sisters and cousins and asked them if they knew Kalungi. Cerinah had mentioned him once, they said. She'd been introduced to him by David Bahati, a senior ruling party official and sponsor of Uganda's notorious anti-homosexuality bill calling for gay people to be imprisoned for life. Bahati had invited her to a Parliamentary Budget Committee workshop on Kalangala, an island in Lake Victoria. He said he had a friend there who could show her around. "I've never been to Kalangala, let me go," Cerinah told her sisters.

Although the nature of Nebanda's relationship with Kalungi is unknown, her MP colleagues told me that in the past, Museveni had frequently used attractive young people to seduce his political enemies and spy on them.

Bahati denied having ever met Kalungi, or introducing him to Nebanda, but he and others did caution her that she was going too far in her criticism of Museveni and his ministers, and that her life was in danger, as did others. Six months before she died, her speechwriter and political strategist Edward Waswa collapsed and died suddenly, just as she would. He was not well-known, so there was no postmortem, but at his funeral, one of Nebanda's friends warned her, "Be careful of your life. They'll poison you next."

Cerinah dismissed these warnings. "If I go, another one will come up," she said. "I will leave my mark before I die."

Nebanda's postmortem was carried out the morning after she died. Two pathologists, one a police surgeon, the other an academic named Sylvester Onzivua who had been retained by Parliament to conduct an independent investigation dissected

her body before 17 witnesses, including police, several MPs, and
family members. Both pathologists concluded that she must
have consumed something toxic that killed her very quickly.
Her pancreas was inflamed and her lungs, which would normally have been spongy, were stiff. But the doctors couldn't
determine what the toxic substance was without further tests.
Since Uganda didn't have a lab capable of such tests, the police
arranged to take one set of Nebanda's tissue samples to a lab in
the UK, and Onzivua arranged to deliver another set to a lab in
South Africa.

As Onzivua's plane to Johannesburg was about to depart a
few days later, security agents rushed onboard, arrested him,
and confiscated Nebanda's tissue samples. Enraged MPs began
speculating in speeches and on TV that the government might
have had a hand in Nebanda's death. Why else would the police
have prevented an independent autopsy? They started a petition calling for a special parliamentary session to investigate.

Museveni told reporters that the MPs spreading such
rumors were "fools" and "idiots," and ordered their arrest. Four
of the MPs spent Christmas and New Years in jail. The president
then summoned the speaker of Parliament to his official residence and informed her that the special parliamentary session
on Nebanda's death would take place "over my dead body."

When the deputy prime minister turned up at Nebanda's
funeral in Butaleja to offer condolences on behalf of the president, Nebanda's mother grabbed the papers he was reading from
out of his hands and tore them to pieces. She then threw the
bits of paper after him as angry mourners chased him to his car.
Afterwards, police swooped in on the town and arrested several
people for what the locals called "over-talking."

Shortly after Nebanda died, Adam Kalungi, her supposed drug dealer boyfriend, was arrested and charged with

manslaughter for causing her death from overdose. There's a video of his confession on YouTube, in which this young Denzel Washington lookalike tells reporters that on the evening she died, he'd come home to find her snorting lines of heroin. She thought it was cocaine, he claimed, which he said she habitually used to boost her self-confidence and lose weight. As he spoke, his eyes darted around the room and his mouth twitched. It seemed to me like a poorly arranged piece of theater intended to persuade the public that this idealistic young woman was just a degenerate.

During his trial, Kalungi said his confession had been forced and that the police offered him a large sum of money. He was neither a drug user nor a drug dealer, he said. He was an IT specialist who worked with international organizations. In January 2014, he was sentenced to four years in prison for delaying taking Nebanda to the hospital when she supposedly became ill at his house. He appealed and was released four months later.

Oddly enough, Nebanda's bladder was empty when the autopsy was conducted the morning after she died and the whereabouts of her urine was a key mystery in the case. At Onzivua's trial, a policeman claimed that before taking Nebanda to the hospital, Kalungi summoned a local doctor to his apartment who—for unknown reasons—infused her with intravenous fluids and then drained her urine into a basin and left it on the floor.

Two toxicology reports on Nebanda's tissue samples were eventually produced, one on the police surgeon's samples that had been sent to England, and another, on the samples said to have been confiscated from Onzivua at the airport and then sent to a lab in Israel. The results made no sense. The two labs had attempted to measure the amount of cocaine, heroin, and alcohol in Nebanda's blood and in a sample of the urine the police

claimed they'd found in Kalungi's apartment. The findings of
the two labs should have been identical, but the levels of the
various substances differed by a factor of ten in some cases.
According to the Israeli lab, the concentration of alcohol in
Cerinah's urine—or whomever it belonged to—was nine times
higher than it was in her blood sample, in which alcohol was
barely detectible. Normally, the blood-urine alcohol ratio is less
than two; a ratio of nine is unknown in the history of toxicology,
suggesting that alcohol may have been poured directly into the
urine sample. None of the samples were tested for any poisons.

Petroleum sector transparency legislation never came up in
Parliament again.

"When Cerinah spoke, you'd see the whole House clapping,"
Cerinah's mother Alice told me when I met her in Entebbe in
August 2016. "She was the mouthpiece saying what others
would like to, but feared." Whoever wanted her dead "must have
thought, 'if this one grows like this she could be a problem.'"

Museveni promised Alice that he would establish a commission of inquiry into Cerinah's death, but it was never convened.
Nor was the family issued a death certificate, which would have
listed the cause of death. "You know it's very political," the clerk
said when Alice tried to obtain it.

"I don't go out," Alice told me. "I just sit in the house doing
nothing. I can't pass thirty minutes without thinking about that
girl. . . . Her room is locked. I left it as it was. I look at it as if she
was on a trip and she'll be coming back."

The General Challenges the Dictator

Let us now imagine that one day something in our greengrocer snaps and he stops putting up the [communist] slogans merely to ingratiate himself. He stops voting in elections he knows are a farce. He begins to say what he really thinks at political meetings. And he even finds the strength in himself to express solidarity with those whom his conscience commands him to support. In this revolt the greengrocer steps out of living within the lie. He rejects the ritual and breaks the rules of the game. He discovers once more his suppressed identity and dignity. He gives his freedom a concrete significance. His revolt is an attempt to live within the truth.

The bill is not long in coming . . .
                                        —Vaclav Havel, *The Power of the Powerless*

If Cerinah Nebanda was assassinated, what would have been the reason? What sort of threat could a 24-year-old woman possibly pose to one of Africa's most powerful dictators?

General David Sejusa had been Uganda's intelligence coordinator before fleeing into exile in the UK in May 2013. A few months later, he told an online Ugandan newspaper that Nebanda, along with several other prominent Ugandans, had been assassinated on orders from "on high." I was therefore eager to meet him.

The enigmatic general had a reputation for being gruff with journalists. In official photographs, he was a stern-faced 60-year-old with a horseshoe mustache, dressed in military garb draped with medals. But when we met at a chain restaurant in a compound of office buildings on the outskirts of a British university town in October 2013, he was wearing a bulky gray sweater and looked like a professor from the nearby university.

The story the general told me would defy belief, if much of it weren't confirmed by contemporary news reports and interviews with other Ugandan political observers.

"There was a movement of elimination," he told me. What worried Museveni even more than the opposition was that discontent was also growing inside his own NRM party. "A meeting was held in Statehouse [the president's official residence] in September 2012 involving key family members." Museveni himself was there, as well as First Lady Janet Museveni, Museveni's then-38-year-old son Muhoozi Kainerugaba, Museveni's half-brother Salim Saleh, and various in-laws. Sejusa wasn't invited to this meeting. By then, he had been put on what is known in Uganda as *katebe*, a state of powerlessness in which officials retain their titles and salaries but are given no tasks and don't receive official reports. Most intelligence work was now carried out by a parallel agency directly under the control of the Museveni family. Nevertheless, Sejusa told me he had built up a strong personal network during his many years in power and he soon found out what took place at that September 2012 meeting.

194 General Sejusa claimed the decision to eliminate the fractious MPs was taken the September before Nebanda died. Shortly after the meeting at the president's office, Sejusa, who was still Museveni's senior adviser and spy chief, wrote a prophetic letter that appeared in several Ugandan newspapers warning of "creeping lawlessness," "sickening robberies of government money," and "murders." "The poor people of Uganda should be treated humanely," he wrote, referring to the crackdown on the street protests, "and should not be flogged on the streets." He named no names, but no informed reader would have had any doubt that he was addressing the president and his family.

Two months after Sejusa's letter warning of murders appeared, Cerinah Nebanda was dead. Three other young outspoken MPs were also slated to be killed, Sejusa told me. One of them, Hussein Kyanjo, maintains he was poisoned but survived. The others publicly expressed fears for their own safety.

**

After Nebanda's death, demands for an end to the Museveni regime grew louder. "Are you stupid [to continue voting for the same leader that cannot pave your road]?" one of the MPs who'd been jailed for speculating that Nebanda had been poisoned asked a cheering crowd shortly after his release.

Then an exasperated President Museveni warned "irresponsible" political leaders that the army might have to take over and restore order. Another letter to the media from General Sejusa followed, urging the government to find another way to handle the forces pushing for genuine democracy in the country.

Soon after this letter appeared in a local newspaper, one of Sejusa's assistants in the intelligence service received a call on his cell phone from a man identifying himself as a major in the Presidential Guard Brigade. "Where do you work?" the major asked. "In the coordinator's office," the employee replied, referring to Sejusa, whose official title was "Coordinator of Intelligence Services."

"You mean that enemy Sejusa? We shall kill him."

"If by killing him, you think you'll take away the problems"—meaning the democratization movement in Uganda—"then you'll have to kill us all," the young man said, according to Sejusa's account.

"You wait," said the major.

Then in early March 2013, a group of gunmen attacked an army barracks in Mbuya, a suburb of Kampala, just before dawn. A soldier on guard shot dead one of the attackers and injured several others. The matter might have ended there, had Sejusa not leaked another letter to the media. This one was addressed to the director of the Internal Security Organization—Uganda's FBI—urging him to investigate the possibility that the attack had been staged as part of what Ugandans call the "Muhoozi Project"—President Museveni's plan to install his son Muhoozi Kainerugaba as his successor.

Sejusa had heard that the barracks had been stormed not by coup plotters, but by security guards assembled from Saracen, a private company co-owned by Museveni's half-brother Salim Saleh. The plan was to blame the "so-called coup" on disgruntled senior army commanders, including Sejusa, who would then be rounded up and charged with treason. Muhoozi's Special Forces Unit—an armed division under his command—was standing by to save the day. If the plan had succeeded, Muhoozi would have looked like a hero, making it easier for Museveni to justify handing over power to him. However, the scheme was thwarted when a sleeping soldier who was supposed to be guarding the

196   barracks and had not been briefed about the plan woke up and roused others who fought off the so-called attackers before Muhoozi arrived.

The contents of Sejusa's letter were reported in two Ugandan newspapers, both of which were shut down for a week by the police immediately afterward, along with two radio stations. Some of the reporters who wrote about the letters were arrested; others received death threats. Sejusa was in England on government business at the time and was preparing to fly home when he learned that a line of tanks had been deployed along a twenty-mile stretch of road leading to the airport where he was to land. The point of this vast deployment was to make it look as though Sejusa was a real threat, with a rebel army standing by to stage a coup. Sejusa would later tell Voice of America the soldiers were to arrest him as soon as he arrived, fly him by helicopter to a prison outside Kampala, arrange a mock attack by his supposed allies, and then kill him in the ensuing chaos. Sejusa canceled his flight and stayed in Britain.

Could this story be true? Government spokesmen claim the Mbuya barracks attack was staged not by the Museveni family but by lower-level officers seeking to gain attention and rewards from their superiors. Sejusa made up his story in order to justify his application for political asylum in Britain, they say.

In December 2013, Sejusa and about 45 other Ugandan exiles gathered in a classroom at the London School of Economics to launch a movement to oust Museveni from power. They said their aim was not to take power themselves, but to remove the Museveni regime—either by force or the threat of it—and then establish institutions to oversee free and fair elections, the restoration of the rule of law, and other freedoms that are currently suppressed in Uganda. Although the invitation-only meeting was small, Sejusa and others told me that the movement, known as the Freedom and Unity Front (FUF) had wide support both among Ugandan émigrés and in Uganda's Parliament, military, security services, and the highest ranks of Museveni's government. Verifying this wasn't possible since even mentioning the names of FUF supporters inside Uganda would put them in obvious danger.

The launch began with the singing of the national anthem, followed by a prayer for peace by a Ugandan princess. During a PowerPoint presentation about the crackdown on democracy activists, a young Ugandan woman who was apparently not on the official guest list sat down in a middle row. A doctor was describing the miserable state of Uganda's health services when she suddenly stood up, pointed at General Sejusa, and began shouting "War criminal! He committed genocide against my people!" Several men rose from the audience and tried to throw her out.

"No, let her stay," Sejusa called out. The other men urged her to sit down and be quiet, but she stormed out anyway.

Soon, it was Sejusa's turn to speak. "It is never too late to do the right thing," he began. "My purpose is not to proclaim my sainthood but it is to undo the wrong I could have participated in."

Sejusa—who was known as Tinyefuza until 2012—joined the NRA in the early 1980s and helped Museveni take power. During the 1970s he'd led student protests against the abuses of then President Idi Amin. He was arrested several times and was once hacked with a machete in the torture cells of Amin's State Research Bureau. He still bears the scars on his head. While fighting with Museveni's NRA he nearly lost both legs in a gun battle with Obote's soldiers, and can barely bend them now.

As a senior officer in Museveni's army, he'd publicly defended many of the regime's worst abuses, including the brutal cordon and search campaigns in northern Uganda, the Ranch Restructuring Scheme invasions in southern Uganda, and a police raid on the High Court in which several Besigye supporters who had just been released from prison were violently rearrested.

When I told Sejusa I wanted to write about him, he sent me his CV. In addition to the usual sections entitled "Education" and "Employment History," there was a long section entitled "Battles"—including several in northern Uganda where the woman heckler said she was from. Sejusa had a major part in the early years of the war, and this is what she was screaming about.

In 1991, a battalion operating in the northern villages around Bucoro rounded up hundreds of civilians and held them in an empty primary school. Thirty-six men spent three days imprisoned in a three-foot-deep pit covered with logs, listening to their screaming wives and daughters being gang-raped by Museveni's soldiers. Several men were raped as well. One night the soldiers burned hot peppers over a fire near the pit and blew the smoke into it. At least six men died of hunger and asphyxiation. When the soldiers finally departed, they took at least eight of the youngest women with them; most have never been heard from again. No senior Ugandan army personnel were ever punished for this crime.

Sejusa was minister of state for defense during the military campaign called Operation North when the Bucoro massacre occurred. Reports by USAID and Amnesty International link him to this and other atrocities. However, human rights investigators were banned from the area at the time, and the reports give no details of Sejusa's involvement. Sejusa says he was in

command of a different division at the time of the Bucoro massacre, and he denied to me that he could have done anything to
stop it.

Lawrence is not one to downplay the misdeeds of
Museveni's officers, so I asked him whether he knew if Sejusa
had ever committed war crimes. "There's an official military
structure in Uganda," he explained, "but there's also a shadow
paramilitary structure consisting of lower-level officers who
were responsible for most of the crimes." Sejusa was a senior
commander in the official structure, but according to Lawrence,
the real brutes were men like Major Reuben Ikondere, who led
the Bucoro massacre, Captain Chris Bunyenyezi, who led the
battalion that killed the people in the train wagon in Mukura,
and Captain "Suicide" Mwesigwa, who was famous for having
shot dead his father's dog and, when the father complained, shot
him dead too. "Most of these men were under Museveni's direct
command," Lawrence said. "There's no way that Sejusa could
have effectively reprimanded them," assuming he'd wanted to.

However, in 1991, Sejusa did order the arrest and severe
beating of 18 northern Ugandan politicians who were angry
that the NRM was failing to negotiate with Joseph Kony, while
doing nothing to stop the massive cattle raids—for which some
believed the army itself was responsible. None died, but Sejusa's
soldiers broke the hand of one of them. When I asked Sejusa
about this, he sighed. "I wasn't stupid. I knew it was wrong.
Museveni had ordered the arrest of those politicians. They
wanted the government to negotiate with Kony, but the policy
was to fight him, and they were slowing down the operation."

In 1992, Sejusa was sacked from the Defense Ministry
when he clashed with Museveni over a British proposal to phase
out half the infantry and use the savings to purchase modern

200   weapons. By then, Kony had been severely wounded and had retreated to Sudan. Sejusa argued that the infantry should be reduced gradually, because the troops were necessary to keep Kony out of Uganda. After Museveni overruled him and reduced the force, Kony recovered and resumed terrorizing northern Uganda.

After returning to the capital Kampala from the LRA front in 1992, Sejusa worked on writing the country's constitution, which guarantees free and fair elections, the rule of law, and other rights that Museveni has since violated. In 1996, he testified to Parliament that the LRA war was being needlessly prolonged, that the military budget had become a source of corrupt gains for the government and army insiders, and that soldiers and civilians were suffering horribly as a result—a claim later backed up by many scholars and journalists who have studied Uganda. He then submitted his resignation from the army, but President Museveni refused to accept it. Sejusa sued and won the right to resign in court. The government appealed. The Supreme Court was, according to Sejusa, also about to rule in his favor, but the decision was reversed on direct orders from the president. Sejusa went on to hold various government positions, and achieved high rank in the army. But because he was unable to resign, he remained subject to military law, and under Museveni's control.

"It was like living your whole life inside a coffin," Sejusa said when I asked him how he felt about that. "We'd discuss it in the high command." The officers would ask each other, "How long can this go on? Is this why we fought to liberate this country?" But then, he said, another internal voice would speak up. "And where will you go if you quit? They'll follow you everywhere. And you have a family. And they could also be hurt."

After Sejusa fled to the UK, Ugandan operatives trailed him everywhere and he was briefly under the protection of Scotland Yard. A procession of beautiful women—a singer, an air hostess, a young helicopter pilot, an MP—was dispatched from Statehouse to seduce, and he says, poison him. Back in Uganda, four members of his staff were arrested and charged with treason; hundreds of villagers from his home area were rounded up and jailed under the same charge. Sejusa's teenage son was removed from his Ugandan boarding school after thugs were found trying to scale the perimeter fence at night and administrators said they could not guarantee his safety. Sejusa's wife narrowly missed being killed in two car accidents, and in November 2013, his brother was found dead at the base of a dam. Sejusa is convinced that all of these incidents were orchestrated by the government, as was the death of Nebanda.

Interrogation

The evil of slavery is in the way it permitted white men to handle Negroes—their bodies, their actions, their opportunities, their very minds and thoughts. To the depths of their souls Negroes feel handled, dealt with ordered about, manipulated—by white men. I cannot overemphasize the tenacity and intensity of this feeling among Negroes, and I believe any fair-minded person pondering the history of the Negroes' enforced posture in a world of white power would concede the justice of this feeling.

—James Farmer

By September 2014, Annet had been out on bail for three and a half years. Since her arrest, she'd lived alone in a small bungalow in a Kampala suburb. Once a month she attended court where her case was mentioned, but there had been no trial and her lawyer had not even seen the evidence against her. Then one night there was a knock on her door. Assuming it was a neighbor, she opened it. Two men she didn't know were standing there. They grabbed her, dragged her to a waiting vehicle, and blindfolded her as they drove away.

"We have information on your husband!" the men shouted.

"Where are the guns?! Who is behind you?!"

The next day, Lawrence, unable to reach Annet by phone, called her brother who began checking in all the police stations. Word soon reached her captors that her family was looking for her. "We better hurry up," Annet remembers one of the men saying.

The following afternoon, the men drove her, blindfolded again, to the village next to hers and left her by the roadside. They hadn't tortured her this time, but they threatened to come back for her.

When Lawrence told me this story, I wondered whether Annet, as the wife of a U.S. citizen, might be entitled to protection from the American embassy. With charges pending, she couldn't leave the country, but she had been mentioned in the State Department's 2012 Human Rights Report as the likely victim of politically motivated persecution. I put Lawrence in touch with a lawyer who did pro-bono work on cases like this. He contacted members of Congress and the State Department, and in due course, Annet received an invitation to meet with a political officer at the embassy.

At the meeting, Annet explained that she was being followed, that her phone was being tapped and that she'd recently been abducted.

Her police file, which neither she nor her lawyers had seen, lay on the American officer's desk.

"I'm told you have arms!" Annet says he exclaimed.

"You are funding terrorist activities! You are planning to bomb Kampala!"

"What?!" said Annet.

"There is no way the United States can help you," he said.

After Lawrence and Annet were charged with terrorism in 2011, he was placed on the FBI's no-fly list. He appealed the decision and was interviewed by two FBI investigators who determined he was not a security threat and allowed him to fly again. If the FBI wasn't convinced of the charges against Lawrence, why was the embassy's political officer taking the charges against Annet so seriously?

Shortly before the 2011 election, Lawrence had drawn up a list of possible ministers in a post-Museveni cabinet. It was just a thought exercise, and he had not sent it to anyone else. However, someone he knew in Uganda's Criminal Investigations Department told him that the list was one of the pieces of evidence in Annet's file. The only way it could have gotten to Kampala was if the men who paid his neighbor $1,000 to break into his Poughkeepsie apartment in November 2010 had been Ugandan government agents.

Another "Election"

Why do others think of grabbing power from him just by using words?

> —Museveni supporter quoted in Jude Kagoro's
> *Militarization in Post-1986 Uganda*

Kizza Besigye launched his fourth presidential run in July 2015. Voting was scheduled for February, and in November, I followed his campaign in Busoga, a particularly destitute rural area not far from the capital. He made eight speeches a day, eschewing many big towns in favor of villages that had been devastated by 30 years of Museveni's corrupt leadership. This region once had a real economy, with factories and shops, now nearly all derelict. There was water six feet underground but barefoot children still hauled it for miles in buckets on their heads. Besigye promised to invest in education and health care, put

206   a stop to rampant land-grabbing, and improve farmers' access to credit. He said he would pay for this in part by enforcing anti-corruption laws and reducing the size of Uganda's bloated Parliament and civil service, which had become huge patronage machines.

Besigye faced the usual obstacles getting his message across. In October, police threw tire-cutters in front of his convoy without warning. Although no one was hurt, several cars collided and were damaged beyond repair. In early January, a group of displaced people invited him to inspect their miserable living conditions, but police blocked the way and fired into the crowd, seriously injuring several people. Social media videos showed police planting mortars and carrying assault rifles at Besigye rallies, presumably to frighten the crowds. Another candidate, former Prime Minister Amama Mbabazi, claimed that his rallies were disrupted by pro-Museveni hooligans, while the police looked on and did nothing. The police denied this.

Besigye's November nomination brought the capital Kampala to a standstill. Hundreds of thousands of people poured into the streets, and it took his convoy five hours to drive a few miles from the Electoral Commission headquarters to a stadium for a rally. Ugandan politicians typically bribe voters at rallies with wads of shilling notes, bars of soap, or other small gifts. President Museveni has been photographed numerous times handing over canvas sacks of cash. But at rallies throughout the country, Besigye's supporters gave him money, as well as live goats and turkeys, pieces of roast chicken, even furniture—and set fire to their ruling party membership cards. A woman named Jane interviewed by journalists from Uganda's *Monitor* newspaper walked 15 miles just to give him 5,000 shillings, or about

$1.50. She had lost her sandals and her feet were bleeding, but she told the reporters she was happy to have given Besigye the money and would now go home. Museveni's rallies also attracted large crowds, but many supporters were paid and bused in. Some complained to journalists that they'd had no idea where the buses were going.

In an attempt to ensure a credible poll, a European NGO offered to co-finance a tallying system that would allow independent verification of the results, but the regime declined and purchased a system that did not allow such verification. A long convoy of tanks and tear gas trucks received much publicity as it traversed the country a week before the election, as did a Youtube video of soldiers from the Special Forces Command, led by Museveni's son Muhoozi, conducting maneuvers in highly technical-looking military gear. "The state will kill your children" should they come out onto the streets to protest the results of the election, NRM chairwoman Justine Lumumba told Uganda's parents in January.

Police Chief Kale Kayihura also recruited hundreds of thousands of volunteer "Crime Preventers" from villages all over the country, many of them young thugs and troublemakers feared by their neighbors. The Crime Preventer initiative was created without legislation and the exact number of recruits and their command structure was unknown. Kayihura claimed it was modeled on Britain's Neighborhood Watch Program, but Neighborhood Watch volunteers merely report suspicious activity in their communities to the local police and are never supposed to intervene. By contrast, many Crime Preventers wore Museveni t-shirts, assaulted opposition supporters, and learned to strip and assemble an AK-47. Human Rights Watch and other groups called for the Crime Preventers to be disbanded.

With the election just one month away, Patricia Mahoney, Charge D'Affaires at the U.S. embassy in Kampala published an opinion piece in Uganda's *Observer* newspaper commemorating Martin Luther King Day. She paid tribute to the slain civil rights leader and expressed concern about election violence. But her article, titled "The Path of Nonviolence is More Powerful," seemed odd to me, given America's long military relationship with Museveni.

Shortly after the polls closed on election day, Besigye led a group of reporters to a large house in Naguru, an upscale Kampala neighborhood near the national police headquarters. Informants had been observing the house for weeks and had seen boxes of ballots and computer equipment as well as large amounts of food being delivered there. Suspecting it was a base for a government-run vote-rigging operation, Besigye banged his fists on the gate and demanded to be admitted. Through the small eye-window in the gate, a reporter saw pot-bellied men in the compound scrambling and hurling boxes over the rear wall and into the house. A young man who was about to enter the building panicked and ran. Besigye's supporters chased him down. In the scuffle, a pistol and handcuffs fell out of the young man's pocket. Three pickup trucks with police bearing machine guns arrived minutes later, sprayed the rapidly gathering crowd with tear gas, arrested several Besigye supporters, and escorted the candidate home.

Besigye claimed the building was a "rigging house" from which government agents were transmitting doctored election results to the main Electoral Commission tally center a couple of miles away. Uganda's police spokesman Fred Enanga dismissed Besigye's claims. The building in question housed one of numerous command centers, Enanga said, and was off-limits to the public. He did not explain why the police did not prove this by allowing Besigye and the reporters to tour the facility.

The following evening, retired Uganda Supreme Court judge George Kanyeihamba was watching the early election returns on TV when he noticed something odd. "The record will show," he wrote in Uganda's *Observer* newspaper, "that initially, presidential candidate Yoweri Museveni was leading with some 56 percent of provisional results so far declared," but as more results came in, "Museveni was going down to 50 percent and Besigye was climbing up to the same number. Suddenly, an invisible hand stopped the process and blackened the TV screen. Within a minute or two, the screen brightened up and showed Museveni with over 60 percent and Kizza Besigye with 32 percent."

The Electoral Commission announced Museveni's victory the next day. A few journalists with cameras turned up to record the proceedings, but otherwise the venue, festooned with bunting in the red, yellow, and black of the national flag had a somber atmosphere. Wearing a black academic-style gown, the 71-year-old chairman of the commission, Badru Kiggundu, slowly read out a section of Uganda's electoral law and then, in alphabetical order, mumbled the names of the candidates and their respective share of the vote. President Museveni had won with 60.62%; Besigye received 35.61%, and six other candidates received much smaller fractions. A few people clapped, and then the only sound on the broadcast, which I watched on Ugandan television in my hotel, was the awkward rustling of Eng. Kiggundu's papers as he shuffled them into a neat pile.

Just hours before Kiggundu's announcement, Eduard Kukan, head of the European Union's Election Observation Mission to Uganda, held a press conference at which he criticized the government for the repeated arrest of Besigye and jailing and teargassing of his supporters, the long delayed arrival of ballot papers in opposition areas on election day, the open endorsement of Museveni by the Electoral Commission chairman, and the planting of tanks and armed soldiers all around the country to intimidate voters. As far as I knew, it was the first time Western observers had ever criticized a Ugandan election.

By law, opposition groups were allowed to post observers at all 28,010 polling stations around the country to witness the voting and counting and sign final tally records known as Declaration of Results forms. Besigye's FDC had such witnesses at most polling stations—and in contrast to the results announced by the Electoral Commission, its officers claimed Besigye won with 52 percent of the vote, despite the delays, intimidation, ballot stuffing, and other obstructions. (Several opinion polls were conducted before Uganda's 2016 election, and a discussion of the findings, controversies and interpretations can be found in the notes on page 260.)

Besigye called a press conference the day after the election to present the FDC's findings, but just as it was getting started, his office was stormed by police who confiscated papers and computers and jailed numerous staff members, including data entry clerks and Besigye himself.

The FDC claimed it was still in possession of 70 percent of the Declaration of Results forms but because so many of its officers were in detention, the party was unable to prepare a petition to challenge the results before the Uganda Supreme Court within 10 days of the election, as required by law. FDC officials then called for an internationally supervised audit of the election—as happened in Afghanistan in 2014, for example—but the international community ignored them.

The day before Museveni's swearing-in, Besigye managed to escape from house arrest and appeared on the streets of downtown Kampala and a video of himself being "sworn in" as president in a mock ceremony was released on the Internet. People gathered around his vehicle to greet and cheer for him, but the police chased them away with bullets, batons, and tear gas. The police shut down Facebook and other social media immediately and then whisked Besigye away to Jinja, a nearby town. He was then taken by helicopter to a police station in the remote Karamoja region, where he was charged with treason and transferred to a prison. Karamoja was once considered a Museveni stronghold, but local people poured out onto the streets singing FDC songs and marched to the prison with gifts of tomatoes, chickens, turkeys, and money for the opposition leader. The army was called in to control the crowds and counter-terrorism police threatened to shoot any journalist who tried to photograph the politician. Besigye was flown back to Kampala in handcuffs, jailed and released two months later.

Museveni's swearing-in ceremony was attended by a rogue's gallery of fellow dictators, including Omar al-Bashir of Sudan, Teodoro Obiang Nguema Mbasogo of Equatorial Guinea, and Robert Mugabe of Zimbabwe. In his speech, Museveni ridiculed his critics as "those stupid ones," and called the International Criminal Court, which had charged some of his guests with crimes against humanity, "a bunch of useless people." The American ambassador walked out when she heard these words, as did diplomats from other Western countries.

212   Museveni had built his career on demonizing Bashir. Behind all the problems in central Africa was "Sudan, Sudan, Sudan, Sudan," he'd told Assistant Secretary of State Jendayi Frazer in 2007. Now he and Bashir were behaving as if they'd been comrades all along. Was it finally dawning on the Americans that the problems in the region were really Museveni, Museveni, Museveni, Museveni?

The General Returns

Because it is a systematic negation of the other person and a furious determination to deny the other person all attributes of humanity, colonialism forces the people it dominates to ask themselves the question constantly: "In reality, who am I?"

—Frantz Fanon, *The Wretched of the Earth*

General Sejusa and I corresponded often by text and email. Whenever I bemoaned the perfidious donors he told me they were not Uganda's real problem. The Ugandan people lacked leadership, he said. They only needed to be organized and the Museveni regime would crumble under the weight of its own contradictions. The donors would then adjust to the outcome. "We'll fight it out ourselves on those dusty streets," he assured me.

But his attempt to mobilize the Ugandan diaspora against Museveni was not a success. Many of the exiles he'd hoped to rally turned out to be regime spies. Others lacked commitment or were in a fragile mental state.

In the summer of 2014 Sejusa met three of Museveni's operatives in the UK. A deal was struck, the details of which have not been divulged by any of the parties, and Sejusa returned to Uganda shortly before Christmas. He and Museveni have both hinted that the U.S. and UK governments were involved in the negotiations. Sejusa's constant railings against Museveni on the BBC and Voice of America were proving embarrassing. He almost certainly knew more about how the West had abetted Museveni's crimes than he was saying publicly. Sending him back to Uganda would presumably help ensure he kept his mouth shut.

Sejusa wanted to go home anyway. The diaspora was hopelessly divided and four of his young aides were languishing in prison in Uganda, charged with being part of his alleged coup plot. If convicted, they could face the death penalty. According to Sejusa, Museveni promised to release them and allow him to retire from the army. After Sejusa returned, Museveni claimed he made no such promises. Sejusa remains technically a serving officer, although he has no uniforms or guns and is not deployed. As I write this, his aides remain behind bars and scores of others have been arrested on similar charges.

Then the noose tightened. On September 15, 2015, Sejusa's friend Interior Minister Aronda Nyakairima died suddenly on an Emirates Airlines plane as he was returning from a business trip to South Korea. He was 56 years old and in perfect health, according to his wife. Two years earlier, Sejusa had named Aronda as a target of assassination, along with himself and another senior government official, for opposing the Muhoozi Project—Museveni's plan to anoint his son as his successor. Museveni claimed that Aronda had become ill in Seoul, but had been denied treatment there because he lacked South Korean health insurance. The South Korean embassy vehemently denied this.

Three weeks before the 2016 election, Sejusa told a local radio interviewer that Museveni's government was a dictatorship and the upcoming election a sham. "You run the whole of this interview," he told the journalist. "Sometimes you just run only parts. You run the whole of it."

Two days later, Sejusa's house was surrounded by police. He was arrested, court martialed, and jailed for two months on charges of insubordination.

No one was quite sure what to make of the mysterious General Sejusa. Had he really returned to Uganda to launch a war of liberation? If so, why were his aides and so many others charged with treason, while he, their alleged master, was charged only with insubordination and then freed? Some Ugandan friends told me they thought the general was a double agent, pretending to be a dissident, but in fact working secretly with Museveni to expose genuine opposition, especially in the army and government.

Over the years, some of Uganda's most courageous journalists have turned to praising Museveni; some of its finest judges have issued decisions that should put them to shame and some of its most respected academics have diverted their interests away from the country's political problems to tangential subjects. What inducements had they been given? What threats did they face? At what price were they willing to settle? And had Sejusa settled too?

I certainly don't know. But I do know that to live in Uganda is to be trapped in a web of lies that challenge the very notion of identity. This is what tyranny is like for the aging general, the portly cabinet minister, and the woman selling tomatoes by the road. All are slaves not just to Museveni, but to the entangled reality he has created. Outsiders cannot possibly judge those who live day to day under such conditions.

Our behavior—yours and mine as well—is influenced by the prevailing moral atmosphere of the political system under which we live. At the end of the Cold War we were promised a new world, governed by an overarching spirit of justice and human rights. Western leaders were the first to break that promise. One abuse led to another and now we must all live together on a globe that has lost its bearings, where in many societies, telling the truth and defending your rights or those of others is so dangerous that the only way to survive is to become like the hare in an African trickster tale.

Shortly before Uganda's election in 2016, one of Lawrence's favorite musicians publicly endorsed Museveni. He asked the musician why and then posted the answer on his Facebook page. I've printed it here, with some corrections and clarifications, as noted.

> Kiwa [Lawrence's nickname] you are in New York and I am in Kampala. There is this pressure from the [other musicians]. That my staying away was going to unleash the [Uganda Revenue Authority] on the whole industry. You here (sic) that you might not be able to perform . . . because they can use security reasons to cancel your shows. If you are far like you at times you can't comprehend how Uganda works. We have to survive; otherwise we are all ending up refugees in New York, and your snow. Seriously you know me, and the history is there for you, do you think I would do it, if they did not lean on me. Naye tulabye [we have suffered], people are insulting us, but they need to be where we are . . . of all people I expect you to understand!

"My heart is with those musicians who went unwillingly!" Lawrence wrote.

Mine is too.

Conclusion

True charity begins where justice ends.

—St. Alberto Hurtado, S.J.

In August 1941, President Franklin Roosevelt told the American people he was going fishing. For four days, a secret service agent sat on the deck of a boat off the coast of Martha's Vineyard puffing on a cigarette holder and pretending to be FDR. Staff onboard issued homey press releases about Roosevelt's Scottish terrier Fala who was "restless for a little shore leave."

The real FDR was with Winston Churchill aboard the HMS *Prince of Wales* off the coast of Newfoundland drafting a five-page statement of the aims of the still nascent alliance between the U.S. and Britain against Hitler. The original Atlantic Charter hangs in the museum on Roosevelt's Hyde Park estate, not far from where Lawrence lives in Poughkeepsie. On a beautiful spring day in 2015, we went to see it.

The document lists eight principles to which the U.S. and Great Britain pledged to abide. The third one reads as follows:

> They respect the right of all peoples to choose the form of government under which they will live; and they wish to see sovereign rights and self government restored to those who have been forcibly deprived of them;

America's new image of itself as a global power was born on that ship. But how would America engage with this new world? Would it seek to transform it by restoring "sovereign rights and self government" to oppressed people? Or would it seek to dominate it, by replacing one form of colonialism with another? After the war, U.S. internationalism would give rise to the UN, the Universal Declaration of Human Rights, the World Bank and countless other promising organizations, conventions, and agreements. Sometimes these entities would work for the benefit of people in foreign lands; sometimes they served as instruments of U.S. power and foils to absorb the blame for disastrous policies implemented on behalf of Washington.

But on that boat, Roosevelt was almost certainly sincere about the sentiments contained in the Atlantic Charter. He'd expressed similar views eight months earlier in his "Four Freedoms" speech, calling for freedom of speech and religion and freedom from fear and want, "everywhere in the world." It was this last phrase that worried FDR's advisers. "That covers an awful lot of territory, Mr. President," speechwriter Harry Hopkins said at the time. "I don't know how interested [the American] people are going to be in the people of Java."

"I'm afraid they'll have to be someday, Harry," the president replied. "The world is getting so small that even the people in Java are getting to be our neighbors now."

Churchill's devotion to the British Empire was "visceral" writes historian James Hubbard, and he never supported self-determination "everywhere in the world." His signature on the original Atlantic Charter document is actually in FDR's handwriting. A month later, he told the House of Commons, "at the Atlantic meeting, we had in mind, primarily . . . the States and nations of Europe now under Nazi yoke."

But neither the Americans nor the British could rein in the ideas contained in the Charter itself. Nelson Mandela was a 23-year-old law clerk when he heard about the shipboard signing of the Atlantic Charter. In his memoir *Long Walk to Freedom*, he writes that it "reaffirmed faith in the dignity of each human being. . . . Some in the West saw the Charter as empty promises, but not those of us in Africa." The African National Congress would soon draw up African Claims, its own civil rights manifesto based on the Charter.

When Harry Truman, standing in the shadow of the atom bomb, launched America's first foreign aid program in 1952, his speech echoed the Charter's sentiments. America's greatest gift to other nations would not be our technology and know-how, Truman said, but "the true secret of our American revolution . . . that the vitality of our science, our industry, our culture is embedded in our political life . . . that only free men, freely governed can make the magic of science and technology work for the benefit of human beings, not against them."

Despite Truman's stirring words, State Department officials were extremely apprehensive about the prospect of African self-government. George Kennan, who helped shape early Cold War U.S. foreign policy, complained privately that non-Europeans were "impulsive, fanatical, ignorant, lazy, unhappy and prone to mental disorders and other biological deficiencies," wrote historian James Hubbard. The mixture

220   of westernized and exotic backgrounds created "embittered fanatics," he wrote in his diary, who would easily succumb to Soviet-inspired demagoguery. "We have to get over our complex that every little black or brown man with a tommy gun in his hand is automatically a 16 carat patriot on the way to becoming the local George Washington," echoed Eisenhower's foreign policy advisor C. D. Jackson. In 1952, the U.S. even opposed, unsuccessfully, including an article on government by the will of the people in a proposed United Nations Declaration of Human Rights. Vice President Richard Nixon put it bluntly: Africans could not be democratic, having only emerged from the trees 50 years earlier.

The Americans would have greatly preferred that the Europeans continue handling the dark continent through their empires, but decolonization was inevitable. The fate of the French, who were being pummeled in Algeria, provided a lesson for what was in store for imperialists who overstayed their welcome. In 1960, British Prime Minister Harold Macmillan spent two months touring Her Majesty's African colonies. Looking back on a decade of pro-independence riots in Malawi, Uganda, Kenya, and elsewhere, and fearing a string of Boston Tea Parties across the Empire, he drafted his famous "Winds of Change" speech announcing his Empire's imminent dismantling. By 1965 it had virtually disappeared.

Washington realized it needed an Africa policy quickly. Diplomats were convinced that the Soviets were already "wooing" African independence activists. This wasn't true, according to numerous national security estimates; most emerging African leaders were concerned with internal and regional politics, and wished to remain neutral in the Cold War. But the Americans saw Marxist conspiracies in every trade deal or contact between African leaders and the USSR and they quietly panicked about what this might mean for control of the newly created United Nations and world supplies of diamonds, gold, uranium, and other strategic resources.

But Africa's soon to be 40-plus independent nations, countless tribes, and numerous clans posed a vexing policy conundrum because few in Washington knew anything about them. To Undersecretary of State George Ball, their names seemed like "typographical errors." America's treatment of its own black population posed serious diplomatic problems. Flummoxed as to what to say to a visiting Ethiopian diplomat, President Dwight Eisenhower said he'd heard that African elephants, unlike their Indian cousins, could not be tamed, a remark the visitor considered racist.

Eventually, Eisenhower arrived at a solution. America would pursue a "two track" approach, professing support for African self-determination, while giving African leaders a stark choice: Side with us or the Soviets. If with us, expect lavish foreign aid and a free rein to control your own people by any means, including harsh repression. If with the Reds, expect no U.S. military or development aid, and risk being overthrown or assassinated by covert CIA operatives or rebels backed by them. In due course, African leaders deemed ambivalent about protecting U.S. interests, including Congo's Patrice Lumumba, Ghana's Kwame Nkrumah, and Uganda's Milton Obote were shown the door, if not by U.S. operatives, then by those of her allies.

When the Cold War ended, the U.S. cautiously began supporting multi-party democracy in some African countries including Ghana, Zambia, Malawi, and eventually, Kenya. But Uganda, poor, landlocked, and wracked with political strife since independence, would not make the list. The Reagan administration and those that followed had other plans for this beleaguered country. Instead, it would become a knight in America's bloody campaign to rearrange the balance of power on the African continent.

Lawrence had never heard of the Atlantic Charter before. As he gazed at the crumpled sheets, typed out on un-headed paper with small corrections penciled in by Roosevelt, he told me he'd always thought of FDR as a violent president. On a previous visit to Hyde Park, he'd seen the study where Roosevelt and Churchill resolved to drop the atom bomb on Japan. That day, he'd brought along a group of DP politicians who were visiting from Uganda. They were feuding about something—he doesn't remember what—and Lawrence decided to use a trick of Eleanor Roosevelt's whose cottage Val-Kill is just down the road from Hyde Park. Rather than let the Ugandan politicians argue all day, Lawrence tried "Picnic Diplomacy." Eleanor's idea was that it's hard for people not to be civil once they've spent a pleasant day together. So he took them to Hyde Park and Val-Kill and the Vanderbilt Mansion and then they all sat by the Hudson and watched the boats go by.

I asked him what the visiting Ugandans thought of the Roosevelt family mansion, with its enormous living room, lavish draperies, table settings and chandeliers and the dramatic naval paintings in the hallway. They didn't comment on those things, Lawrence said. What amazed them was that the building was standing at all. Why didn't the Republicans burn it down after Eisenhower won in 1952? The former residences of Uganda's ex-leaders Obote and Amin were in ruins.

Lawrence continues to teach political science at Dutchess County Community College. His courses stress the importance of political participation. All U.S. citizens who enroll in them must vote in order to pass, and students regularly read and debate newspaper articles on politics. "Student involvement is important," he says. "We are leaving the government to a few crazy people, and that's how we've ended up where we are."

And one more thing. Lawrence and Annet have a little boy named Chris. He was conceived using a mail order insemination service and born in 2015. He lives with Annet in Uganda, and Lawrence very much hopes to meet him one day.

FURTHER READING

UGANDA

Ogenga Otunnu's masterful two-volume *Crisis of Legitimacy and Political Violence in Uganda, 1890 to 1979* (Palgrave Macmillan, 2016) and *1980 to 2016* (Palgrave Macmillan, 2017) appeared just as I was completing the manuscript of this book, necessitating many last-minute corrections. It is the only comprehensive political study of Uganda, and one of the few covering the entire history any African country.

Adam Branch's *Displacing Human Rights: War and Intervention in Northern Uganda* (Oxford University Press, 2011) provides valuable insights into the LRA war and the shielding of abuses by Museveni's army from international scrutiny. For another scholarly overview of the war in northern Uganda and its many misrepresentations, see *The Lord's Resistance Army: Myth and Reality*, Tim Allen and Koen Vlassenroot, editors (Zed Books, 2010).

Chris Dolan's *Social Torture: The Case of Northern Uganda, 1986-2006* (Berghahn Books, 2009) and Carlos Rodríguez Soto's *Tall Grass: Stories of Suffering and Peace in Northern Uganda* (Fountain Publishers, 2009) shed valuable light on the crisis in Northern Uganda. For a more light-hearted but no less chilling account, see *The Worst Date Ever: or How It Took a Comedy Writer to Expose Africa's Secret War* by Jane Bussmann (Pan, 2010). See also *A Brilliant Genocide* (2016), Atlantic Star Production's haunting documentary on this subject.

Amii Omara-Otunnu's classic *Politics and the Military in Uganda, 1890-1985* (Palgrave Macmillan, 1987) traces the militarization of Ugandan politics from colonial times through the Obote II regime. Aili Tripp's *Museveni's Uganda: Paradoxes of Power in a Hybrid Regime* (Lynne Rienner, 2010); Olive Kobusingye's *The Correct Line? Uganda Under Museveni* (AuthorHouse, 2010), Daniel Kalinaki's *Kizza Besigye and Uganda's Unfinished Revolution* (DominantSeven, 2014) and Henry Ford Mirima's *Oil Discovery January 2006: The Role Ugandans Played* (Marianum Press, 2016) provide vivid accounts of corruption and repression in Museveni's Uganda.

THE BRITISH IN EAST AFRICA

Sadly out of print, Charles Miller's *The Lunatic Express: An Entertainment in Imperialism* contains an amusing, if overly forgiving account of Britain's takeover of Uganda. A more academic account can be found in James

Hubbard's *The United States and the End of British Colonial Rule in Africa, 1941-*   225
1968 (McFarland, 2010). For colonial atrocities, see the first volume of Ogenga
Otunnu's *Crisis of Legitimacy*.

RWANDA

Andre Guichaoua's *From War to Genocide: Criminal Politics in Rwanda,*
1990–1994 (University of Wisconsin Press, 2015) is probably the most
comprehensive history of Rwanda genocide. Mahmood Mamdani's *When*
Victims Become Killers: Colonialism, Nativism, and the Genocide in Rwanda
(Princeton University Press, 2001) explores the historical antecedents of the
crisis, while Filip Reyntjens's *Political Governance in Post-Genocide Rwanda*
(Cambridge University Press, 2013) describes the human rights abuses and
entrenchment of repression that followed the RPF takeover.

Barrie Collins's *Rwanda 1994: The Myth of the Akazu Genocide Conspiracy*
and Its Consequences (Palgrave Macmillan, 2014) mistakenly equates the
revenge killings of Hutus with the attempted extermination of the Tutsis,
which he argues was not a planned genocide. Sadly, these considerable flaws
overshadow more convincing sections of the book dealing with Uganda-
U.S. relations and the emergence of the Rwandan Patriotic Front, which are
corroborated by human rights organizations, contemporary news sources and
diplomatic and UN sources cited in the notes of this book.

CONGO/ZAIRE

The overthrow of Mobutu Sese Seko and the brief reign of Laurent Kabila
are covered by Filip Reyntjens's *The Great African War: Congo and Regional*
Geopolitics, 1996-2006 (Cambridge University Press, 2009), Gerard
Prunier's *From Genocide to Continental War: The Congolese Conflict and the*
Crisis of Contemporary Africa (Hurst, 2005) and Jason Stearns's *Dancing in*
the Glory of Monsters: The Collapse of the Congo and the Great War of Africa
(Public Affairs, 2011), the latter being the most accessible to non-specialist
readers. Philip Roessler and Harry Verhoeven's *Why Comrades Go to War:*
Liberation Politics and the Outbreak of Africa's Deadliest Conflict (Hurst, 2016)
is especially valuable for the light it sheds on the involvement of the U.S. in
preparation for the war and the foibles of rebel leader and erstwhile Congolese
President Laurent Kabila. Michela Wrong's *In the Footsteps of Mr. Kurtz: Living*
on the Brink of Disaster in Mobutu's Zaire (Harper, 2002) traces Mobutu's
extraordinary life up until his overthrow in 1997.

SUDAN/SOUTH SUDAN

Deborah Scroggins's *Emma's War: A True Story* (Vintage, 2004) provides an accessible introduction to Sudan's harrowing history, and Hilde Frafjord Johnson's *South Sudan: The Untold Story from Independence to the Civil War* (I.B. Tauris, 2016) recounts the heartbreaking collapse of South Sudan.

SOMALIA

Mai Harper's *Getting Somalia Wrong? Faith, War and Hope in a Shattered State* (Zed Books, 2012) sheds valuable light on the colossal blunders of the George W. Bush administration in that country.

The following PhD theses are also highly recommended:

Jonathan Fisher, *International Perceptions and African Agency: Uganda and Its Donors 1986-2010*. University of Oxford, 2011.

Kenneth Kresse, *Containing Nationalism and Communism on the 'Dark Continent': Eisenhower's Policy toward Africa, 1953-1961*. University of Albany, 2006.

John A. Rowe, *Revolution in Buganda 1856-1884*. University of Wisconsin, 1966.

NOTES

INTRODUCTION

20 denied sufficient food aid:
*Development Without Freedom. How
Donor Aid Underwrites Repression
in Ethiopia*. Human Rights Watch.
October 19, 2010.

21 meant to pay for medicine:
Anthony Wesaka. "Mukula: I paid
Gavi Money to Janet Team." *The
Monitor*. November 14, 2012.

**21 underground trade in
yellowcake:** Princeton N.
Lyman and J. Stephen Morrison.
"The Terrorist Threat in Africa."
Foreign Affairs. January/February
2004; Joseph P. Wilson. "What I
Didn't Find in Africa." *The New York
Times*. July 6, 2003; *Parameters*. U.S.
Army War College. Winter 2000–01;
Ann Mezzell. *U.S. Policy Shifts on
Sub-Saharan Africa: An Assessment of
Contending Predictions*. ASPJ Africa &
Francophonie. 4th Quarter 2010.

22 ably covered by others: Among
them: Filip Reyntjens. *Political
Governance in Post-Genocide Rwanda*.
Cambridge University Press, 2015;
*The Great African War: Congo and
Regional Geopolitics, 1996–2006*.
Cambridge University Press, 2010;
Gerard Prunier. *From Genocide to
Continental War*. Hurst, 2005; Jason
Stearns. *Dancing in the Glory of
Monsters: The Collapse of the Congo
and the Great War of Africa*. Public
Affairs, 2012; Philip Gourevitch. *We
Wish to Inform You that Tomorrow
We Will Be Killed with Our Families:
Stories from Rwanda*. FSG, 1999;

Mahmood Mamdani. *When Victims
Become Killers: Colonialism,
Nativism, and the Genocide in Rwanda*.
Princeton University Press, 2002.
Tim Allen and Koen Vlassenroot.
*The Lord's Resistance Army: Myth
and Reality*. Zed Books, 2010; Caros
Rodriguez Soto. *Tall Grass. Stories
of Suffering and Peace in Northern
Uganda*. Fountain Publishers, 2009;
Robert O. Collins. *A History of
Modern Sudan*. Cambridge University
Press, 2008; Adam Branch.
*Displacing Human Rights: War and
Intervention in Northern Uganda*.
Oxford University Press, 2011; Hilde
Johnson. *South Sudan: The Untold
Story from Independence to Civil
War*. IB Taurus, 2016; Mary Harper.
*Getting Somalia Wrong? Faith,
War and Hope in a Shattered State*.
Zed Books, 2012; Philip Roessler
and Harry Verhoeven. *Why Comrades
Go to War*. Hurst, 2016.

**22 deemed unfriendly to the
regime:** Jude Kagoro. *Militarization
in Post-1986 Uganda: Politics,
Military and Society Interpretation*. Lit
Verlag, 2015.

23 commit terrorist acts:
Sulaiman Kakaire. "Terrorism
Redefined as Opposition Smells a
Rat." *The Observer* (Uganda): May 4,
2015.

**24 operatives who alter vote
counts:** For sources, see Chapter 10.

**24 two researchers presented
data:** Roberto Stefan Foa and
Yascha Mounk. "The Signs of
Deconsolidation." *The Journal of
Democracy*. January 2017.

228   25   **$24 trillion worth:** Paul Trustfull. "A Man with a Vision: President Joseph Kabila Kabange."

25   **expand their own sphere of influence:** Harry Verhoeven. *Water, Power and Civilization in Sudan: The Political Economy of Military-Islamist Statebuilding.* Cambridge, Cambridge University Press, 2015; Richard G. Catoire. "A New CINC for Africa?" *Parameters.* Winter 2000–01, pp. 102–117.

26   **Africans needed to fight their own battles:** Jendayi Fraser. "Reflections on U.S. Policy in Africa 2001–9." *The Fletcher Forum of World Affairs.* Vol. 34, No. 1. Winter 2010.

26   **export Islamic revolution across Africa:** David Ignatius. "U.S. Fears Sudan Becoming Terrorists' 'New Lebanon.'" *The Washington Post.* January 31, 1992.

27   **compared to the Nazi Holocaust:** Gourevitch.

28   **crimes in RPF occupied areas:** Alison Des Forges. *"Leave None to Tell the Story": Genocide in Rwanda.* Human Rights Watch: 1999, p. 701.

28   **beating them like donkeys:** Jason Clay. "The eviction of the Banyarwanda. The story behind the refugee crisis in southwest Uganda." Annex 3 in "The Human Rights Situation in South Africa, Zaire, the Horn of Africa and Uganda." Hearings before the Sub-Committee on Human Rights and International Organizations and the Subcommittee on Africa of the Committee on Foreign Affairs, House of Representatives, 98th Congress, 2nd Session. June 21, 1984.

28   **Those who refused:** Clay op. cit. and Ogenga Otunnu. "Rwandese Refugees and Immigrants in Uganda." Chapter 1 in *The Path of a Genocide: From Rwanda to Zaire.* Howard Adelman and Astri Suhrke eds. Transaction Publishers, 2000.

29   **negotiated return of the refugees:** Andre Guichaoua. *From War to Genocide: Criminal Politics in Rwanda, 1990–1994.* University of Wisconsin Press: 2015, p. 24.

29   **Museveni's own promises:** Ogenga Otunnu. "An Historical Analysis of the Invasion by the Rwanda Patriotic Army (RPA)." *The Path of a Genocide,* p. 45.

29   **U.S. foreign aid to Uganda nearly doubled:** Robert E. Gribbin (former U.S. ambassador to Rwanda). *In the Aftermath of Genocide: The U.S. Role in Rwanda.* iUniverse: 2005, p. 67; Ellen Hauser. "Ugandan Relations with Western Donors in the 1990s: What Impact on Democratisation?" *The Journal of Modern African Studies,* vol. 37, no. 4, (Dec., 1999), pp. 621–641.

29   **Uganda purchased ten times more U.S. weapons:** Defense Security Cooperation Agency: Foreign Military Sales, Foreign Military Construction Sales and other Security Cooperation Historical Facts, as of September 30, 2015.

29   **CIA accurately predicted:** Statement of Alison Des Forges submitted to the Hearing before

the Subcommittee on International Relations and Human Rights of the Committee on International Relations, House of Representatives, 105th Congress, Second Session, May 5, 1999, p 52.

30 **President Clinton has repeatedly apologized:** William J. Clinton. Address to Genocide Survivors at the Airport in Kigali, Rwanda. March 25, 1998.

30 **Sudan-backed anti-Museveni rebels:** "Hutu Comeback Plans Go Under Gear, but Sweden-based Rebel Group Is Disowned." *The Exposure.* September 1994.

30 **herded most of the refugees back to Rwanda:** Filip Reyntjens. *Political Governance in Post-Genocide Rwanda.*

31 **tracked thousands of them down in the jungles of Congo:** Roessler and Verhoeven, Chapter 6.

31 **U.S. Special Forces:** Jihan El-Tahri. *Afrique en Morceaux. La Tragedie de Grands Lacs.* Arte France Canal, 2000; Roessler and Verhoeven, p. 211. And Chapters 8 and 9 in this book.

31 **hundreds of thousands— perhaps millions:** The numbers are controversial. See James Butty. "A New Study Finds Death Toll in Congo War too High." Voice of America News. January 20, 2010.

32 **massacred and raped thousands of Congolese:** International Court of Justice, Reports of judgments, advisory opinions and orders case concerning armed activities on the territory of the Congo (*Democratic Republic of the Congo v. Uganda*). Judgment of 19 December 2005.

32 **Uganda joined the South Sudan civil war:** Helen Epstein. "The Lost Hopes for South Sudan." *New Yorker* online. January 18, 2016.

32 **on the brink of genocide:** Dominique Rowe. "The World's Youngest Country Is 'on the Brink' of Genocide, Says U.N. Commission." *Time.* December 02, 2016.

32 **Between 1987 and 1989:** "Presidents Museveni and Reagan talk for peace, friendship, better relations." *The Afro American.* November 14, 1987; Jane Perlez. "Uganda After Its Years of Terror: A New Political Stability Emerges." *The New York Times.* June 15, 1989.

33 **his army wreaks havoc:** Jonathan Fisher. International Perceptions and African Agency: Uganda and Its Donors 1986–2010. Ph.D. diss. University of Oxford, p. 24.

33 **"Muddling in Bumbledom":** Christopher Hamlin. "Muddling in Bumbledom: On the Enormity of Large Sanitary Improvements in Four British Towns, 1855–1885." *Victorian Studies.* vol. 32, no. 1 (Autumn, 1988), pp. 55–83.

33 **The stories are rooted:** Alice Werner. *Africa: Myths and Legends.* Senate, 1995. African slaves brought these stories to America with them, and over time the zoology changed.

230   We know them today as the stories of Bre'er Rabbit, Bre'er Fox, Bre'er Bear, etc.

34   low priority in Washington: Ann Mezzell. "U.S. Policy Shifts on Sub-Saharan Africa: An Assessment of Contending Predictions." *ASPJ Africa & Francophonie*. 4th Quarter 2010.

34   Africa staff of the National Security Council has tripled: Fisher. *International Perceptions and African Agency*, p. 287.

34   from Somalia to Senegal: Richard G. Catoire. "A CINC for Sub-Saharan Africa? Rethinking the Unified Command Plan." *Parameters*, Winter 2000–01, p. 102-117.

34   They conduct drone strikes: Nick Turse. "The U.S. Carried Out 674 Military Operations in Africa Last Year. Did You Hear About Any of Them?" *The Nation*. April 14, 2015.

35   "the free flow of natural resources": William Minter and Daniel Volman. "Making Peace or Fueling War in Africa." *Foreign Policy in Focus*, March 13, 2009, see also Branch. *Displacing Human Rights*, p. 223.

35   crushing nascent democracy movements: Helen Epstein. "The Lost Hopes for South Sudan." *New Yorker* online. January 18, 2017.

35   "through protests and struggle": Barak Obama. "A More Perfect Union." Speech before the National Constitution Center. Philadelphia, Pennsylvania, March 18, 2008.

37   deployment of Ugandan troops: Harry Verhoeven. "South Sudan Conflict Destabilizes Ethiopia's Regional Strategy." *World Politics Review*. May 29, 2014.

38   quadruple in the next 90 years: World Population Prospects. UN Population Division. 2015 Revision.

39   numerous multi-million dollar scandals: "Letting the Big Fish Swim. Failures to Prosecute Corruption in Uganda." *Human Rights Watch*. October 2013.

40   less likely to report on human rights abuses: Nancy Qian and David Yanagizawa. "Watchdog or Lapdog? Media and the U.S. Government." Working Paper 15738 http://www.nber.org/papers/w15738 National Bureau of Economic Research. February 2010.

40   deny the existence of Museveni's torture chambers: "Open Secret: Illegal Detention and Torture by the Joint Anti-terrorism Task Force in Uganda." *Human Rights Watch*. April 2009.

40   2001 and 2006 were uncontroversial: George Kanyeihamba. *The Blessings and Joy of Being Who You Are*. Self published, 2012, p. 184 ff. Koen Vlassenroot and Sandrine Perrot. "Ugandan Military Entrepreneurialism on the Congo Border." *African Conflicts and Informal Power: Big Men and Networks* ed. Mats Utas. Zed Books, 2012, p. 51.

41   no legitimate grievances: Janet I. Lewis, Janet Ingram. *How Rebellion Begins: Insurgent Group Formation*

and Viability in Uganda. Ph.D. diss., Harvard University, 2012.

41 **Joseph Kony alone:** *Kony 2012*. A documentary film produced by Invisible Children, Inc., 2012. For a corrective, see *A Brilliant Genocide*. A documentary film produced by Atlantic Star Productions, 2016.

41 **Salva Kiir Mayardit's ethnic reign of terror:** Helen Epstein. The Lost Hopes for South Sudan. *New Yorker* online. January 18, 2017.

CHAPTER 1

44 **"Wachusetts Mills":** John A. Rowe. "The Reign of Kabaka Mukabya Mutesa 1856–1884." *Revolution in Buganda 1856–1900*. Ph.D. diss. University of Wisconsin, 1966, p. 78; Charles Miller. *The Lunatic Express: An Entertainment in Imperialism*. Macmillan, 1971.

45 **inordinate respect for their military heroes:** Jude Kagoro. *Militarization in post-1986 Uganda*. Lit Verlag, 2015.

45 **Mutesa was worried about Egyptian garrisons:** John F. Faupel. *African Holocaust: The Story of the Ugandan Martyrs*. Literary Licensing, 2011, p. 11.

45 **subjects in awe of him:** Rowe. *Revolution in Buganda 1856–1900*, p. 48.

45 **growing power of the Christians:** Faupel. *African Holocaust*, p. 20.

46 **The Arabs stoked the young Kabaka's fears:** Edward Mutesa

II. *The Desecration of My Kingdom*. Constable, 1967; Faupel. *African Holocaust*, p. 40.

46 **45 Christian pages put to death:** Thomas Packenham. *The Scramble for Africa*. Avon Books, 1992, p. 314.

46 **new religious faith was stronger:** Faupel. *African Holocaust*, p. 115.

46 **The causes remain poorly understood:** John A. Rowe. *Lugard at Kampala*. Longmans of Uganda, 1969, p. 6. For the best explanation, see Ogenga Otunnu. *Crises of Legitimacy and Political Violence in Uganda 1890 to 1979*. Palgrave, 2016.

47 **lowered him head first into a pit latrine:** See Chapter 3, and Otunnu, p. 122.

47 **"such was the enormity of the slaughter":** Michael Twaddle. *Kakungulu and the Creation of Uganda 1968-1928*. James Currey, 1993, p. 91.

47 **70 percent of all Africans enlisted for the Allies:** Amii Omara-Otunnu. *Politics and the Military in Uganda, 1890—1985*. Palgrave Macmillan, 1987, p. 37.

48 **Yusufu, Yacobo and Yokosofati:** Rowe. *Lugard at Kampala*.

48 **folk hero was the hare:** Charles Onyango-Obbo. "Congo-Kinshasa: Back Home, Wolves Await Congo's Hares." *The East African*. December 16, 1999.

49 **Life at the Palace:** Albert Bade. *Benedicto Kiwanuka: The Man and His Politics*. Fountain Publishers, 1996,

232   p. 27. Barbara Kimenye. "Working and Partying at Mengo with Kabaka Mutesa." *The Monitor* (Uganda) October 11, 2015.

50   periphery of cocktail parties: Carol Summers. "Radical Rudeness: Ugandan Social Critiques in the 1940s." *Journal of Social History*. Vol. 39, no. 3, Spring 2006, pp. 741–770. Barbara Kimenye. "Working and Partying at Mengo with Kabaka Mutesa."

50   hand-picked Buganda legislature: Nominally, the Baganda voted directly for their Lukiiko representatives; in reality, the Kabaka influenced the choice of candidates so that whoever was elected was loyal to himself. If someone he disliked won, he sometimes simply changed the results or found some other reason to disqualify him.

50   "selfish political racketeers": Bade. *Benedicto Kiwanuka: The Man and His Politic*, p. 42.

50   Kabaka out of national affairs: Sarah Stockwell. "'Splendidly Leading the Way'? Archbishop Fisher and Decolonisation in British Colonial Africa." *The Journal of Imperial and Commonwealth History*. Vol. 36 , no. 3, 2008; Kevin Ward. "The Church of Uganda and the Exile of Kabaka Mutesa II 1953–55." *The Journal of Religion in Africa*. Vol. 28. no. 4, pp. 411–449.

51   His parents had named him Apollo: Ali A. Mazrui and Lindah L. Mhando. "On Poets and Politicians: Obote's Milton and Nyerere's Shakespeare." Chapter 12 in *Julius Nyerere, Africa's Titan on a Global Stage: Perspectives from Arusha to Obama*. Carolina Academic Press, 2013.

51   snobbery toward Catholics: Ward. "The Church of Uganda"; Samwiri Lwanga-Lunyiigo. *A History of the Democratic Party of Uganda. The First Thirty Years (1954–1984)*. Fountain Publishers, 2015.

52   killed a woman during an anti-Catholic riot: Faustin Mugabe. "11-Year-Old Mutebi Taken to Exile in London." *The Monitor* (Uganda) August 27, 2016.

52   "temper of mind": James Ocitti. *Political Evolution and Democratic Practice in Uganda, 1952–1996*. Edwin Mellen Press, 2000.

53   Obote bided his time: Godfrey Nsubuga. *The Person of Dr. Milton Obote*. Nissi Publishers, 2012, p. 44.

54   Precious artifacts: Mutesa. *The Desecration of My Kingdom*, p. xv.

54   The 10,000 Tanzanian troops: Nsubuga. *The Person of Dr. Milton Obote*, p. 103.

54   Muwanga declared Obote the winner: Commission of Inquiry into Violations of Human Rights in Uganda. Findings, Conclusions and Recommendations. October 1994, p. 34.

56   On the way back to Kayiira's basecamp: According to Museveni, the driver, fearing his booty would fall into government hands, summoned the NRA to collect the weapons; confidential sources in the Democratic Party and the NRA told me that Museveni's men ambushed Ssonko and took the weapons. Joshua Kato. "Did Museveni Take Kayiira's Guns?" *New Vision* (Uganda). January 13, 2007.

56 **known as the National Resistance Army:** The truck carried lawnmowers. When it was captured by NRA, a rumor began circulating that Kayiira's troops had brought them to scare away the government troops—who'd be duped into mistaking the noise for gun fire. (See Pecos Kutesa. *Uganda's Revolution 1979–1986: How I Saw It.* Fountain Publishers, 2006.) It's a funny story, but apparently not true.

56 **tipped off by Museveni:** Andrew Mwenda. The *Clash of Two Warlords. The Monitor* (Kampala). October 12, 2007.

57 **"Detainees Brutally Buttered in Central Police Post":** *The Citizen.* May 10, 1995.

57 **"dust to down curfew":** *The Citizen.* October 10, 1990.

58 **most widely read newspaper in Uganda:** Hans Peter Schmitz. *Transnational Mobilization and Domestic Regime Change.* Palgrave Macmillan, 2006, p. 79.

58 **Obote's spies:** Pecos Kutesa. *Uganda's War of Liberation,* p. 148; Mwenda. *Clash of Two Warlords.*

58 **wearing a necktie:** Kutesa. *Uganda's War of Liberation,* p. 3.

59 **"One cannot really describe the awe":** Kutesa. *Uganda's War of Liberation,* p. 12.

59 **pretending to be a field marshal:** Amii Omara-Otunnu. "Yoweri Museveni." *Political Leaders in Contemporary Africa South of the Sahara: A Biographical Dictionary,* edited by Harvey Glickman. Greenwood, 1992.

59 **concerned weapons and military strategy:** Anonymous interview. Kampala, February 2016.

59 **led a radical student group:** Karim F. Hirji. *Cheche: Reminiscences of a Radical Magazine.* Mkuki Na Nyota, 2010.

59 **Museveni's senior thesis:** "Fanon's Theory on Violence: Its Verification in Liberated Mozambique," reprinted in *Essays on the Liberation of Southern Africa,* edited by Nathan M. Shamuyarira (Dar es Salaam: Tanzania Publishing House, 1971).

60 **"It was easier to describe him":** Akena Adoko. *From Obote to Obote.* Vikas Publishing House, 1983.

61 **"the war of the flea":** Robert Taber. *War of the Flea: The Calssic Study of Guerrilla Warfare.* Potomac Books, 2002.

61 **in action in Mozambique:** Stephen Ellis. *Comrades Against Apartheid.* Indiana University Press, 1992, p. 45.

61 **Dead bodies appeared in forests:** A. B. Kasozi *The Social Origins of Violence in Uganda*

234   *1964-1985.* McGill-Queens University Press, 1994, p. 146 ff.

61   **"We beat the truth out of him":** *Commission of Inquiry into Violations of Human Rights in Uganda. Findings, Conclusions and Recommendations.* October 1994, Chapter 6.

61   **failed to elicit condemnation:** Schmitz. *Transnational Mobilization and Domestic Regime Change*, p. 80. At a donors meeting in January 1984, little was said about the human rights situation, Obote's government was granted $430 million in aid, and the UK continued to train Obote's army.

62   **Elliott Abrams called for:** Ibid. p. 115.

62   **Some killings were reprisals:** John Kazoora. *Betrayed by My Leader.* Self published, 2011, p. 83.

62   **the work of the NRA:** Anonymous interviews August 2013, Kampala; A. J. McIlroy. "Uganda Killers 'Are Disguised as Soldiers.'" *Daily Telegraph*, August 16, 1984, p. 5. The Telegraph Historical Archive, tinyurl.galegroup.com/tinyurl/4ANAb1. Accessed 25 Dec. 2016; Frederic Musisi. "Bitter Tales From Luwero Triangle." *The Monitor* (Kampala), January 30, 2013; See also China Keitesi. *Child Soldier.* Souvenir Press, 2003, a memoir by a young woman who claims to have been forced to join the NRA at age nine, was repeatedly raped and forced to kill others. However, it is difficult to verify her claims and the Uganda government disputes them; see also Kassim Kiggundu, as told to Maggie Black. "I Was a Child Soldier for Uganda's President." *The New Internationalist.* May 9, 2011.

62   **Paul Lubwana:** Frederic Musisi. "Bitter Tales from the Bushes of Luwero Triangle." *The Monitor* (Kampala), January 30, 2013.

62   **Several NRA veterans confirmed:** Ibid.; A. J. McIlroy. "Uganda Killers 'Are Disguised as Soldiers.'"

62   **"who is a soldier, who is a guerrilla":** Michael Twaddle. "Political Violence in Uganda," *Political Violence.* Collected Seminar Papers No. 30. Institute of Commonwealth Studies, University of London, 1982: 89. Referred to in Otunnu, *Crises of Legitimacy.*

63   **"We don't possess the power to prevent accidents":** Reuters. "Foreigners Urged to Quit Uganda." *Daily Telegraph*, March 5, 1983.

63   **Canadian engineer was gunned down:** UPI. "Uganda Rebels 'First' Victim." *Daily Telegraph*, 22 Mar. 1983.

63   **European aid workers were killed:** The Associated Press. "4 Europeans Killed by Ugandan Rebels." *The New York Times*, January 24, 1984; J. Rodrigues. "Kampala Killings 'By Rebels.'" *Daily Telegraph*, January 26, 1984.

63   **killers were never definitively identified:** Ibid.; the killings were also mentioned in Elliot Abrams' "Testimony in The Human Rights

Situation in South Africa, Zaire, the Horn of Africa and Uganda." Hearings before the Sub-Committee on Human Rights and International Organizations and the Subcommittee on Africa of the Committee on Foreign Affairs, House of Representatives, 98th Congress, 2nd Session. June 21, 1984, p. 113.

63 **"well-informed" U.S. sources:** Caryl Murphy. "New Ugandan crackdown Said to Kill Thousands." *The Washington Post.* August 5, 1984.

63 **army probably killed 300,000 people:** William Pike. "The Killing Grounds of Kapeka." *The Observer.* August 19, 1984.

64 **"nothing to support [these] claims":** McIlroy. "Uganda Killers 'Are Disguised as Soldiers.'"

64 **locals recognized them:** Musisi. "Bitter Tales from the Bushes of Luwero Triangle."

64 **"They were dressed halfway":** Michael Mubangizi. "Uganda: Otafiire Backs Otunnu Luwero Bush War Probe." *The Observer (Kampala)* April 21, 2010.

64 **not hundreds of thousands:** Amnesty International, 1992, p. 4.

64 **donors soon began pulling out:** Schmitz. *Transnational Mobilization and Domestic Regime Change,* p. 79.

64 **Okello's men offered:** Otunnu, *Crises of Legitimacy.*

65 **shredded an agreement:** Bethuel Kiplagat. "Reaching the 1985 Nairobi Agreement." *Accord* 11. 2002;

Timothy Kalyegira. "25 Years Since the 1985 Coup d'état in Uganda." *The Monitor* (Kampala). August 1, 2010.

65 **glowing tributes to Museveni:** William Pike. "Peasant Army Pacifies Uganda." *The Observer.* October 24, 1985.

65 **"The Pearl of Africa Shines Again,":** Cameron Doudu. "Pearl of Africa Sets a Shining Example." *The Observer.* May 18, 1986.

65 **Museveni was Robin Hood:** "Guerrrilla Who Ended a Nightmare." *The Observer.* February 9, 1986.

66 **The holdings of his vast Lonrho Company:** Andrew Sardanis. *Zambia: The First Fifty Years.* I. B. Taurus, 2015.

66 **Sudan People's Liberation Army:** Scroggins' op cit.

66 **"150 million pounds into national liberation movements":** Deborah Scroggins. *Emma's War: A True Story.* HarperCollins, 2003, Chapter 15.

66 **Obote reportedly rebuffed Rowland's request:** Robert Young Pelton. "Saving South Sudan: Unholy Alliances." *Vice.* May 28, 2014; Joseph Ochieno. "Liberty—44 Years of Retarded Growth." *The Monitor* (Kampala), October 20, 2006.

66 **Rowland began assisting Museveni:** Martin Aliker interview with Sue Onslow. Institute of Commonwealth Studies. University of London, May 22-23, 2013.

236

66 **the stuff of myth:** Kagoro. *Militarization in post-1986 Uganda.*

66 **In two damning reports:** Amnesty International reports, 1989 and 1992.

67 **covered by *Citizen* reporters:** See for example: "Resistance Committees Brutalities Condemned." *The Citizen.* July 18, 1986; "NRA Officers Locked Prisoners in Cupboard." *The Citizen.* November 23, 1988; "Detainees Die in Army Barracks." *The Citizen.* May 17, 1989; "NRA Canes Hundreds in Mpigi Operation." *The Citizen.* August 9, 1989; "Security Men Torture Prisoners." *The Citizen.* March 9, 1989; "Torture Cold Blood (sic) Killings in Lubiri Barracks." *The Citizen.* July 22, 1992; "Tortue Remains Rampant in Basiima House." *The Citizen.* August 26, 1992.

67 **beaten with iron rods:** Amnesty International, 1989, p. 29.

67 **nails drilled into their heads:** Amnesty International, 1989, p. 34.

67 **genitals electrocuted:** Amnesty International, 1989, pp. 20, 34.

67 **"suitcase style":** Ibid.

67 **"Many victims were tied up 'three-piece' with ropes":** Jimmy Kwo. "Remembering NRA's massacre at Namokora." *The Monitor* (Uganda). February 16, 2014.

67 **"stories of harassment and abuse":** *Sowing the Mustard Seed*, p. 177 and Branch, p. 65.

68 **Lawrence published part one:** "What happened at Namkora (sic)?" *The Citizen.* November 5, 1986.

69 **35th Battalion was simply disbanded:** Kutesa. *Uganda's Revolution*, p. 255.

69 **caused gangrene:** Wikileaks cable: Ambassador Robert Houdek. Meeting with Museveni. January 21, 1987.

69 **told the Uganda Law Society:** David Kibirige. "Who Killed Kayiira?" *The Monitor* (Uganda). March 7, 2004.

70 **on welfare in Poughkeepsie:** Diane Pomello, "Kayiira Reported Better; Family Back in Poughkeepsie." *The Circle*, Marist College, vol. 33 no. 11. January 1987, p. 3.

70 **a report which has yet to be released:** Paul Lewis. "I'm the Fall Guy for Ugandan Murder, Says ex-BBC Man." *The Guardian.* January 20, 2007.

70 **human right performance continued to deteriorate:** "West Gives Virtual Ultimatum to Kenya on Multipartyism." *The Exposure.* July 1990; Jennifer Windsor, "Democracy and Development: The Evolution of U.S. Foreign Assistance Policy." *Fletcher Forum*, vol. 27, no. 2 (2003), pp. 141–150.

71 **full honors on Capitol Hill:** "Presidents Museveni and Reagan Talk for Peace, Friendship, Better Relations." *The Afro American.* November 14, 1987; Perlez. "Uganda After Its Years of Terror."

71 **charm decision-makers in the U.S.:** Jonathan Fisher. *International Perceptions and African Agency: Uganda and Its Donors, 1986–2010.* Ph.D. diss., Department of Politics

and International Relations, University of Oxford, 2011, p. 150.

71   spend time at Reagan's ranch: Perlez. "Uganda After Its Years of Terror."

72   "a bunch of useless people": For references, see Chapters 15 and 19.

CHAPTER 2

74   tied by the wrists: Lawrence told me about this in September 2013. While I was unable to verify it, similar cases have since been reported in Uganda. See for example: Andrew Bagala. "UPDF to Probe Soldier Torture Claim, Says CDF." *The Monitor* (Kampala). December 29, 2016.

74   crushed the testicles: Amnesty International also reported incidents of testicle crushing. See *Uganda: The Human Rights Record, 1986–1989.* Amnesty International, 1989, p. 34.

74   lost some 300,000 animals: Chris Dolan. *Social Torture: The Case of Northern Uganda, 1986–2006.* Berghahn Books, 2011.

74   find all their animals gone: Ben Jones. "Remembering the Teso Insurgency." *The Guardian.* February 24, 2009.

74   his favorite bull: Norah Tamale. "Teso to be Ruled by Cattle Rustlers." *The Citizen.* March 20, 1989.

75   Museveni's soldiers also took their share: Amnesty International, 1992. "Uganda: The Failure to Safeguard Human Rights," p. 8.

75   Now they carried machine guns: Dolan. *Social Torture: The Case*

of Northern Uganda, 1986–2006, p. 178; Ogenga Otunnu. "We See Nothing, We Hear Nothing, We Do Nothing: Conspiracy and Concealment of Genocide in Acholiland, Northern Uganda, 1986–2006." Chapter 1 in *Crisis of Legitimacy and Political Violence in Uganda, 1979–2016.* Palgrave Macmillan, 2017.

75   acquire helicopter gunships: Peter Otai. "Uganda: The Hidden Tyrrany." Uganda People's Front mimeo. November 1991; Anonymous interviews in Soroti, Uganda, 2010.

75   allowing the Karamojong to keep their weapons: Larry Kelen and Asiya Vura. "Mafia Like Arms Dealers Threat to Africa Democracy." *Crested Journal,* vol. 1 no. 5, September 2004.

75   NRA always withdraw: Tamale. "Teso to be Ruled by Cattle Rustlers." Otai. "Uganda: The Hidden Tyranny."

75   18 Acholi politicians: "Uganda: Human Rights Violations by the National Resistance Army." Amnesty International, December 1991.

76   She fled to Kenya: Tim Allen and Koen Vlassenroot; Alice Lakwena obituary. *The Economist.* January 25, 2007.

76   burned alive in their huts: "Ugandan Exiles Plot to Oust Museveni." *Africa Analysis.* September 6, 1991; Amnesty International. "Uganda: The Human Rights Record, 1986–1989"; Amnesty International. "Uganda: The Failure to Safeguard Human Rights." 1992. See also *A Brilliant Genocide,* Ebony Butler's 2016 film about NRA atrocities in northern Uganda.

238   76   **taking down the names of victims:** "Terrible things are Happening in Northern Uganda." *The Citizen.* January 18, 1989.

76   **criticizing religious leaders:** "Politicians Religious Leaders: Don't Abandon Uganda." *The Citizen* January 25, 1989.

76   **Uganda's bishops:** "Uganda Catholic Bishops Reject Violence." *The Citizen.* February 1, 1989.

78   **The chopping off of ears and lips:** "NRA Soldiers Profit from Kony's War." *The Monitor* (Kampala) September 2-5, 1994; "NRA Men Blamed for Karuma Ambush." *The Monitor* (Kampala) August 30–September 2, 1994; "Rebel Col. Kawuma Says He Was on Government Mission." *The Monitor* (Kampala) August 28–30, 1995; "NRA Rapped for 'Fearing' Kony's Rebels." *The Monitor* (Kampala) August 23–25, 1995. See also *A Brilliant Genocide.*

78   **eyewitness reports:** Before Kony, the cutting off of lips and ears had never been reported in Uganda. It had been used by RENAMO, a right-wing militia group in Mozambique, where both Museveni and then-Deputy NRA commander Fred Rwigyema had trained in the 1960s and 70s. See Elizabeth Lunstrom. *The Making and Unmaking of Sovereign Territory—From Colonial Extraction to Post-colonial Conservation in Mozambique's Massingir Region.* Ph.D. diss. The University of Minnesota, 2007.

79   **Uganda's much larger army:** Allen and Vlassenroot.

79   **According to NRA commander David Sejusa:** Richard Dowden. "A Convenient War: Britain's Mistake in Backing Uganda." *Prospect Magazine.* September 2014.

79   **gave Kony an ultimatum:** Billie O'Kadameri. LRA/government negotiations 1993/4. Accord 11. 2002.

79   **the army would track her phone:** Jane Bussman. *The Worst Date Ever: Or How it Took a Comedy Writer to Expose Africa's Secret War.* Pan, 2010.

79   **Throughout the 20-year Kony war:** Els de Temmerman. *Aboke Girls. Children Abducted in Northern Uganda.* Fountain Publishers, 2001; Dolan. *Social Torture: The Case of Northern Uganda, 1986—2006*; Carlos Rodriquez Soto. *Tall Grass: Stories of Suffering and Peace in Northern Uganda.* Fountain Publishers, 2009; Adam Branch. *Displacing Human Rights: War and Intervention in Northern Uganda.* Oxford University Press, 2011.

80   **permission to travel there:** Rodriguez Soto. *Tall Grass.*

81   **"who were trying to make us fail":** Ibid.

81   **inflate his defense budget:** *Our Friends at the Bank.* A film by Peter Chappell, 1998.

81   **"ghost soldiers":** Andrew Mwenda. "Uganda's Politics of Foreign Aid and Violent Conflict: The Political Uses of the LRA Rebellion." Chapter 2 in *The Lords' Resistance Army: Myth and Reality*, Allen and Vlassenroot eds.

CHAPTER 3

82   **small pot of hybrid maize seedlings:** Swaib Nsereko. *Africa Hand America Loves*. Rosedog Books, 2011.

83   **Young ex-convicts lined the main thoroughfares:** Judith Miller. "Sudan." Chapter 3 in *God Has Ninety-Nine Names: Reporting from a Militant Middle East*. Simon and Schuster, 1996.

84   **breaking of the Egypt–Israel peace deal:** Miller. "Sudan," p. 142.

84   **"Holiday Inn" for terrorists:** Timothy Carney. "The Sudan: Political Islam and Terrorism." Chapter 6 in *Battling Terrorism in the Horn of Africa*. Robert I. Rotberg, editor. Brookings Institution Press, 2005.

84   **Museveni had known John Garang:** Pagun Amum, former Secretary General of the Sudan Peoples Liberation Movement. Personal communication, August 2016. Historian Gerard Prunier denies that the two men knew each other in Dar es Salaam, but Amum says both Garang and Museveni confirmed to him that they did.

85   **In 1991 Garang:** Herman Cohen. *Intervening in Africa*. St. Martin's Press, 2000, p. 68; anonymous interviews Kampala, 2010, 2013, 2016.

85   **State Department officials met with Garang:** Cohen. *Intervening in Africa*, p. 72; "U.S. Officials Encourage Sudan Opposition." *Africa Analysis*. September 20, 1991.

85   **smuggling 400 anti-tank missiles:** "Rebel Armies Seek Unity to Oust Bashir." *Africa Analysis*. November 15, 1991. Cohen. *Intervening in Africa*, pp. 81-84. Milton Allimandi. "Indictment expected soon in attempt to smuggle missiles from the US." *Journal of Commerce*. September 8, 1992. Milton Allimadi. "Uganda aide cooperates in US smuggling case." *Journal of Commerce*. December 30, 1992.

85   **delivered to the SPLA:** "Ugandan Caught in Saudi-Cairo Plot." *Africa Analysis*. September 1992; New Front Line. *The Indian Ocean Newsletter*. October 24, 1992.

85   **approved this mysterious deal:** John J. Fialka. "Operation Loose Cannon: U.S. Arms-Trade Stings Attacked After Backfiring." *The Asian Wall Street Journal*. March 21, 1994.

85   **another shipment of U.S. weapons:** "Israeli Weapons Bound for Rebels in Southern Sudan: Arms May Be Destined for SPLA Fight Against Khartoum." *The Independent* (UK). March 18, 1994. John Prendergast. *Crisis Response: Humanitarian Band-Aids in Sudan and Somalia*. Pluto Press, 1997. Prendergast speculates that the U.S. and Israel were supplying the SPLA with "non-humanitarian" assistance before Khartoum began assisting Joseph Kony in 1994, and also that Operation Lifeline Sudan humanitarian aid was diverted by the SPLA. pp. 64, 66–67, 77.

240

86 **canned beans and corned beef:** Herman Cohen. Intervening in Africa p. 88; "Ugandan Security in Thrall to Rebellions." *Africa Analysis.* March 21, 1997; "Hopes for Eritrea-Sudan Peace Deal." *Africa Analysis.* November 27, 1998; Anonymous interviews, Arua, Kampala 2010.

86 **U.S. military assistance to Uganda soared:** Ellen Hauser. "Ugandan Relations with Western Donors in the 1990s: What Impact on Democratisation?" *The Journal of Modern African Studies,* vol. 37, no. 4, (Dec., 1999), pp. 621–641.

86 **greatly escalating the war:** Ruddy Doom and Koen Vlassenroot. "Kony's Message: A New Koine? The Lord's Resistance Army in Northern Uganda." *African Affairs,* Vol. 98, No. 390 (Jan., 1999), pp. 5-36.

86 **overcrowded camps:** "1,000 Displaced Die Every Week in War-torn North—Report." IRIN News. August 29, 2005.

86 **Jan Egeland:** Associated Press. "Northern Uganda 'world's biggest neglected crisis.'" *The Guardian.* October 22, 2004.

87 **U.S. media downplayed atrocities:** Nancy Qian and David Yanagizawa. "Watchdog or Lapdog? Media and the U.S. Government Working Paper." NBER Working Paper Series 15738, February 2010; Nancy Qian and David Yanagizawa. "The Strategic Determinants of U.S. Human Rights Reporting: Evidence from the Cold War." *The Journal of European Economic Association Papers and Proceedings,* 7(2-3), 2009 May-June, pp. 446-457.

87 **overlooked the suffering:** There were exceptions. See for example Elizabeth Rubin. "Our Children Are Killing Us." *The New Yorker.* March 23, 1998.

CHAPTER 4

89 **ethnic anger and fear:** Andre Guichaoua. *From War to Genocide: Criminal Politics in Rwanda.* University of Wisconsin Press, 2015, Chapter 1.

89 **"Where will I fix them?":** "Habyalimana (sic) Orders Rwandese to Stay Where They Are." *The Citizen.* September 27, 1989.

89 **They wanted power:** Kuperman. "Explaining the Ultimate Escalation in Rwanda."

89 **take over Rwanda by force:** Stephen Kinzer. *A Thousand Hills: Rwanda's Rebirth and the Man Who Dreamed It.* Wiley, 2008, p 50; Faustin Mugabe. "Was Rwigyema Assassinated?" *The Monitor* (Uganda). October 1, 2014; Alan J. Kuperman. "Explaining the Ultimate Escalation in Rwanda: How and Why Tutsi Rebels Provoked a Retaliatory Genocide." Speech prepared for the 99th Annual Meeting of the American Political Science Association, Philadelphia, PA, August 28–31, 2003; Timothy Kalyegira. "RPF Invasion of Rwanda and Denials." *The Monitor.* December 18, 2012.

90 **Basima House:** Amnesty International. Uganda. Human

Rights Violations by the National Resistance Army. December 4, 1991.

90 **Corner Kilak:** Timothy Kalyegira. "Insurgency in the Northern and Eastern Regions in 1986." *The Monitor* (Uganda). December 12, 2012.

90 **Bunyenyezi:** The Mukura Massacre of 1989. Justice and Reconciliation Project. Field Note 12, March 2011.

90 **"These Rwandans":** Ogenga Otunnu. "An Historical Analysis of the Invasion by the Rwanda Patriotic Army (RPA)." Chapter 2 in *The Path of a Genocide: From Rwanda to Zaire.* Howard Adelman and Astri Suhrke eds. Transaction Publishers, 2000, pp. 22–23.

90 **open borders program:** Timothy Kalyegira. "RPF invasion of Rwanda and Denials." *The Monitor.* December 18, 2012.

91 **Habyarimana told U.S. State Department:** Herman Cohen. *Intervening in Africa,* p. 166.

CHAPTER 5

94 **Africa's most brutal dictators:** Webster Griffin Tarpley and Anton Chaitkin. *George Bush: The Unauthorized Biography.* Progressive Press, 2004.

95 **when they became too critical:** "Uganda: The Failure to Safeguard Human Rights." Amnesty International, 1992.

95 **"orders from above":** Perez Rumanzi. "I work on orders from

Museveni says Kayihura." *The Monitor* (Kampala). December 18, 2016.

95 **Museveni justified the ban:** Yoweri K. Museveni. *What Is Africa's Problem?* "Chapter 20: Political Substance and Political Form." University of Minnesota Press, 2000; Nelson Kasfir. "'No-party Democracy' in Uganda." *Journal of Democracy* 9.2 (1998), pp. 49–63.

96 **When he took over in 1986:** Yoweri K. Museveni. *Sowing the Mustard Seed.* Palgrave Macmillan, 1997.

96 **proved a fiasco:** George Kanyeihamba. *The Blessings and Joy of Being Who You Are.* Self published, 2012.

96 **castoffs from China:** Ibid.

96 **others disappeared completely:** "Uganda: The Failure to Safeguard Human Rights." Amnesty International, 1992.

96 **Robert Wasswa-Lule:** "State Admits Arresting DP Leaders for No Reason." *The Citizen.* May 6, 1992; "Law Society Accuses Government of Persecuting Ugandans." *The Citizen.* June 3, 1992.

97 **Three months later he was fired:** "Wasswa-Lule Sacked." *The Citizen.* August 26, 1992.

97 **no police investigation:** "Who Burnt the DP Offices?" *The Citizen.* May 27, 1992.

97 **the Russians not the Americans:** "American Ambassador

242   Calls for Democracy." *The Citizen*. October 20, 1992.

97   **The audience roared with applause:** "American Ambassador Pins Down Katageya." *The Citizen*. November 10, 1992.

98   **"grooming a dictatorship":** "Donors Threaten Aid Cuts if Tricks Are Detected in Democratization Exercise." *The Exposure*. October 1994; "A Yardstick to Declare Elections Free, Fair or Unfair and Rigged." *The Exposure*. December 1993; "EC in Dilemma to Please Both Museveni and Donors." *The Exposure*. December 1993.

98   **Some UN diplomats agreed:** "Museveni Commits Yet Another Grave Error." *The Exposure*. December 1993.

99   **a donor report:** Ellen Hauser. "Ugandan Relations with Western Donors in the 1990s: What Impact on Democratisation?" *The Journal of Modern African Studies*, vol. 37, no. 4 (Dec., 1999), p. 627; "U.S. Endorses Elections, Snubs Mobilizers." *The Citizen* Apr 20, 1994.

99   **said they'd attend:** "European Community to Attend DP Rally." The Citizen. November 10, 1993.

99   **"I don't want to have to shoot you":** "Museveni's Dictatorship Proved Beyond Doubt." *The Citizen*. November 24, 1993.

100   **Why was America using sanctions:** "Democracy Is Like a Five Gear Car, Says U.S. Ambassador Johanny (sic) Carson." *The Exposure*. December 1993.

CHAPTER 6

101   **Kampala's largest shoe store:** Kalyegira. "RPF invasion of Rwanda and Denials."

102   **all taken from NRA arsenals:** Otunnu. "An Historical Analysis of the Invasion by the Rwanda Patriotic Army (RPA)," p. 40.

102   **true purpose of the mobilization:** Ibid., p. 42.

103   **The ranchers protested:** Mahmood Mamdani. *When Victims Become Killers: Colonialism, Nativism and Genocide in Rwanda*. Princeton University Press, 2001, Chapter 6; Expedit Ddungu. *The Other Side of Land Issues in Buganda: Pastoral Ciris and the Squatter Movement in Sembabule Sub-district*. Kampala, Center for Basic Research, 1994.

103   **Museveni refused the ranchers:** Godfrey Serwada. "Mawagola Squatters Resort to Stealing." *The Citizen*. September 12, 1990; "Now Government deals with Ranchers Militarily." *The Citizen*. June 26, 1990; "Rwandese Grabbing Our Land." *The Citizen*. June 20, 1990.

104   **Most of the men were occupied:** Ibrahim Ssemujju Nganda. "This Is Not the Museveni I Fought With." *The Observer* (Uganda) June 10, 2009; "Rwandese Refugee Army Overruns Four Garrisons." *Weekly Topic*. October 12, 1990; Ibrahim Ssemujju Nganda. "OPEN SECRETS: Museveni's Untold Role in RPF War." *The Observer* (Uganda). July 9, 2009; Mulwanyamuli interview with author. Kampala. February 2016.

104   **"I would like to make it very clear":** Otunnu. "An Historical Analysis of the Invasion by the Rwanda Patriotic Army (RPA)," p. 44.

104   **Museveni must have been lying:** Cohen. *Intervening in Africa*, p. 164.

105   b**reach of the United Nations Charter:** See for example, The United Nations Charter: Principle VI.a "Crimes against Peace."

105   **Organization of African Union rules:** See for example Founding Charter of the Organization of African Unity. Article III, principles 3 and 4.

105   **"stiff talking points":** Gribbin. *In the Aftermath of Genocide: The U.S. Role in Rwanda*, p. 66.

105   **seal all Uganda–Rwanda border-crossings:** Otunnu. "An Historical Analysis of the Invasion by the Rwanda Patriotic Army (RPA)," pp. 44–45.

105   **Kagame flew in to Entebbe Airport:** Kinzer. *A Thousand Hills: Rwanda's Rebirth and the Man Who Dreamed It*, p. 64; Gribbin. *In the Aftermath of Genocide: The U.S. Role in Rwanda*, p. 66.

105   **For the next three and a half years:** Otunnu. "An Historical Analysis of the Invasion by the Rwanda Patriotic Army (RPA)," p. 43; "Arming Rwanda: The Arms Trade and Human Rights Abuses in the Rwandan War." Human Rights Watch Arms Project. January 1994.

105   **Museveni threatened to charge the journalist:** "Uganda: The

Failure to Safeguard Human Rights." Amnesty International, 1992, p. 31.

106   **inspection team was denied access:** "RPF Keeping Uganda/Rwanda Border Closed." *The Exposure.* August 1991.

106   **U.S. officials met quietly with RPF leaders:** Cohen. *Intervening in Africa*, p. 168.

106   **Western donors doubled aid:** Hauser. "Ugandan Relations with Western Donors in the 1990s: What Impact on Democratisation?" p. 626.

106   **what the RPF was fighting for:** Guichaoua. *From War to Genocide: Criminal Politics in Rwanda*, p. 24.

106   **Flaten urged the Bush Sr. Administration:** Gribbin. *In the Aftermath of Genocide: The U.S. Role in Rwanda*, p. 64.

107   **it was far too late:** Cohen. *Intervening in Africa*, p. 178.

108   **economic inequalities in the country:** Cohen. *Intervening in Africa*, p. 169.

108   **"demon Tutsis":** Guichaoua. *From War to Genocide: Criminal Politics in Rwanda.*

108   **Scores of non-RPF Tutsis were rounded up:** Guichaoua. *From War to Genocide: Criminal Politics in Rwanda*, p. 24.

109   **"What to do about the Tutsis?":** Alison Des Forges. *"Leave None to Tell the Story": Genocide in Rwanda.* p. 73.

109   **the Ugandans insisted:** Roméo Dallaire. *Shake Hands with the Devil:*

244   *The Failure of Humanity in Rwanda.*
Random House, 2003, pp. 95–96.

110   **NRA refused to allow the peacekeepers:** Dallaire. *Shake Hands with the Devil: The Failure of Humanity in Rwanda*, p. 96.

110   **"of course we did support the [RPF invasion]":** Rwanda's Genocide: Looking Back. Hearing before the Sub-Committee on Africa. April 22, 2004.

110   **the CIA predicted:** Statement of Alison Des Forges, May 5, 1998, p. 52.

111   **riots at academic conferences:** Jonathan Fisher. "Writing about Rwanda since the Genocide: Knowledge, Power and 'Truth,'" *Journal of Intervention and Statebuilding*, 9:(1) 134-145.

111   **"anyone in the media":** William Wallis. "Lunch with Paul Kagame." *The Financial Times.* May 13, 2011.

111   **RPF had fired a similar missile:** Filip Reyntjens. *Trois Jours qui ont Fait Basculer l'Histoire.* Harmattan, 1995, p. 45; Anonymous interview with Ugandan security official, New York, 2015. Jean-Louis Bruguiere. *Deliverance de Mandats D'Arret Internationaux* (Report of Judge Bruguiere on the assassination of President's Juvenal Habyarimana and Cyprien Ntyaramira.) November 17, 2006.

112   **sold to Uganda by the USSR:** Bruguiere. *Deliverance de Mandats D'Arret Internationaux.*

112   **details of these investigations:** In 1997, investigators working for the United Nations International Criminal Tribunal for Rwanda interviewed three senior RPF informants who said they participated in the attack on the plane and gave highly detailed accounts of their own and Kagame's involvement. One offered to link the investigators to the soldier who fired one of the SAMs from Masaka Hill, and all three offered to provide documentary evidence of the plot. The leader of the investigation team, Australian lawyer Michael Hourigan transmitted this information to his superiors via a secure phone in the U.S. Embassy in Kigali. A few days later, the tribunal's chief prosecutor, Louise Arbour, who had been supportive of the plane crash investigation until then, ended it, claiming that it was not in the tribunal's mandate. From Nick McKenzie, "Uncovering Rwanda's Secrets," *The Age* (Australia), February 10, 2007. The online version of this article contains links to Hourigan's original report to the tribunal: National Team Enquiry, Internal Memorandum created by UN investigator Michael Hourigan in January 1997 in order to brief Louise Arbour, head of the International Criminal Tribunal for Rwanda. See also Affidavit of Michael Andrew Hourigan, The International Criminal Tribunal for Rwanda, Arusha, Tanzania, November 27, 2006. And Mark Doyle, "Rwanda Plane Crash Probe Halted," BBC News, February 9, 2007.

According to French sociologist Andre Guichaoua, who served as an expert witness on the tribunal, and whose book From War to Genocide: Criminal Politics in Rwanda, 1990–1994 contains what is probably the most comprehensive account yet of what happened when the plane went down, two additional independent investigations point in the same direction as Hourigan's. Guichaoua was in Rwanda on that fatal night, and was struck by the panic the crash triggered in Hutu elite circles. By contrast, the RPF troops stationed in Kigali seemed highly regimented and alert. Guichaoua also noted the silence of the embassies. In the years that followed, several Rwandan government insiders confided in Guichaoua that they believed the RPF was responsible for the crash. Then in 1998, the families of the French flight crew who were killed along with Habyarimana opened a formal investigation of the crash, overseen by French judge Jean-Louis Brugiere. In 2004, Brugiere issued arrest warrants against nine of Kagame's associates. Rwanda broke diplomatic relations with France one week later.

Meanwhile, a Spanish judge who was investigating war crimes in Rwanda independently of Hourigan and Brugiere came to the same conclusion they did concerning responsibility for the crash. According to Guichaoua, dozens of witnesses who gave testimony to these various investigators paid with their lives as the RPF attempted to "conceal or suppress incriminating evidence from dossiers relating to

political assassinations, explosions and massacres...as well as the attack on the presidential plane." Guichaoua, *From War to Genocide*, p. 147.

In 2008, Kagame's government released two reports of its own on the crash. In one of them, the authors announced that 33 arrest warrants against French politicians and military officers would soon be issued. Diplomatic meetings were held and all investigations—French, Spanish, Rwandan and otherwise— were suspended.

112 **supposedly exonerated the RPF:** "Rwanda Genocide: Kagame 'cleared of Habyarimana Crash.'" BBC News. January 10, 2012.

112 **margin of error:** Filip Reyntjens. "Attentat de Kigali: 'la vérité a gagné'?" *Le Monde*. January 31, 2012.

112 **"He knew full well":** Dallaire. *Shake Hands with the Devil: The Failure of Humanity in Rwanda*, p. 327.

113 **"If we'd gone in sooner":** "Bill Clinton: We Could Have Saved 300,000 Lives in Rwanda." CNBC Meets. March 13, 2013.

113 **Kagame told him:** Dallaire. *Shake Hands with the Devil: The Failure of Humanity in Rwanda*, p. 342.

113 **The UN estimated later:** Mark Prutsalis. "Sitrep 10: Rwandan Refugees in Tanzania New Arrivals Report." FAX. May 17, 1994.

114 **tied "three-piece":** See also "Hutu Comeback Plans Go Under

246   Gear, but Sweden-based Rebel Group Is Disowned." *The Exposure*. September 1994. Filip Reyntjens. *Political Governance in Post-Genocide Rwanda*. Cambridge University Press, p. 100.

114 **honorary doctorate:** Frank Wright. "'U' presents Ugandan President with Degree, Humphrey Medal." *Star Tribune*. June 24, 1994.

114 **"the future of black Africa":** Frank Wright. "Museveni's Tenacity Has Served His Struggling Nation Well." *Star Tribune*. January 9, 1995.

114 **to Nelson Mandela:** James C. McKinley Jr. "Uganda Leader Stands Tall in New African Order." *New York Times*. June 15, 1997.

114 **"herdsman philosopher":** Johanna McGeary and Sally B. Donnelly. "An African for Africa." *Time*. September 1, 1997.

114 **they found Museveni charming:** "Museveni Amuses the Crowd at Davos." *Africa Analysis*. February 6, 1998.

114 **National Security Advisor Anthony Lake:** Visits by foreign leaders of Uganda. Office of the Historian. The White House. https://history.state.gov/departmenthistory/visits/uganda.

CHAPTER 7

115 **$15 million each year to spend:** Michela Wrong. *In the Footsteps of Mr. Kurtz: Living on the Brink of Disaster in Mobutu's Congo*. Harper Perennial, 2002, p. 206.

115 **roughly $10 billion more:** Wrong, p. 196.

115 **siphoned $100 million a year:** Wrong, p. 115.

116 **raped the man's wife and daughter:** Wrong, p. 207.

116 **"Go ahead and steal":** Wrong, p. 99.

118 **stop counting:** Reyntjens. *Political Governance in Post Genocide Rwanda*, p. 105.

118 **especially returned refugees:** The Gersony Report referred to in Reyntjens. *Trois Jours qui ont Fait Basculer*, Chapter 4; see also Alison Des Forges. *"Leave None To Tell The Story": Genocide in Rwanda*, pp. 726-34.

119 **acrobats and a Zairean singing and dancing troupe:** Daniel Kalinaki. *Kizza Besigye and Uganda's Unfinished Revolution*. DominentSeven Publishers, 2014, p. 92.

119 **It turned out to be a bomb:** Ibid., p. 92.

119 **their sights on Museveni:** "Ganging Up Against Militant Islam." *Africa Analysis*. January 27, 1995; "Hutus Join Ugandan Rebels to Oust Museveni." *The Exposure* (Uganda). March 1995.

119 **meeting in Kampala:** Prunier, p. 67.

120 **"lack of revolutionary seriousness":** Che Guevara. *The African Dream: The Diaries of the Revolutionary War in the Congo*. Grove Press, 2001, p. 69.

120   **kidnapped four university students:** Brian Aronstam. "Out of Africa." *Stanford Magazine*. July/ August 1998.

120   **"make the whole operation look Congolese":** Stearns, p. 87.

120   **260,000 remain unaccounted for:** Roessler and Verhoeven, p. 210.

CHAPTER 8

121   **"We members of ESO":** "ESO Operatives Cry to Museveni over Discrimination." *The Citizen*. March 16, 1995.

122   **"The Cuban trainers":** "Report on ESO Enraged Government." *The Citizen*. April 20, 1995.

123   **police burst into Lawrence's house:** "Kiwanuka's Agony Since Arrest." *The Citizen*. April 20, 1995.

123   **didn't know what the charges were:** Ibid.

123   **Ugandan spies were tracking:** "I Would Have Died in Prison— Kiwanuka." *The East African*. May 22-28, 1995.

124   **to assassinate Lawrence:** "Suspect Arrested in Plot to Kill Kiwanuka." *The East African*. June 19-25, 1995.

124   **Daniel Arap Moi:** "Moi Meets Team from Uganda." *The East African*. June 19–25, 1995.

124   **Joseph was brutally beaten:** "Editor's Father Attacked." *The New Vision*. July 1, 1995.

CHAPTER 9

126   **Daniel Simpson:** Quoted in El-Tahri, *Afrique en Morceaux*.

127   **unless Rwanda and Uganda pulled their troops:** Filip Reyntjens. *The Great African War: Congo and Regional Geopolitics, 1996–2006*. Cambridge University Press, 2005, p. 60.

127   **airports were being used to ship equipment:** El-Tahri. *Afrique en Morceaux*.

127   **greeted warmly by the Americans and Europeans:** Steven Erlanger. "U.S. Decides Time Is Ripe to Elbow Mobutu Aside." *The New York Times*. April 30, 1997.

127   **"engine of regional growth":** Howard French. "On Visit to Congo, Albright Praises the New Leader." *The New York Times*. December 13, 1997.

128   **"The U.S. government has decided to support Kabila":** Aronstam. "Out of Africa."

128   **Millions would die:** Chris McGeal. "War in Congo Kills 45,000 People Each Month." *The Guardian*. January 23, 2008.

128   **Villagers were raped:** Kirsten Johnson; Jennifer Scott; Bigy Rughita; Michael Kisielewski; Jana Asher; Ricardo Ong; Lynn Lawry. "Association of Sexual Violence and Human Rights Violations with Physical and Mental Health in Territories of the Eastern Democratic Republic of the Congo." *The Journal of the*

248   *American Medical Association*, 2010, 304 (5), pp. 553–561; L. Melhado. "Rates of Sexual Violence Are High in Democratic Republic of the Congo." *International Perspectives on Sexual and Reproductive Health*, 2010, 36 (4), p. 210.

128   **10 different militant groups:** Suliman Baldo. "Covered in Blood: Ethnically Targeted Violence in Northern DRC." *Human Rights Watch.* July 7, 2003.

128   **recruited hundreds of child soldiers:** International Court of Justice. "Armed Activities on the Territory of the Congo (*Democratic Republic of the Congo v. Uganda*)" press release, December 19, 2005, p. 2.

128   **Ugandan military planes ferried gold:** ICJ; Final Report of the Panel of Experts on the Illegal Exploitation of Natural Resources and Other Forms of Wealth of the Democratic Republic of the Congo. United Nations, 2002.

128   **the Victoria Group:** See also: Peter Danssaert & Brian Johnson Thomas. *Greed & Guns: Uganda's Role in the Rape of the Congo*. International Peace Information Service, 2006, and references therein.

129   **Salim Saleh**: Koen Vlassenroot, Sandrine Perrot & Jeroen Cuvelier. "Doing Business Out of War: An Analysis of the UPDF's Presence in the Democratic Republic of Congo," *Journal of Eastern African Studies*, 2012, 6:1, 2-21; Final Report of the Panel of Experts on the Illegal Exploitation of Natural Resources and Other Forms of Wealth of the Democratic Republic of the Congo, United Nations, 2002; Timothy Raeymaekers, "Protection for Sale? War and the Transformation of Regulation on the Congo–Ugandan Border," *Development and Change*. Volume 41, Issue 4, July 2010, pp. 563–587.

129   **Viktor Bout:** Final Panel of Experts Report; Madeleine Drohan. *Making a Killing*. The Lyons Press, 2003.

129   **use dangerous methods involving explosives:** Anneke Van Woudenberg. "The Curse of Gold." *Human Rights Watch.* June 1, 2005.

129   **"rape capital of the world":** International Court of Justice. Judgment of "Case Concerning Armed Activities on the Territory of the Congo (*Democratic Republic of the Congo v. Uganda*)." December 19, 2005.

129   **Rwanda-backed Tutsi rebels mutilated the same women:** United Nations High Commissioner for Human Rights. Report of the Mapping Exercise documenting the most serious violations of human rights and international humanitarian law committed within the territory of the Democratic Republic of the Congo between March 1993 and June 2003. August 2010.

129   **Roughly one woman in five:** Kirsten Johnson et al; Melhado, p. 210.

129   **including M23:** Gregory Wallance. "The Real Reason Susan Rice Didn't Deserve to Be Secretary

of State." Forbes.com. December 14, 2012.

129   **900kg of gold:** UN Group of Experts on the Democratic Republic of Congo Report. United Nations Security Council May 23, 2016 paragraph 158 and footnote 31. May 23, 2016.

130   **helicopter attacks on elephants:** Final report of the Group of Experts on the Democratic Republic of Congo. United Nations Security Council. January 23, 2014, Annex 102, p. 235.

130   **overlook crimes committed by the RPF:** Roessler and Verhoeven, p. 159.

130   **200 U.S. Special Forces troops:** Roessler and Verhoeven, pp. 158–9.

130   **U.S. also gave Rwanda aerial reconnaissance and radio intelligence:** Roessler and Verhoeven, p. 203.

130   **the Clinton Administration:** John F. Clark. "The Clinton Administration and Africa: White House Involvement and the Foreign Affairs Bureaucracies." *Issue: A Journal of Opinion*, Vol. 26, No. 2, (1998), pp. 8-13.

131   **defend themselves against terrorist incursions:** Roessler and Verhoeven, p. 188.

131   **with U.S. approval:** Adam Branch. *The Political Dilemmas of Global Justice: Anti-Civilian Violence and the Violence of Humanitarianism, the Case of Northern Uganda*. Ph.D. diss. Columbia University, 2007, p.

186; "Kabila's Jackson Rebuff May Sour U.S. Relations." *Africa Analysis*. February 20, 1998.

131   **Pentagon officials:** Roessler and Verhoeven, pp. 204–5.

131   **contact with Peter Whaley:** Peter Whaley obituary. *The Washington Post*. February 5, 2005.

131   **"Whaley's War":** Ibid.

131   **Etienne Tshisekedi:** Testimony of Peter Rosenblum. Submitted to the Congressional Record. July 8, 1997.

132   **"disengagement from Zairean civil society":** Rosenblum personal communication, October 2016.

132   **Susan Rice:** Peter Roseblum, personal communication January 2017; see also Armin Rosen. "The Controversial Africa Policy of Susan Rice." *The Atlantic*. November 29, 2012.

132   **overtures to Sudan's Bashir:** "U.S. Links Lose Museveni Credibility." *Africa Analysis*. November 13, 1998; Reyntjens. *The Great African War*, Introduction and Chapter 2: The War of Liberation.

133   **teaming up with the Rwandan Hutu militants:** "Hutu Comeback Plans Go Under Gear, but Sweden-based Rebel Group Is Disowned." *The Exposure*. September 1994.

133   **outlandish terror plots:** David Rose. The Osama Files. *Vanity Fair* January 2002; Ambassador Timothy Michael Carney. Interview with Charles Stuart Kennedy. The Association

250   for Diplomatic Studies and
Training Foreign Affairs Oral
History Project. June 24, 2002.

133 **"pygmy despot":** Robert O.
Collins. *A History of Modern Sudan.*
Cambridge University Press, 2008,
p. 216.

134 **By early 1998:** Howard French.
*A Continent for the Taking: The
Tragedy and Hope of Africa.* Knopf,
2004, p. 246.

134 **Madeleine Albright:**
Quoted in Peter Rosenblum.
"Irrational Exuberance: The Clinton
Administration in Africa." *Current
History.* May 2002.

134 **"Every country's human
rights record can be improved":**
Peter Bouckaert. "Hostile to
Democracy: The Movement System
and Political Repression in Uganda."
Human Rights Watch. September
1999, p. 147.

134 **John Ashcroft:** Democracy
in Africa: The New Generation of
African Leaders. Hearing before the
Subcommittee on African Affairs of
the Committee on Foreign Relations.
United States Senate. 105th
Congress, Second Session. March
12, 1998.

135 **special envoy Jesse Jackson:**
Onyango-Obbo. "Poor in Money, But
Even Poorer in Democracy." *The New
York Times.* July 12, 2003.

135 **apologized for slavery:**
James Bennet. "Clinton in Africa:
The Overview; In Uganda, Clinton
Expresses Regret on Slavery in U.S."
The New York Times. March 25, 1998.

CHAPTER 10

138 **Robert Felkin:** Robert Felkin.
Notes on Labour in Central Africa.
Edinburgh Medical Journal. Vol. 29,
part 2, 1984, p. 922 ff.

139 **Mulago Hospital:** According
to Dr. Anthony Mugasa, reproductive
health adviser of the Uganda
Ministry of Health, the maternal
mortality rate at Mulago in 1972 was
71 per 100,000 live births. Interview
with Dr. Mugasa, July 2013. In 1970,
it was about 60 for blacks in the
US. Maternal Mortality and Related
Concepts. Vital and Health Statistics
Series 3, number 33. National Center
for Health Statistics. Centers for
Disease Control and Prevention. U.S.
Department of Health and Human
Services. February 2007.

139 **can't diagnose pneumonia:**
Education and Health Services in
Uganda. A Report by the World
Bank. November 2013; Anthony
Wesaka. "Nambooze Attacks Doctors
Who Steal Patients." *Daily Monitor.*
October 23, 2013.

139 **seven times more likely to
die in childbirth:** According to Dr.
Anthony Mugasa, reproductive
health adviser of the Uganda
Ministry of Health, the maternal
mortality rate at Mulago in 1972 was
71 per 100,000 live births. Interview
with Dr. Mugasa, July 2013. It is now
498 per 100,000. Interview with Dr.
Mugasa, July 2013.

139 **During a drought in 2017:**
Anonymous interview. New York
City March 2017.

139   **spent $150 million a year:** Andrew Mwenda. "Health Care for the Rich." *The Independent.* May 6, 2012; Yasiin Mugerwa. "State House Budget Shoots to Shs160b." *The Monitor* (Kampala) January 6, 2011; Emmanuel Ayeibona. "State House Report Reveals Rot in Wakiso Hospitals." *The Monitor* (Kampala) August 14, 2016.

139   **complete primary school:** Uganda National Commission for UNESCO. "Count down to 2015: Is Uganda on track? Assessment of progress to attainment of EFA goals in Uganda final report." June 29, 2012.

139   **Eighty percent of their teachers:** Patricia Ahimbisibwe. "80 pc of Teachers Can't Read." *The Monitor.* September 21 2016. The World Bank claims Uganda's Primary School Completion Rate is 50 percent, still one of the lowest in the world, but the rate is in fact much lower than this, according to raw data collected from the Uganda Bureau of Statistics by the Great Lakes Institute for Strategic Studies and shown to this author.

139   **nearest water source:** World Bank. October 2016 report.

140   **"The valley dams":** "Kazibwe Ready To Resign Over Dams." *The New Vision* (Kampala), January 14, 1999.

140   **In 1995, the World Bank:** Joel D. Barkan et al., "The Political Economy of Uganda," a background paper commissioned by the World Bank, July 6, 2004, p. 64.

140   **sold it to a consortium:** Roger Tangri and Andrew Mwenda. *The Politics of Elite Corruption in Africa: Uganda in Comparative African Perspective.* Routledge, 2013, p. 58.

140   **Belorussian junk helicopters:** "Besigye Wants Independent Inquiry into Junk Helicopter Deal." *The New Vision.* November 7, 2000.

140   **number of scandals:** See for example: Ambassador Jerry Lanier to U.S. Secretary of State Hillary Clinton. CABLE: Uganda's all you can eat corruption buffet. Wikileaks cable. January 10, 2010; Human Rights Watch. "Letting the Big Fish Swim: Failures to Prosecute High Level Corruption in Uganda." October 2013; Anthony Wesaka. "Mukula Claims Giving Gavi Fund Money to Janet Museveni." *The Monitor* (Uganda). November 13, 2012; Dear Jeanne, How Soldiers Stole State House Money. *The Monitor* (Uganda). November 24, 2013.

141   **worse shape than the LRA:** Allen and Vlassenroot.

141   **new private jet:** Ian Drury. "UK Aid Cash Helped African Dictator Buy Himself a £30m Jet." *The Daily Mail.* June 10, 2011.

141   **purchased four Russian fighter jets:** Julius Barigaba. "$740m Fighter Jets Scam Sneaks Under the Radar." *The East African.* April 4, 2011.

141   **handed out to voters as bribes:** *Letting the Big Fish Swim: Failures to Prosecute High Level Corruption in Uganda.* Human Rights Watch, 2013.

252   141   **five million dollars each month:** Anthony Wesaka. "Mukula: I paid Gavi Money to Janet Team." *The Monitor* (Uganda). November 14, 2012; Henry Ford Miriima. *Oil Discovery January 2006: The Role Ugandans Played*. Marianum Press (Uganda) 2013. Chapter 17; Milton Allimadi. "I Discovered 5 Million Dollars Were Being Stolen Every Month in Uganda." Zoe Bakoko. Interview with Zoe Bakoko. Bakoru, former Minister of Gender, Labor and Social Development. Sahara TV, February 18, 2013.

141   **repeated break-ins:** Fisher. *International Perceptions and African Agency*, p. 182; see also Letter from 31 Ugandan and International Organizations. RE: Break-ins targeting offices of Ugandan human rights organizations. Human Rights Watch. June 13, 2016.

141   **Western diplomats:** Fisher, p. 140.

142   **"Auntie Lynda":** Fisher. *International Perceptions and African Agency*, p. 143, 148. After leaving office, Chalker lobbied for Museveni through her firm Africa Matters. So did President George W. Bush's Assistant Secretary of State for African Affairs Jendayi Frazer at the lobbying firm The Whitaker Group.

142   **Clare Short:** Fisher, p. 142; Steve Crawshaw. "Chalker in Lonely Fight for Aid to Third World." *The Independent*. February 16, 1996.

142   **"disappointed" by atrocities:** Fisher, pp. 282, 319.

142   **19 percent poverty rate:** The Uganda Poverty Assessment Report: Farms Cities and Good Fortune: Assessing Poverty Reduction in Uganda from 2006 to 2013. World Bank 2016.

142   **70 percent of Ugandans think they are poor:** Ibid. p 42.

142   **multinational companies:** "iDroid USA to Leave Kampala Just Six Months After Arriving." *The Indian Ocean Newsletter*. September 25, 2015; James Anyanzwa. "No Payment Deal for Uchumi Creditors, Employees in Uganda." *The East African*. May 14, 2016; "British Airways Stops Flights to Uganda's Entebbe airport." BBC. July 24, 2015; Lerato Mbele. "Why Is Britain's Barclays Bank Pulling Out of Africa?" BBC. March 1, 2016.

143   **Ugandan Health Ministry official:** Demographic and Health Surveys (DHSProgram.com). Comparison of unmet need for family planning in 17 Sub-Saharan African countries. By author. November 21, 2016.

CHAPTER 11

145   **Kalangala Action Plan:** Charles Onyango-Obbo. "Inside the Mind of President Museveni." *The East African*. February 7, 2011; Chris Kibirige. "Museveni Leader of Kalangala Action Plan." *The Monitor* (Uganda). March 7, 2002.

145   **Court originally decided 4-1:** Charles Onyango-Obbo, "'Crown Prince' Museveni, and 'Queen' Janet," *The Monitor*. May 9, 2001; George Kanyeihamba. *The Blessings and Joy of Being Who You Are*, p. 184.

146 **"Successful societies limit the power of the state":** Remarks by President George W. Bush at the 20th anniversary of the National Endowment for Democracy, United States Chamber of Commerce, Washington, D.C. November 7, 2003.

146 **dragged him off airplanes:** Kalinaki. *Kizza Besigye: Uganda's Unfinished Revolution*. Chapter 9.

147 **Powell said:** Charles Onyango-Obbo. "Is the Kampala Government's Last Meal Being Cooked? And When Besigye Met Colin Powell." *The Monitor* (Uganda). 25 July 2001.

147 **Museveni flew to Washington:** Reed Kramer. "Bush to Visit Africa in Early July; Three Countries on Current Itinerary." AllAfrica.com. June 9, 2003.

147 **Bush asked Ambassador Kolker:** Interview with Ambassador Jimmy Kolker, Washington DC, October 2015.

148 **Constitutional Review Commission:** Kalinaki. *Kizza Besigye*, p. 226.

148 **stage-managed assassination:** Ibrahim Ssemujju Nganda. "The Mystery of Ayume's death." *The Observer* (Uganda). May 27, 2004.

148 **Pro-Kisanja agents:** Olive Kobusingye. *The Correct Line? Uganda under Museveni*. Author House, 2011, Chapter 10.

148 **Teodoro Obiang:** Joshua Norman. "The World's Enduring Dictators: Teodoro Obiang Nguema Mbasogo, Equatorial Guinea." CBS News, June 19, 2011.

149 **diverted to the war chest:** James Ogoola et al. "The Report of the Judicial Commission of Inquiry into the Mismanagement of the Global Fund. Submitted to the President of Uganda." May 30, 2006.

149 **Richard Feachem:** John Donnelly. "Global Fund Director Under Fire." *Boston Globe*. February 5, 2007.

150 **malaria incidence increased:** Helen Epstein. "The Politics of malaria." Harpers. February 2011.

150 **never punished:** "Uganda Shaken by Fund Scandal." *The Washington Times*. June 15, 2006.

150 **Luis Moreno-Ocampo:** Jess Bravin. "For Global Court, Ugandan Rebels Are Proving a Tough Test— Prosecutor Is Hampered by African Politics, Tactical Fights; No Trial Date in Sight." *The Wall Street Journal Europe*. June 9, 2006.

151 **Joel Barkan:** "Uganda Military Allocated $200m as Donors Protest," *East African* (Nairobi), June 20, 2005; Fisher, p. 180; Richard Banégas. "Democracy, Security and Governance in Uganda: The Contradictions of Post-Conflict Reconstruction." In Jean-Pierre Chrétien and Richard Banégas (eds), *The Recurring Great Lakes Crisis: Identity, Violence and Power*. Hurst, 2006. Referred to in Fisher, p. 110; Barkan et al. *The Political Economy of Uganda*. (*The Art of Managing a Donor-Financed Neo-Patrimonial State*). Final draft July 2004; John V. Sserwaniko. "Uganda's Mysterious Deaths." *The Monitor*. May 20, 2007.

254

152 **$4 billion in debt relief:** The International Monetary Fund. "IMF to Extend 100 Percent Debt Relief to Uganda under the Multilateral Debt Relief Initiative." Press release. December 23, 2005.

152 **watered-down version:** The World Bank. "The Political Economy of Uganda: The Art of Managing a Donor-Financed Neo-Patrimonial State." November 2005.

152 **Six Uganda Caucus members:** Fisher, p. 156. Scribe Strategies. "Supplemental Statement submitted to the Department of Justice in compliance with the Foreign Agents Registration Act," October 20, 2005. www.fara. gov/docs/5673-Supplemental-Statement-20051020-1.pdf.

152 **Congolese rebel group:** Louis Charbonneau and Michelle Nichols. Rwanda, Uganda arming Congo rebels, providing troops - U.N. panel. Reuters. October 17, 2012.

152 **ICC declined to investigate:** Armin Rosen. The Controversial Africa Policy of Susan Rice. *The Atlantic*. November 29, 2012.

153 **ICC prosecutions sends a message:** For example, Helen Epstein, "The Lost Hopes for South Sudan." The *New Yorker* Online. January 18, 2017.

CHAPTER 12

155 **67 people were dead:** Tristan McConnell. "Close Your Eyes and Pretend to Be Dead: What Really Happened Two Years Ago in the Bloody Attack on Nairobi's Westgate Mall." *Foreign Policy*. September 20, 2015.

156 **Al Qaeda operatives:** James Gordon Meek. "'Black Hawk Down' Anniversary: Al Qaeda's Hidden Hand." ABC News. October 4, 2013.

156 **Rosa Whitaker:** Ken Silverstein. "Connections Work for Ex-Trade Official: Public and Private Dealings with African Governments Highlight Revolving-door Issue." *The Los Angeles Times*, March 2, 2004. Risdel Kasasira and Frederic Musisi. "How the railway project slipped off." *The Monitor* (Kampala). August 31, 2014.

157 **by $450 million:** Yasiin Mugerwa. "Railway Inquiry Takes Ugly Turn." *The Monitor* (Uganda). January 18, 2015; "Obama Renews Agoa that Failed in Uganda." *The Insider* (Uganda). July 23, 2015; Wikileaks cable: UGANDA: PARLIAMENT INVESTIGATES AGOA ISSUES. From U.S. Embassy Kampala to U.S. Secretary of State, October 31, 2007.

157 **"strongly supporting the U.S.":** Jonathan Fisher. "Managing Donor Perceptions: Contextualizing Uganda's 2007 Intervention in Somalia." *African Affairs*. May 9, 2012.

157 **Bush and Museveni were speaking frequently:** Fisher. *International Perceptions and African Agency*, p. 168.

157 **chair-throwing brawl erupted in Parliament:** Ken Menkhaus. "The Crisis in Somalia: Tragedy in Five Acts." *African Affairs* 106/204, pp. 357–390.

157   **Alliance for the Restoration of Peace and Counterterrorism:** Menkhaus.

157   **Islamic Courts Union:** Mary Harper. *Getting Somalia Wrong.* African Arguments/ Zed Books, 2012, p. 81.

158   **streets were safe:** Harry Verhoeven. "The Self-fulfilling Prophecy of Failed States: Somalia, State Collapse, and the Global War on Terror," *Journal of Eastern African Studies*, vol. 3, no. 3, November 2009, pp. 405–25.

158   the **George W. Bush administration:** Menkhaus.

159   **"keeping Somalia out of terrorist hands":** Fisher, "Managing Donor Perceptions"; Risdel Kasasira. "How UPDF Somalia Mission Was Planned." *The Monitor.* August 14, 2016; Harry Verhoeven, personal communication.

159   **Frazer brooded:** Menkaus.

159   **accused the group of declaring war:** Verhoeven. "The Self-fulfilling Prophecy of Failed States."

159   **weak, disorganized TFG:** Kasasira. "How UPDF Somalia Mission Was Planned"; Verhoeven. "The Self-fulfilling Prophecy of Failed States."

159   **The Pentagon assisted:** David Axe. "U.S. Weapons Now in Somali Terrorists' Hands." *Wired.* August 2, 2011; Menkhaus.

159   **Al-Shabaab:** Colum Lynch. "Qatar's Support for Islamists

Muddles its Reputation as Neutral Broker in Mideast." *The Washington Post.* November 28, 2012.

160   **Stonings, hangings, and amputations:** "Whipped for Wearing a 'Deceptive' Bra: Hardline Islamists in Somalia Publicly Flog Women in Sharia Crackdown." *The Daily Mail.* October 16, 2009.

160   **training Museveni's troops:** Kasasira; Xan Rice and Suzanne Goldenberg. "How U.S. Forged an Alliance with Ethiopia over Invasion." *The Guardian.* January 13, 2007.

160   **trainload of food:** Kasasira.

160   **Al-Shabaab suicide bombers:** Risdel Kasasira. "How the 2010 Kampala Bombings Broke the Back of al-Shabaab." *The Monitor.* August 19, 2016.

161   **Museveni told the Americans:** Ibid.

161   **Osama bin Laden:** David Smith. "Al-Shabaab: From al-Qaida Rejects to a Fighting Force of Thousands." *The Guardian.* April 2, 2015.

162   **aren't paid for months:** Risdel Kasasira. "UPDF in Somalia Not Paid for Nine Months." *The Monitor* (Uganda). September 6, 2015; Deo Walusimbi. "UPDF in Somalia Unpaid for 7 Months." *The Observer* (Uganda). December 23, 2015; Joachim Buwembo. "Poor Mutebile, Look What Became of That Orphan He Brought Up." *The East African.* November 22, 2014.

256

162 **When a soldier questioned:** Edward Ssekika. "Soldiers Shock Museveni with More Leaks." *The Observer* (Kampala). October 19, 2013; "Editorial. Promotions in the Army Raise Valid Concerns." *The Observer* (Kampala). October 13, 2013.

162 **sentenced to twenty years in prison:** Ivan Okuda. UPDF Tortures Soldiers, Jails Him for 20 Years. *The Monitor* (Kampala) March 14, 2017.

162 **ammunition delivered to AMISOM:** Robert Young Pelton. "Does the U.S., UN and Amisom supply Al-Shabaab?" *The Somalia Report.* July 30, 2011; United Nations, Report of the Monitoring Group on Somalia and Eritrea pursuant to Security Council resolution 1916 (2010), p. 44.

162 **arming both sides of the conflict:** Axe, "U.S. Weapons Now in Somali Terrorists' Hands"; Pelton, "Does the U.S., UN and Amisom Supply Al-Shabaab?"

162 **single embassy bombing suspect:** Chris Reinolds Kozelle. "American Killed in Uganda Was Dedicated to Service." CNN. July 14, 2010.

CHAPTER 13

167 **another Besigye housekeeper:** Kalinaki. *Kizza Besigye,* p. 267.

167 **23 opposition activists were killed:** Andrew Mwenda. "The Dynamics of Election Violence in Uganda." *The Independent* (Uganda). November 2, 2015.

168 **Mulenga told him:** Kanyeihamba. *Blessings and Joy,* Chapter 39.

169 **4–3 in favor of Museveni:** Republic of Uganda, in the Supreme Court of Uganda at Mengo. Presidential Election Petition NO. 01 OF 2006. (CORAM: Odoki, CJ, Oder, Tsekooko, Karokora, Mulenga, Kanyeihamba and Katureebe, JJ.SC.) *Rtd. Col. Dr. Kizza Besigye vs. Electoral Commission and Yoweri Kaguta Museveni.* January 31, 2007. Two years later, the Ugandan government declined to renew Kanyeihamba's appointment to the African Court on Human and People's Rights, and replaced him with Mulenga. Michael Mubangizi. "Critical Judge Loses African Court Job to Friendlier Joseph Mulenga." *The Observer* (Uganda). August 13, 2008.

169 **Besigye won the 2006 election:** Frederic Musisi and agencies. "Besigye Won 2006 Polls— Sejusa." *The Monitor* (Kampala) December 17, 2013; Anonymous. "I have stolen votes for Museveni for 30 years—former ISO boss." *The Monitor* (Kampala). February 6, 2015.

169 **"Because I rigged it!":** Interview with David Sejusa, London, October 2013.

169 **European Union election observer:** EU Election Observation Mission, Uganda, February 23, 2006. Final Report on the Presidential and Parliamentary Elections. The British election monitoring NGO NEMgroup was far more critical, but British government officials reportedly pressured it to tone down its final report. Fisher. *International Perceptions and African Agency,* p. 283.

170 **land is a source of identity:** Faupel. *African Holocaust,* p. 20.

170 **"investment zones":** Robert Mwanje. "Kabaka Responds to Museveni's Letter." *The Monitor* (Uganda). December 23, 2007; Josephine Maseruku. "New Land Law Not Needed—Kabaka." *New Vision* (Uganda). December 23, 2007.

170 **Museveni blamed the evictions:** Edris Kiggundu. "Mengo Loses Battle on Land Bill." *The Observer*, November 19, 2009.

170 **Three other Baganda officials:** Robert Mwanje and Risdel Kasasira. "Buganda Officials Narrate Their Ordeal in Detention." *The Monitor.* August 2, 2008.

171 **"divide and rule" strategy:** "Kabaka's Response to Museveni Letter on Land." *The Monitor.* January 8, 2008.

171 **manipulated by Museveni:** Edris Kiggundu. "Uganda: I Can Abolish Kingdoms, Says Museveni." *The Observer.* September 11, 2009.

171 **"Your Royal Highness":** Charles Jjuuka. "President Museveni Backs Banyala Chief." *New Vision* (Uganda). December 14, 2008.

171 **Denis Walusimbi Ssengendo:** Sadab Kitatta Kaaya. "Strict Rules for Kabaka's Kayunga Visit." *The Observer.* January 23, 2104.

172 **40 people had been killed:** Human Rights Watch. Uganda: Investigate 2009 Kampala Riot Killings." Press Release. September 10, 2010.

173 **Lawrence sent smaller tranches of money to Annet:** Simon Musasizi. "Annet Namwanga:

Terrorist or Activist?" *Observer.* February 7, 2011.

174 **three men in plain clothes:** Annet told me they were plainclothes, but according to *The Monitor* they were in uniform. John Njoroge. "Mao Campaign Official Goes Missing." *The Monitor* (Uganda). January 24, 2011.

174 **"involuntarily dragged":** Ibid.

174 **Joint Anti-Terrorism Task Force:** Human Rights Watch. "Uganda: End Torture by Anti-Terror Unit." Press Release. April 8, 2009.

174 **a captive managed to escape:** Maria Burnett. "Open Secret: Illegal Detention and Torture by the Joint Anti-terrorism Task Force in Uganda." *Human Rights Watch.* April 8, 2009.

175 **Ruhakana Rugunda:** Wendy Glauser. "Evidence Points to Routine use of Torture by Uganda Government." *World Politics Review.* May 16, 2008.

175 **"Mummy and daddy are in such pain":** "Editorial: Please Produce Annet Namwanga." *The Monitor.* January 25, 2011.

175 **"We also read about her in the papers":** Norbert Mao. "Release Annet Namwanga or Produce Her in Court." *The Monitor* (Kampala). January 27, 2011.

175 **would not say where:** Anonymous interviews with author. Kampala. November 2015, February 2016.

176 **conspiracy to commit terrorist acts:** Adante Okanya

258   and Edward Anyoli. "DP Woman
Charged with Terrorism." *New Vision.*
February 6, 2011.

176   **$350 million:** Human Rights
Watch. "Letting the Big Fish Swim:
Failures to Prosecute High Level
Corruption in Uganda." October 21,
2013.

176   **stuffed into huge potato
sacks:** Kalinaki. *Kizza Besigye*, p. iv.

177   **"Return our Money"
campaign:** Helen Epstein. "What the
U.S. Is ignoring in Uganda." *New York
Review of Books* Daily. July 19, 2011.

177   **including a two-year-old:**
Human Rights Watch. Uganda Civil
Society Seeks Independent Inquiry
into April Killings. June 15, 2011.

178   **sprayed in the face:** The video
of the assault on Besigye can be
viewed at http://www.youtube.com/
watch?v=ZoNt_RKhIdk.

178   **U.S. State Department report:**
Dicta Asiimwe. What Next After
Clinton's Damning Uganda Report.
The Independent (Kampala). May 10,
2010.

179   **Carson deemed the election
"successful":** Reed Kramer. "Obama
will promote 'strong democratic
agenda'—Carson." AllAfrica.com.
March 15, 2011.

179   **$600 million:** Richard
Wanambwa. "Uganda: UK
Minister Tells Museveni to Wear
a Statesman's Cloak." *The Monitor*
(Uganda), May 26, 2011.

CHAPTER 14

182   **"orders from on high":**
Henry D. Gombya, "Nebanda, Wapa,
Mugalu & Others Died from Orders
on High," *The London Evening Post*,
August 29, 2013.

182   **discovery of oil:** Nicholas
Shaxson. "Oil, Corruption and
the Resource Curse." *International
Affairs*, 83: 6, 2007.

183   **Irish firm Tullow and Italian
firm ENI:** Henry Ford Miirema.
"Oil Discovery: The Role Ugandans
Played." Marianum Press. August
2013; Tabu Butagira. "Wiki Reveals
Claims of Massive Oil Bribes." *The
Monitor* (Uganda), September 14, 2011;
Rob Davies. "William Hague Dragged
into Tullow Oil Court Row." *The Daily
Mail*, March 15, 2013; "Museveni
'$50m bribe': The Inside Story." *The
Observer* (Uganda), March 17. 2013;
Tabu Butagira. "Uganda Scoffs at
$50m Museveni Oil Bribery Claim."
The Monitor (Uganda), March 19, 2013.
"Uganda: Security Report Details Oil
Sector Corruption." WikiLeaks cable,
January 13, 2010.

183   **continued making deals:**
Mirema.

185   **"like a poultry house":**
Parliamentary Hansard (Uganda)
December 21, 2012. Testimony of
Hon. MP Mr. Milton Muwuma;
"Latrine": *Parliamentary Hansard*
(Uganda) December 21, 2012,
Testimony of Hon. MP Mr. Peter
Ogwang.

185 **multi-million dollar bribe:** Ambassador Jerry Lanier to U.S. Secretary of State Hillary Clinton. CABLE: Uganda's all you can eat corruption buffet. Wikileaks cable. January 10, 2010.

186 **"You go back to your districts":** "Nebanda Was Right: Editorial. Find Lasting Solution to Drug Shortage." *The Monitor* (Kampala). January 15, 2017.

188 **"Be careful of your life":** Anonymous interviews, Kampala 2015, 2016.

188 **"I will leave my mark before I die":** *Parliamentary Hansard* (Uganda) December 21, 2012. Testimony of Hon. MP Sanjay Tannah.

189 **"over my dead body":** Museveni attacks MPS as idiots and fools: https://www.youtube.com/watch?v=WI5PftLdLYs; Yasin Mugerwa and Mercy Nalugo. "Museveni, Kadaga clash in Rwakitura." *The Monitor* (Kampala). January 2, 2013.

189 **"over-talking":** Julius Odeke. "I was emotional when I tore up Museveni's speech." *The Independent* (Kampala). January 25, 2013.

189 **Adam Kalungi:** Kalungi speaks out on Nebanda's death: https://www.youtube.com/watch?v=iweS2rCLwhs; Anthony Wesaka. "Nebanda's death: Adam Kalungi is a free man." *The Monitor* (Kampala) July 4, 2014.

190 **autopsy:** Sylvester Onzivua, personal communication. Benon Tugumisirize. "Uganda: Nebanda Trial—Witness Makes Key Confession." *New Vision.* April 8, 2013; Shifa Mwesigye and Benon Tugumisirize. "Mukwaya Hospital Staff Recount Nebanda Death." *The Observer* (Kampala). January 10, 2013; Haggai Matsiko. "Uganda: Nebanda's Death Reports." *The Independent* (Kampala). August 23, 2013.

191 **nine times higher:** Haggai Matsiko, "Nebanda's Death Reports," *The Independent* (Uganda), August 23, 2013.

CHAPTER 15

194 **"creeping lawlessness":** Richard Wanambwa. "Tinyefuza Warns on Impunity, Arrogance." *The Monitor.* October 1, 2012.

194 **Hussein Kyanjo:** Deo Walusimbi. "Kyanjo—Sejusa Is Wrong Man Saying the Right Things." *The Observer* (Kampala). October 20, 2013.

194 **fears for their own safety:** "Wolokoso—Kabaka Snubs MP Karuhanga Handshake." *The Observer* (Kampala) January 6, 2013.

196 **kill him in the ensuing chaos:** https://www.youtube.com/watch?v=7ENc_O3DBr0.

196 **Sejusa made up his story:** Edris Kiggundu & Emma Mutaizibwa. "Uganda: How Mbuya Attack Was Stage-Managed." *The Observer* (Kampala). March 28, 2013.

198 **Reports by USAID and Amnesty International:** "Uganda: The Failure to Safeguard Human Rights." Amnesty International. May 1992.

198 **no details of Sejusa's involvement:** "Uganda Exiles Plot to Oust Museveni." *African Analysis.* September 6, 1991.

198 **Bucoro:** "The Beasts at Burcoro Recounting Atrocities by the NRA's 22nd Battalion in Burcoro Village in April 1991." Justice and Reconciliation Project. Field Note 17, July 2013, p. 5.

199 **Mukura:** "The Mukura Massacre of 1989." Justice and Reconciliation Project. Field Note 12, March 2011, p. 7.

200 **LRA war was being needlessly prolonged:** Branch. *The Political Dilemmas of Global Justice*; Allen and Vlassenroot. *The Lord's Resistance Army: Myth and Reality.*

CHAPTER 16

203 **2012 Human Rights Report:** U.S. Department of State. Bureau of Democracy, Human Rights and Labor. Country Reports on Human Rights Practices for 2012.

204 **"There is no way the United States can help you":** The lawyer who helped Annet told me he received the same message from the political officer.

CHAPTER 17

207 **where the buses were going:** Julius Ocungi. Crime preventers duped to attend Museveni rally. *The Monitor* (Kampala). November 6, 2015.

207 **a European NGO:** Stephen Kafeero. "Donors, EC disagree on results gadgets." *The Monitor* (Kampala). January 25, 2016.

207 **tanks and tear gas trucks:** Helen Epstein. "When Democracy Doesn't Count." NYR Daily. January 25, 2016.

207 **"The state will kill your children":** Nelson Wesonga. "Lumumba shoot-to-kill threat sparks outrage." *The Monitor.* February 1, 2016.

207 **Crime Preventers:** "Uganda: Suspend Crime Preventers." *Human Rights Watch.* January 12, 2016.

208 **Patricia Mahoney:** Patricia Mahoney. "The Path of Nonviolence Is More Powerful." *The Observer* (Kampala) January 18, 2016.

208 **Besigye led a group of reporters:** Anonymous interview. New York, February 2017.

209 **George Kanyeihamba:** George Kanyeihamba. "Nepotism and Corruption Sustain Governance in Uganda." *The Observer.* May 9, 2016.

210 **Besigye won with 52 percent:** According to three opinion polls conducted in November and December 2015, Museveni was ahead with roughly 60 percent of the vote, while Besigye, his closest challenger, trailed with 24 percent.

In Uganda, researchers intending to conduct political opinion polls must be licensed by the National Council for Science and Technology—or UNCST, a body in the President's Office that reviews the questionnaire and sampling strategy. Because pollsters can't interview everyone, they select a random sample of "Enumeration Areas"—clusters of 30–100 households roughly equivalent to a village—and interview a randomly selected handful of people—usually three to five—in each one.

Government agents, with a natural interest in the outcome of any poll, should never be informed in advance of which villages pollsters are planning to visit because they could coach or bribe respondents to answer questions in the government's favor. But when I called the UNCST in April 2016 pretending to be a researcher seeking instructions on how to obtain permission to conduct a political opinion poll, a police officer told me I must identify in advance the enumeration areas I intended to visit, and notify both her office and the police and local government officials in those areas before arrival. When one pollster neglected to do this, local officials refused to let the survey proceed.

Patrick Wakida, whose company Research World International conducted one of the four pre-election polls, told me that "experience has taught us that if government people know in advance that pollsters are coming, there's no way you can avoid contamination." Wakida claims his firm obtained a government license before the new rules came into effect and was not required to

submit a list of Enumeration Areas to the UNCST. However, half the respondents on his poll believed that the government, not RWI, was running the poll, and Wakida admits this would have skewed their answers in favor of Museveni. When I asked a representative from a second pollster whether she had submitted the names of enumeration areas in advance, the line broke off. Repeated callbacks and emails went unanswered. According to news reports, a third poll conducted by three British academics in December 2015 found Museveni leading with 66 percent of the intended vote. However, when I phoned one of the researchers, he denied to me that he had conducted a poll at all. A fourth poll was conducted by the reputable research group Afrobarometer, whose representatives also denied informing the government of where their researchers were going in advance. I had no way of verifying whether this was true, but this poll was conducted in May 2015, before Besigye had declared his candidacy. At the time, he was under constant military surveillance, followed everywhere by truckloads of heavily armed soldiers and forbidden from holding public gatherings. So it is possible the poll was accurate.

212   **"Sudan, Sudan, Sudan, Sudan":** Wikileaks cable. The international component of Museveni's in-box. October 16, 2007.

262   CHAPTER 18

214   **U.S. and UK governments were involved:** Richard Wanambwa and Frederic Musisi. "US, UK Pressure Cited in Sejusa Return." *The Monitor* (Kampala). December 16, 2014.

214   **Aronda Nyakairima died suddenly:** "Aronda's wife doubts Gov't post-mortem report. Says the deceased never had a heart attack in 20yrs." WBS TV, September 20, 2015.

215   **South Korean embassy:** Frederic Musisi. "South Korea Protests Aronda Death Blame." *The Monitor* (Kampala). September 22, 2015.

215   **local radio interviewer:** Edward Ssekika. "Interview that Doomed Sejusa." *The Observer*. February 3, 2016.

CONCLUSION

217   **Roosevelt's Scottish terrier Fala:** Elizabeth Borgwardt. *A New Deal for the World: America's Vision for Human Rights*. Harvard University Press, 2005, p. 2.

218   **Harry Hopkins:** Quoted in Borgwardt. *A New Deal for the World*, p. 21.

219   **James Hubbard:** James Hubbard. *The U.S. and the End of British Colonial Rule in Africa 1941–1968*. McFarland, 2011, p. 8.

219   **Harry Truman:** Address before the National Conference on Social and Economic Development. April 8, 1952.

219   **George Kennan:** Hubbard. *The U.S. and the End of British Colonial Rule in Africa 1941–1968*, p. 59.

220   **C. D. Jackson:** Kenneth A. Kresse, *Containing Nationalism and Communism on the 'Dark' Continent: Eisenhower's Policy toward Africa, 1953–1961*, Ph.D. diss., State University of New York, Albany, 2003, p. 171.

220   **United Nations Declaration of Human Rights:** Hubbard. *The U.S. and the End of British Colonial Rule in Africa 1941–1968*, p. 78.

220   **Harold Macmillan:** Harold Macmillan. "Wind of Change." Speech delivered to the Parliament of South Africa, Cape Town February 3, 1960.

220   **remain neutral in the Cold War:** Kresse, pp. 188–89.

221   **George Ball:** Thomas Noer. *Soapy: A Biography of G. Mennon Williams*. University of Michigan Press, 2009, p. 229.

221   **Dwight Eisenhower:** Kresse.

221   **"two track" approach:** For a fascinating account of this, see the essays collected in *Dirty Work 2: The CIA in Africa*. Ellen Ray et al, eds. Lyle Stuart, 1980.

221   **African leaders:** Ibid.

222   **Roosevelt and Churchill resolved:** David McCullough. *Truman*. Simon & Schuster, 1992, p. 379.

Columbia Global Reports is a publishing imprint from Columbia University that commissions authors to do original on-site reporting around the globe on a wide range of issues. The resulting novella-length books offer new ways to look at and understand the world that can be read in a few hours. Most readers are curious and busy. Our books are for them.

globalreports.columbia.edu

Subscribe to Columbia Global Reports and get six books a year in the mail in advance of publication.

globalreports.columbia.edu/subscribe